50 HIKES

IN KENTUCKY

50 HIKES
IN KENTUCKY

SECOND EDITION

Hiram Rogers

From the Appalachian Mountains to the Land Between the Lakes

COUNTRYMAN
PRESS

THE COUNTRYMAN PRESS

A division of W. W. Norton & Company

Independent Publishers Since 1923

To Jack and Rose
for letting me loose in the woods,
and to Jean for joining me there.

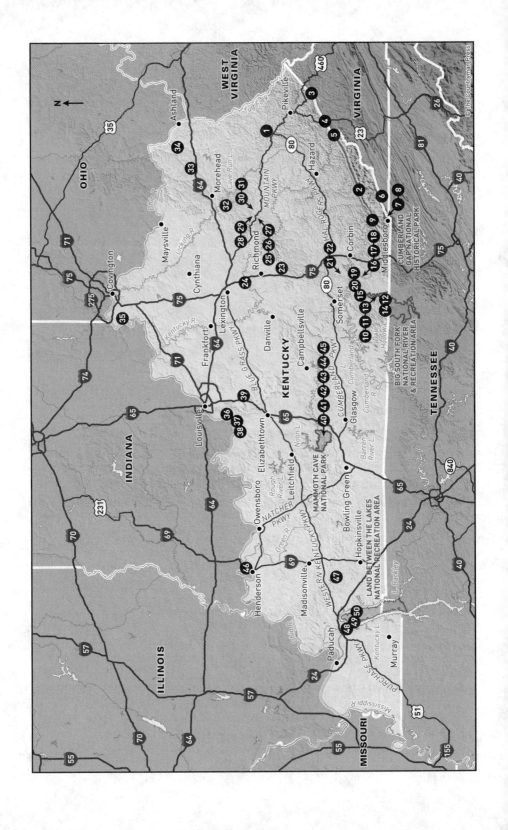

CONTENTS

50 Hikes in Kentucky at a Glance

Hike	Area	Fee?	Difficulty
1. Lakeshore-Moss Ridge Loop	Jenny Wiley State Resort Park		Easy
2. Blanton Forest	Blanton Forest		Moderate
3. Prospector-Geology-Overlook Loop	Breaks Interstate Park		Moderate
4. Pine Mountain Trail-US 23 to Bryant Gap	Pine Mountain Trail		Difficult
5. Bad Branch Trail	Bad Branch State Nature Preserve		Moderate to Difficult
6. Sand Cave and White Rocks	Cumberland Gap National Historical Park		Moderate to Difficult
7. Harlan Road-Sugar Run Loop	Cumberland Gap National Historical Park		Moderate
8. Cumberland Gap	Cumberland Gap National Historical Park		Easy
9. Chained Rock Trail	Pine Mountain State Resort Park		Easy to Moderate
10. Blue Heron	Big South Fork National River and Recreation Area	$***	Moderate
11. Yahoo Falls and Yahoo Arch	Big South Fork National River and Recreation Area	$***	Moderate
12. Kentucky Trail, Ledbetter Trailhead to Troublesome Creek	Big South Fork National River and Recreation Area	$***	Moderate to Difficult
13. Koger-Yamamcraw Loop	Big South Fork National River and Recreation Area	$***	Difficult
14. Gobblers Arch and Mark Branch Falls	Stearns Ranger District		Moderate to Difficult
15. Natural Arch Scenic Area	Somerset Ranger District	$	Easy to Moderate
16. Blue Bend Trail	Cumberland Falls State Resort Park		Moderate
17. Eagle Falls Trail	Cumberland Falls State Resort Park		Easy
18. Cumberland River Trail	Cumberland Falls State Resort Park		Difficult

Distance (in miles)	Views	Waterfall	Arches	Camping	Back-packing	Kids	Notes
3.2				✓		✓	Part of loop circles Dewey Lake
5.3	✓					✓	Knobby Rock and the Maze
3.7	✓			✓		✓	The Breaks
7.6	✓		✓		✓	To Raven Rock	Raven Rock and Skyview Caves
7.4	✓	✓				to falls	Bad Branch Falls and High Rocks Overlook
8.7	✓			✓	✓	✓	White Rocks Overlook and Sand Cave
6.5	✓			✓	✓		Historic Harlan Road and views from Pinnacle Overlook
3.0	✓			✓		✓	Cumberland Gap and the KY-TN-VA marker
3.4	✓		✓	✓		✓	The unique Chained Rock and great views
6.4	✓			✓	✓	✓	River Overlooks and Crack-in-Rock
9.7	✓	✓	✓	✓	✓	to Arch	KY's highest waterfall and two arches
9.4					✓		Through the wild core of the Big South Fork
11.1			✓	✓	✓		Challenging loop past Koger Arch
6.1		✓	✓	✓	✓	✓	Mark Branch Falls and Gobbler Arch
6.8	✓		✓			✓	Short hike to arch plus longer loop
4.7				✓			Cumberland River and Cliffs
2.2	✓	✓		✓		✓	Two beautiful waterfalls
7.1	✓	✓		✓	✓		Cumberland River and Falls

Hike	Area	Fee?	Rating
19. Bark Camp Trail	London Ranger District		Moderate
20. Beaver Creek Wilderness	Stearns Ranger District		Easy to Moderate
21. Bee Rock Loop	Stearns Ranger District	$	Moderate
22. Rockcastle Narrows	London Ranger District	$	Difficult
23. Indian Fort Mountain	Berea College Forest		Easy to Moderate
24. Raven Run-Red Trail	Raven Run		Easy
25. Original Trail	Natural Bridge State Resort Park		Easy to Moderate
26. Hood's Branch and Sand Gap Trails	Natural Bridge State Resort Park		Difficult
27. Whittleton Arch	Red River Gorge Geological Area	$**	Easy to Moderate
28. Courthouse Rock and Double Arch	Red River Gorge Geological Area	$**	Moderate to Difficult
29. Grays Arch Loop	Red River Gorge Geological Area	$**	Difficult
30. Swift Camp-Wildcat Loop	Clifty Wilderness	$**	Moderate
31. Gladie Creek Loop	Clifty Wilderness	$**	Difficult
32. Cave Run Lake Loop	Cumberland Ranger District		Difficult
33. 4C's Trail	Carter Caves State Resort Park		Moderate to Difficult
34. Michael Tygart Loop Trail	Greenbo Lake State Resort Park		Difficult
35. Main Trail	Boone County Cliffs State Nature Preserve		Easy
36. Scott's Gap Loop Trail	Jefferson County Memorial Forest		Moderate
37. Tioga Falls Trail	Fort Knox		Easy
38. Otter Creek Trail	Otter Creek Park	$	Moderate to Difficult
39. Millennium Trail	Bernheim Arboretum and Research Forest	$*	Difficult

Distance (in miles)	Views	Waterfall	Arches	Camping	Back-packing	Kids	Notes
5.4		✓			✓	✓	Rockhouses and cascades along creek
1.9	✓				✓	✓	Overlook above Three Forks
3.9	✓			✓	✓	✓	Overlook and Rockcastle Narrows
9.4		✓		✓	✓	To creek	Rockcastle River and Cane Creek
3.3	✓					✓	Great vistas and intricate rock formations
4.8						✓	Flower Bowl and Kentucky River Overlook
3.8	✓		✓	✓		✓	Shortest route to Natural Bridge
10.4	✓		✓	✓			Natural Bridge and Nature Preserve
4.4			✓	✓	✓	✓	Whittington Arch
6.4	✓		✓	✓	✓	To vistas	Unusual Double Arch and vistas
9.1			✓	✓	✓	to Arch	The huge expanse of Grays Arch
5.5				✓	✓	✓	Wilderness and Swift Camp Creek
9.2				✓	✓		Wilderness area around Galdie Creek
10.2	✓			✓	✓		Popular trails around Cave Run Lake
8.3	✓		✓	✓	✓	✓	Three arches and Smokey Valley Lake
10.1				✓	✓		Wildlife and Pruitt Fork Creek
1.7						✓	Quiet nature preserve
3.5						✓	Spring and summer wild flowers
2.0		✓				✓	Tioga Falls and historic railroad trestles
9.3	✓				✓	✓	Morgan's Cave, River Overlook, and Otter Creek
13.7							Long loop through research forest

Hike	Area	Fee?	Rating
40. Echo River Loop	Mammoth Cave National Park		Easy to Moderate
41. White Oak Trail	Mammoth Cave National Park		Easy to Moderate
42. Mammoth Cave Railroad Trail	Mammoth Cave National Park		Moderate
43. Big Hollow Trail	Mammoth Cave National Park		Moderate to Difficult
44. Historic Tour	Mammoth Cave National Park	$	Easy
45. Grand Avenue Tour	Mammoth Cave National Park	$	Easy to Moderate
46. Backcountry Loop	Audubon State Park		Easy to Moderate
47. Macedonia Trail	Pennyrile State Forest		Easy
48. Canal Loop B	Land Between the Lakes National Recreation Area		Easy
49. North/South Trail-North Welcome Station to Gray Cemetery	Land Between the Lakes National Recreation Area	$***	Difficult
50. Honker Lake Trail	Land Between the Lakes National Recreation Area		Easy to Moderate

$*   Fee for non-members on weekends
$**   Fee for overnight use
$*** Fee for backcountry camping
Bp   Backpacking

Distance (in miles)	Views	Waterfall	Arches	Camping	Back-packing	Kids	Notes
3.3	✓			✓		✓	Scenic front country trails and Mammoth Cave entrance
5.0				✓	✓	✓	Historic ferry route
8.2				✓		✓	Front country railroad bed
12.4				✓			Beautiful trails for hikers and bikers
2.0				✓		✓	Original cave entrance
4.0				✓		✓	Cave formations
4.2				✓		✓	Beautiful forests around Wilderness Lake
3.6				✓		✓	Unusual pine forest
3.0			✓	✓		✓	Flat, easy walking
11.1	✓			✓			Views of Pisgah Bay and swimming beaches
4.6	✓		✓			✓	Views of Honker and Barkley lakes

Introduction

From the natural arches of Eastern Kentucky, across the magnificent caves that underlie the heartland, to the shimmering lakes and rivers of Western Kentucky, the Bluegrass State offers a rich and varied landscape for those willing to explore it on foot. Each region of the state has its own characteristic landscape, and each holds unique surprises, just waiting to delight those who venture around the next bend.

In every season, the trails of Kentucky beckon. In winter, when the leaves have fallen and the underbrush has subsided, evidence of earlier visitors often emerges from the forest. Low walls of stone mark the boundaries of fields, and clusters of rusted artifacts mark long-abandoned homesites. Spring signals the rebirth of the landscape. An explosion of wildflowers carpets the floor of forest and glade, while birds brighten the air with song. In summer, it's time to head for the cool, clear waters of streams and lakes, or climb to wind-swept mountaintops. Fall signals a break from summer's heat. Autumn's patchwork of colors demands appreciation from overlooks high in the mountains.

Eastern Kentucky is known for coal mines and rugged, hard-to-reach mountains. But here at the western edge of the Appalachians are the long, high ridges of the Pine and Cumberland Mountains. Tucked along these scenic mountaintops are the Pine Mountain Trail, Cumberland Gap National Historical Park, Pine Mountain State Resort Park, Breaks Interstate Park, Blanton Forest, and Bad Branch State Nature Preserve.

The Daniel Boone National Forest protects a million-acre strip across the eastern part of the state, stretching from the Tennessee border nearly to the Ohio River. This is a land of delicate waterfalls, quiet forests, and massive sandstone arches. This rocky wonderland contains the Red River Gorge Geologic Area, two designated Wilderness Areas, Cave Run Lake, the Big South Fork National River and Recreation Area, and state parks at Cumberland Falls, Natural Bridge, Carter Caves, and Greenbo Lake. Here are trails suitable for anything from a short stroll to a weeklong wilderness adventure.

Kentucky's fertile Bluegrass Heartland lacks large expanses of public spaces. But a fine assortment of well-located state, county, city, and private parks contain trails ideal for an escape into the woods. Areas such as Fort Knox, Otter Creek, Jefferson County Memorial Forest, the Bernheim Arboretum and Research Forest, and Raven Run Sanctuary have extensive trail systems. Here the urban landscape quickly fades away and quiet, peaceful nature reigns.

Mammoth Cave is the Mecca of Kentucky's Cave Country. The tours of its seemingly endless underground passages are among the wonders of the National Park system. But some people still overlook the park's surface features. Aboveground, and across the Green River, is a spacious backcountry area and natural sanctuary ignored by most park visitors.

In Western Kentucky, it is access to lakes and rivers that makes hiking special. There's perhaps nowhere better suited to this landscape than the Land Between the Lakes, a long narrow peninsula between Kentucky Lake and Lake Barkley. Here are a variety of trails designed for anything from casual strolls to long-distance excitement.

THE HIKES

Choosing 50 hikes from all the trails across Kentucky remains a daunting task. Rather than choose only my personal favorites, I tried to select a variety of trails spread throughout the state. There are trails from the Land Between the Lakes, from along the Ohio River and the borders of Tennessee and Virginia. There's a variety in hike difficulty too: the shortest hike in the guide is less than two miles long, and the longest is nearly 14 miles.

All the hikes in this guide have a few things in common. I was looking for great trails and great destinations: trails that lead to arches, waterfalls, or spectacular overlooks. I am biased toward trails that passed along mountain streams, through awe-inspiring forests, or visited the home of beautiful wild flowers. Though a few crowded trails (the Original Trail at Natural Bridge State Resort Park and the front country trails at Mammoth Cave National Park, for example) are included, I wanted to expose hikers to some less-used routes where they have better opportunities for solitude. I also looked for variety in landscapes: this isn't a book about 50 hikes to arches.

Finally, I looked for hikes on trails built for hikers. There are no long stretches here of eroded horse trails or raceways for speeding mountain bikers. Some of the routes here are multi-use, but I tried to select those which few hikers

would object to. Several of the loops do use small parts of low-use public roads, I assume most hikers would rather do a bit of road walking than backtracking a long hike. I've done my best to steer you clear of areas frequented by ORV's, but these pesky machines occasionally can be found on trails where they are not allowed.

I've also got to admit toward a bias for loop hikes. I know I would rather see new terrain on every mile of a hike, and suspect many others would also. Car shuttles for one-way hikes are another means to avoid retracing your route, but these require at least one other person and are often impractical. I also tend to favor hikes that use part of the Sheltowee Trace Trail (STT). Kentucky's longest trail is literally the backbone for the hiking trails in the Daniel Boone National Forest. Ten of the hikes in the guide use some part of the STT, including those in the Big South Fork National River and Recreation Area, Cumberland Falls State Park, and Natural Bridge State Park.

Finally, I've included two unconventional routes, which are tours through Mammoth Cave. These "underground hikes" can't be matched by trails anywhere else on the face of the earth, or under it. Both the Grand Avenue and Historic tours will be easy walks for most hikers. For the most part, both require simply walking through broad passages and up and down stairs. Mammoth Cave varies its tour schedule by season. Summer visitors may find themselves limited to the high-capacity tours as park rangers are stretched to their limits coping with the summer crowds, and visitors during other seasons should realize that not all tours are offered year-round. Don't expect solitude, or even quiet, on these two outings. However, even in the peak of summer heat and humidity, the temperature inside the cave hovers near a refreshing 54 degrees.

Backpackers have fewer options in Kentucky than do day hikers. Much of the land in the Daniel Boone National Forest is too fragmented to make long-distance hikes practical. However, in addition to the Sheltowee Trace Trail, there are large trail systems at Cave Run Lake, Clifty Wilderness, the Red River Gorge Geological Area, and around the Rockcastle River and Cumberland Falls that are used by overnight hikers. The forest service also manages the Land Between the Lakes National Recreation Area, where the 60-mile North/South Trail is that region's only backpacking trail.

Three areas managed by the National Park Service at Mammoth Cave, Big South Fork, and Cumberland Gap all offer superb backcountry camping. Backcountry camping is prohibited at most Kentucky State Parks. Carter Caves and Greenbo Lake are exceptions where backpacking is allowed.

USING THIS BOOK

Your first stop should be the "50 Hikes at a Glance" table and the location map, which provide quick summaries of the locations of the hikes and their important features. The statistics at the head of each description provide important information concerning each hike. Under "Total Distance" I give the length, type of hike, and what other user groups are allowed on the trail. Many of the trails described here are multiple use, meaning that they are open to other users such as horses, mountain bikes, or even vehicles. On multi-use trails, all users must cooperate so as not to adversely impact the experience of

others. In this section, you'll also learn if there is any road walking needed to complete the hike.

I pushed a measuring wheel along most of the trails, particularly the longer ones, and measured the rest by GPS. The wheel is a great conversation starter; almost every hiker I met wanted to know how far I'd gone. I also measured a few of the trails that were open to mountain bikes with my bike odometer. I used these measurements in my descriptions, except when they differed only slightly from the "official" miles. GPS mileages are commonly used now by hikers, but these are less reliable than wheeled measurements and tend to overestimate distance, and even more so tend to exaggerate elevation gained.

Most of the hikes described here are loops. Some are round-trip hikes, where you hike to a point and return by the same route. One-way hikes do not return to the starting point, and thus require a car shuttle. Semi-loops occur where part of the hike is round-trip, and the rest is a loop; these are also called lasso or loli-pop hikes by some.

"Hiking Time" is a rough estimate of how much walking time will be needed for the average group to complete the loop. This time does not include any stops, and so it is the minimum time a group can expect to be out on the trail. In general, the average group will walk about 2 miles per hour. Obstacles such as long climbs, steep descents, stream crossings, rough footing, or hard-to-find trails will add extra time. Anyone hiking with small children should ignore the time estimates and just make sure the kids enjoy the hike.

"Location" provides a reference point for the hike that anyone can find on a state highway map. Here you'll also find the name of the park or organization that administers the land. Contact information for the organizations is listed in the appendix. I recommend stopping by the visitor center of any area you visit to check the latest trail conditions.

I have listed the USGS quadrangle map(s) for each hike, along with any other useful maps. For many of the hikes, the trails are new or are not shown on the original quadrangle. Information for many trails is available for more popular routes online, but in the backcountry there is no substitute for a map you can hold in your hand. When you're hiking in the state parks, keep in mind that many of the official park trail maps, particularly for the longer trails, are schematic. The National Geographic/Trails Illustrated maps for the Big South Fork and Mammoth Cave are prepared in cooperation with the National Park Service. These waterproof maps are well worth their cost. Outragegis.com is another source of reliable, accurate, and artistic maps for hiking areas in Kentucky.

A one-paragraph overview of the trip's highlights is given next. This is also the place to check for hazards, such as rough stream crossings, or administrative hurdles such as permits or fees. Use this information, along with the table "50 Hikes at a Glance," to find which hike is right for you.

Unlike many states, the Kentucky State Parks do not yet charge entrance fees. The National Park Service units in the state also are among the few in the system that do not charge. However, the United States Forest Service is moving toward a system of user-based fees. Some areas in the Daniel Boone have begun charging entry or parking fees. These fees will support local programs and services, and they should help to improve recreation in the forest.

"Getting There" provides detailed directions for driving to the trailhead, often the trickiest part of any hike. I've tried to pick the most direct routes to trailheads while at the same time minimizing the amount of driving on dirt roads. GPS coordinates for each trailhead are provided.

Some suggestions for other hikes are offered, following the main trail narrative. While many experienced hikers like the challenge of a long walk, many others crave a shorter, high-payoff trip into the woods. I've listed a "short and sweet" version of every hike that shows the easiest way to get straight to the good stuff. There are more and more families on the trails these days; the short and sweet hikes should be suitable for trail-tested kids. The other hiking options are briefly described and are often shown on the same map as the main hike.

SAFETY ON THE TRAIL

This is not a "how-to" guide for safe hiking. Nonetheless, there are several simple safety hints that all hikers should keep in mind. First of all, drive safely on the way to the trailhead. I know of more hiking trips ruined by car accidents on the way to the trail than accidents endured during a hike. Also, be careful where you leave your car. The trailheads described here should be safe, but never assume that a trailhead will be patrolled. Don't tempt thieves by leaving valuables visible. If you are unsure about security, leave your vehicle somewhere else. Include a small first aid kit in your pack for unexpected emergencies.

Though it sounds obvious, the key to staying found is paying attention to your surroundings. The descriptions and maps in this book should guide you safely around the trails, but this only works if everyone is paying attention. Many lost hikers I've encountered had no idea of the name of the road they started from and only a vague idea of their destination.

Poison ivy can be a major problem on many trails, both growing on the ground and climbing trees as a vine. I've tried to note the worst patches of ivy along the trail, but no doubt there are many others. The best way to avoid poison ivy is to recognize it. (Remember: Leaves of three, let it be.) If you expect to hike in an area where poison ivy is abundant, wear long pants. Commercial ivy-block products also work for some people. Poison ivy is also more reactive in the spring, when there is more of the plant's oil on the leaves. If you suspect that you have come into contact with the plant, a vigorous wash with water, as hot as you can stand, as soon as you can, is the best remedy. Some commercial products such as Tech-Nu are effective at breaking down poison ivy oils.

I scouted many of the trails for this guide in mid-summer, when biting insects are at their most voracious. The best way to avoid ticks and chiggers is to wear long pants tucked into your socks and use insect repellent. Flying insects, such as gnats and mosquitoes, can also be annoying. Again, commercial repellents using deet or citronella are effective. The best way to avoid mosquitoes is to avoid trails through low, swampy places in midsummer. People who are allergic to gnats or stinging insects might want to carry an antihistamine with them. Ticks and chiggers are most common in areas frequented by wildlife, as that is their preferred feeding source. Edge areas between forest and openings are the favorite routes for deer, and thus for ticks and chiggers as well. This is one reason the pests are so common in power line cuts and road shoulders.

More people fear snakes than any other creature in the forest. However, encounters with snakes on Kentucky trails are uncommon, and encounters with poisonous snakes even rarer. The eastern diamondback rattlesnake lives in the state. You can recognize this snake by its arrowhead-shaped head and by its distinctive rattle. The copperhead is also found here, but neither species is very common.

Heat is another of the dangers that summer hikers face. To avoid it, stay in the forest versus the open sun, wear a brimmed hat, rest often, and carry more water than you think you will need.

Winter hikers can face problems from hiking in colder temperatures. The key to staying warm in winter is staying dry. Wear clothing that wicks moisture away from the body, rather than cotton clothing, which stays cold and clammy when wet. Avoid overdressing to the point that you sweat. Wearing clothing in layers rather than a single bulky garment allows you to adapt as your effort and conditions change throughout a hike. Finally, it helps to have plenty to eat and drink on those cold days.

Treat all water you find along the trails. Even if the water looks clean, it may not be. If you are out for the day, plan to bring all the water you will need with you. If you are backpacking, you will need to treat your water by boiling, filtering, or using a chemical treatment such as iodine tablets.

Water crossings are another potential hazard faced by hikers. Most large streams crossed by the trails described here have bridges, but some do not. Rock Creek, on the Koger-Yamacraw hike, is an example of an unbridged crossing that may be difficult or dangerous in high water. I've tried to describe typical conditions for any unbridged crossings in this book. A rock hop means that if you have good balance and are lucky, you can get across with dry feet. A ford means that you'll be walking through the water. Of course, conditions can be more severe on any creek after a hard rain, and hikers should use their own judgment to determine if any stream is safe for them to cross. It is better to turn around than to put yourself at risk.

GIVING BACK

With the pleasure of walking Kentucky's trails also comes some responsibility. Each of us needs to leave a trail in as good, or better, shape than when we found it. Mostly this will involve simple measures, such as not littering, controlling campfires, and protecting water sources. But often we can greatly improve an area with a relatively modest amount of work. Many of the people who visit our trails haven't yet learned not to litter. You can help by packing out litter that less thoughtful visitors have left behind. Since places that start clean tend to stay clean, and places that have litter can get worse fast, a little bit of litter cleanup can go a long way.

Park and forest managers across the country are increasingly strapped for funds to maintain trails, and so they increasingly rely on volunteer labor, especially for routine work. Many parks have "Friends of" groups that support parks both financially and through volunteer work. Other environmental and trail groups, such as the Sierra Club, sponsor trail work trips. For those with more time to donate, the American Hiking Society organizes volunteer vacations to places such as Jenny Wiley

State Park and the Pine Mountain Trail, where volunteers work for a week on trail projects.

If you do find hazards or other problems on a trail, please report them to the agency that administers the trail. Trail managers can be surprisingly responsive to trail problems, so you might just prevent the next hiker from encountering the same problem that you did. Of course, if you find something along the trail that you really appreciate, let the manager know that, too. Everyone likes positive feedback.

Trails and trail conditions are always evolving. Should you find things different than the way they are described to be in this guide, please let me know by contacting the publisher, so that new conditions can be described as the guide is updated.

Kentucky offers a multitude of riches to those that explore the Commonwealth on foot. I hope that this guide prompts you step onto the trails and to enjoy them with the help of this guide.

WHAT'S NEW IN THE SECOND EDITION

Much has changed on the Kentucky trails since the first edition of this guide was published. Surprisingly, much of this change has occurred in the areas managed by the National Park Service. Since the release of the first edition, the Big South Fork (BSF) National River and Recreation Area, Mammoth Cave National Park, and Cumberland Gap National Historical Park all either changed their Trail Management Plans or their entire park General Management Plan. On the Kentucky side of the Big South Fork, the changes were relatively minor, the allowed users on some trails changed, mostly to provide more access for horses and mountain bikes and less access for motorized vehicles. Luckily, horse use has increased only slightly and vehicle use has declined significantly. There is little change in the remote character of backcountry areas such as Koger-Yamacraw and the Kentucky Trail, while the more popular areas such as Blue Heron and the Yahoo Falls Loop remain some of the best day hikes in the region.

At Mammoth Cave, most of the changes have occurred on the backcountry trails north of the Green River and west of the main park road. After several years of experimentation with trail use (and maintenance) by mountain bikers, the park kept all trails in this area open to horses and hikers only. Through the early 2000s, these trails saw limited use by horses and maintenance on the trails was adequate. However, the establishment of several commercial horse camps on the north edge of the park has led to a huge increase of horse traffic on trails that were built to handle foot traffic only. The NPS has made considerable effort to rebuild the most vulnerable trails, but a recent spring time visit showed that heavy horse traffic in these wet conditions has degraded many of the trails to the point that they are no longer enjoyable for hikers. Luckily, the park has built two new trails open to hikers and mountain bikers in areas where horse traffic is not allowed, and these two hikes were substituted for the two loops which now see heavy horse traffic.

The Cumberland Gap area is almost unrecognizable, compared to when I first saw it. The former route of US 25 over the Gap has been reclaimed, recontoured, and engineered to resemble the Gap in its 1800s heyday. A new network of trails and trailhead facilities has been constructed around the Gap, leading to a bounty of new trails for hikers to explore. Park favorites such as Sand Cave and White Rocks have remained intact.

In the Cave Run Lake area, the Daniel Boone National Forest also completed a planning process designed to manage the competing needs for trail access among hikers, bike riders, and horses. This process led to a plan that allows hikers access to all trails and tries to separate areas used by bikes from those used by horses. This plan is still in its implementation phase, and several new additions to the Cave Run trail system are planned over the next few years.

With all the changes in the trail systems described above, one would expect that several of the hikes themselves would be new in this edition. In Mammoth Cave, two hikes in the backcountry area were removed due to damage by horses. Luckily for hikers and mountain bikers, two new trails, the Mammoth Cave Railroad Hike and Bike Trail and the Big Hollow Loop, are ready to replace them. At Cumberland Gap, the Shillalah Trail to Hensley Settlement was closed due to flooding for the entire length of this guide's revision and has been replaced by the Sugar Run and Harlan Road loop. In a couple of other cases, I simply found hikes that I preferred over those in the first edition and added the new trail to Cumberland Gap as well as new hikes at Blanton Forest and Raven Run Sanctuary to the guide.

Several other hikes have also changed significantly. At Breaks Interstate Park, the River Trail has proved too steep and rocky for adequate maintenance, and so this edition describes a shorter, but safer and more enjoyable, route. I changed the Bee Rock Loop in the Daniel Boone National Forest so that it now visits the overlook, a route most hikers will prefer. A conversion of road to trail on Tunnel Ridge in Red River Gorge has led to a reroute of the Courthouse Rock Loop, making one of the state's most scenic trails even better. The new management plan for Cave Run Lake eliminated a key connection of the long loop hike described in the first edition, resulting in a similarly lengthy hike on the east side of the area. For the Land Between the Lakes entry, I changed the coverage of the section of the North-South Trail to allow for the possibility of a loop on the northern end of the hike.

Two areas near Louisville came out of long closures to remain in the second edition. The immensely popular Otter Creek Park was closed by the City of Louisville and sat idle before falling under the management of the Kentucky Department of Fish and Wildlife. There are more options for horse riders at Otter Creek now, but a relocation of the the old route steers past some of the areas more frequented by horses. The trail to Tioga Falls was re-opened in 2015 after a closure to rebuild the railroad trestle that crosses the route. The trail reopened without the little-used return route and is now an out-and-back hike.

The first edition of this guide was written before GPS technology was available to consumers. GPS and the availability of online trail information have made hiking guidebooks less dispensable, but there is still a place for a one-stop source for good directions, a reliable map, and descriptions of the natural and cultural history of a beautiful hiking trail. I've added GPS coordinates gathered in the field for trailheads, trail intersections, and other key features along the way. Keep in mind that GPS is not always accurate, and that reception in canyons or covered areas can be unreliable.

Finally, I've noted another welcome change on the trails in Kentucky, lots more hikers! Granted I scouted most of the hikes for the first edition midweek in the heat of the summer, but even then the trails seemed sadly underused. For this edition, most of my hikes were on weekends spread throughout the year. I got my first indication that I would be seeing lots more hikers when I drove past a totally full trailhead for Dog Slaughter Falls on my way to Bark Camp Creek. The Kentucky Trail Town initiative has helped publicize the rich inventory of hiking opportunities throughout the state and has helped more locals discover great walking virtually in their backyard.

I.

EASTERN HIGH LANDS

Lakeshore— Moss Ridge Loop

TOTAL DISTANCE: A 3.2-mile loop on hiking trails

HIKING TIME: About 2 hours

DIFFICULTY: Easy

LOCATION: Jenny Wiley State Resort Park, 3 miles northeast of Prestonburg

MAPS: USGS Lancer and Jenny Wiley State Resort Park Visitor's Guide

Jenny Wiley State Resort Park is centered around the fishing and boating opportunities at 1,100-acre Dewey Lake. The park offers other amenities, including a golf course, the May Lodge, cottages, camping, restaurant, and a surprisingly fine network of hiking trails. A loop combining three trails at the eastern end of the park offers a good sample of what Jenny Wiley trails have to offer; lakeside vistas, quiet woods, and abundant wildlife.

GETTING THERE

From the junction of US 23 and KY 302 south of Prestonburg, drive 4.3 miles north on KY 302 into Jenny Wiley State Park. Turn right on the road that leads to May Lodge and park in the lodge parking area at 4.6 miles (37.69777N & 82.72507W). You can get maps and other park information at the front desk of the lodge.

THE TRAIL

You'll begin the loop with a pleasant walk along the shore of Dewey Lake. From the far left end of the parking loop at May Lodge, start by a sign indicating the boat dock is 0.1 mile and the Lakeshore Trail is 2.5 miles long. At the base of the stairs near the boat dock at 0.1 mile, turn right and follow an asphalt road past the marina. Below the lodge, the trail turns to dirt and has blue blazes. While it hugs the lakeshore, the trail is wide, smooth, and easy.

After a short climb, at 0.9 mile, a side trail leaves right to Cottage 123, offering an opportunity to cut the loop short (37.69368N & 82.7158W). Stay left on the Lakeshore Trail to complete the full loop. Some of the trees along the lakeshore include white oak, red maple, American

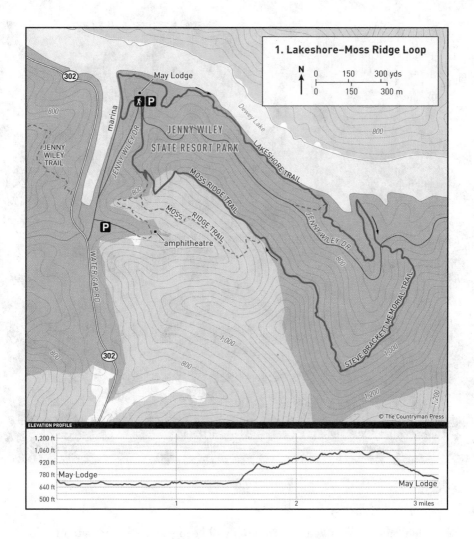

1. Lakeshore–Moss Ridge Loop

ELEVATION PROFILE

hornbeam, pignut hickory, persimmon, and sassafras. Keep your tree finder handy and see if you can identify more. Reach another small ridge and a sign indicating that there is no more hiking allowed along the lakeshore (37.69381N & 82.71414W) at 1.3 miles. Turn right and climb the ridge on a wide path lined with grass and moss. At 1.5 miles, reach a trailhead at the end of a paved road (37.69226N & 82.71302W). This trailhead marks both the end of the Lakeshore Trail and the start of the Steve Brackett Memo-

rial Trail. Beyond the end of the pavement, a gravel road leads left 3.5 miles to a Youth Camp. The paved road to the right offers another short-cut opportunity; it's only a one mile walk back to May Lodge from here.

Brackett was the forester for ten years at the park, and the Eastern Division Forester for the Kentucky Division of Forestry. He built and marked most of the park's trails. To continue on the loop, follow the Steve Brackett Memorial Trail as it climbs further up

THE MOSS RIDGE LOOP IN JENNY WILEY STATE RESORT PARK

the ridge, on a trail marked with green blazes, then turns right to contour along the middle of a steep slope. You'll cross one gas pipeline before reaching a second pipeline at the base of a set of stairs and then reaching a split with a faint roadway at 2.2 miles (37.68947N & 82.71583W). The roadway is closed to hiking, so go right at this junction. After finally gaining the crest of the ridge, reach the junction with the red blazed Moss Ridge Trail at 2.5 miles (37.69246N & 82.71889W).

Either leg of the Moss Ridge Trail will lead to May Lodge, but the right fork will keep you on the ridge top the longest, giving you better views and cooler breezes. The ridge is a better place to spot the wild turkey who roam the woods and enjoy the late blooming fire pinks alongside the trail. Just remember that pink is just the family name for this flower; the flowers are actually a bright red. The flower contains five petals, each of which is "pinked" or notched at the tip. Red blazes on the trees along the trail mark the boundary of US Army Corps of Engineers property. After some wonderful ridgetop walking, begin a steep descent. At 3.0 miles join the other fork of the Moss Ridge Loop (37.6947N & 82.72437W). To the left it is 0.25 mile to the park amphitheatre. Your route goes right, toward the Moss Ridge Trailhead located on the cottage road. To reach May Lodge, continue down the cottage road to the lodge parking area at 3.2 miles.

The legend of Jenny Wiley is a sad one, indicative of troubled times on the American frontier in the late 1700s. Wiley's troubles began in 1789 when her neighbor shot and killed two Cherokee Indians. When a war party returned for vengeance, they found the Wiley homestead undefended. The Indians killed Wiley's brother and three children, capturing the pregnant Wiley and an infant. The infant, and later the newborn, died in captivity, but Wiley survived and was able to escape one night. Her flight from her captors was epic; she had no idea of either her location or the direction of her home. However, she was able to reach the settlements, just ahead of the pursuit of her former captors. In the fall of 1790, she was reunited with her husband. They started another family, and Wiley lived to the age of 71 in the Big Sandy Valley of Kentucky, just north of the present day park.

To honor the journey of Jenny Wiley, the state of Kentucky opened the Jenny Wiley Hiking Trail in 1980. However, much of the trail was on private land, and management issues became rather complex. The foot trail was abandoned in 1998. In its place now is the Jenny Wiley Heritage Byway, a 155-mile road loop that traces the path taken by Wiley in her captivity and on her escape.

OTHER HIKING OPTIONS

1. Short and Sweet. In addition to the several short cuts on the route described here, the Sassafras Trail is a self guided, 0.75-mile interpretive loop occupying a small peninsula jutting into Dewey Lake. Volunteers from the American Hiking Society built the trail in 1995. Look for the trailhead, just 0.1 mile east of the campground entrance on KY 302.

2. The Jenny Wiley Trail extends 4.5 miles from Cottage 132, near the marina, west to approach the junction of with KY 321/KY 460/US 23. You can also access the trail at the campground check-in station, or at the base of the sky lift.

3. Three miles of mountain bike trails near Arrowhead Point are also open to hikers. These trails follow the route formerly used by guided horseback trips in the park.

4. 14 miles from the park is Kentucky's first significant rails to trails project. An 18-mile leg of the Dawkins Line Rail Trail between Hagerhill and Royalton was opened in 2013 and additional 18 miles is planned.

Blanton Forest

TOTAL DISTANCE: A 5.3-mile hike to Knobby Rock, Sand Cave, the Maze, and along the Watts Creek Trail

HIKING TIME: About 3 hours

DIFFICULTY: Moderate

LOCATION: Blanton Forest State Nature Preserve, 3 miles west of Harlan

MAPS: USGS Harlan and Blanton Forest State Nature Preserve

The name Harlan, Kentucky brings to mind images of grim-faced coal miners working far underground or of huge mining machines stripping the earth to reach coal seams from the surface. But thanks to the foresight and generosity of one local family, Harlan is the site of one of the most remarkable forests in the region. The Blanton Forest State Nature Preserve protects the largest old growth forest remaining in Kentucky. The trails at Blanton Forest do not pass by any remarkably large trees, but instead they offer a visit to Sand Cave, the incredible rock garden of The Maze, and mountain views from the unique Knobby Rock.

GETTING THERE

From the junction of US 119 and KY 840, drive two miles north on KY 840 to a sign for Camp Blanton (36.85894N & 83.38207W). The trailhead for Blanton Forest and its prominent signboard is not along the road to the privately owned camp, but it is visible just past the road and through a cable gate. The US 119 junction is about three miles west of the west side of Harlan and 23.3 miles east of the junction of US 119 and US 25.

THE TRAIL

From the trailhead parking area, a short path leads up to the gravel Camp Blanton Road, which winds above a small lake and some cabins. Just before reaching the camp swimming area at 0.3 mile, a yellow blazed trail splits off to the left (36.86171N & 83.37889W). This feeder trail passes under a powerline and over a wooden bridge before reaching the first of two closely spaced junctions with the Knobby Rock Trail at 0.7 mile (36.86222N & 83.37383W). Numerous

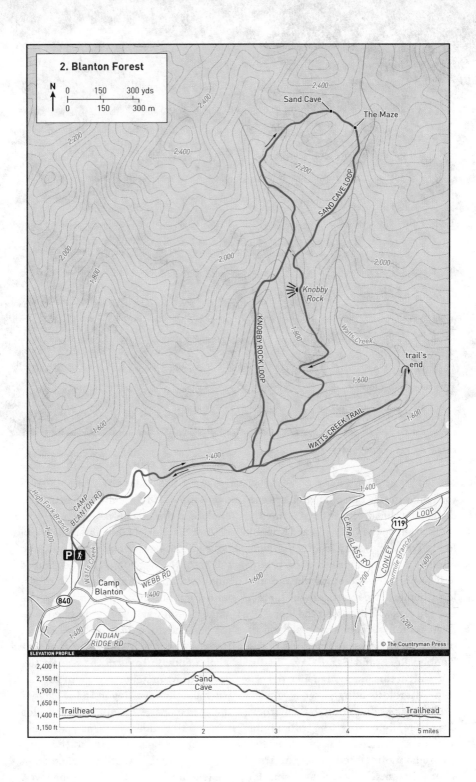

2. Blanton Forest

N

| 0 | 150 | 300 yds |
| 0 | 150 | 300 m |

2,400

Sand Cave

The Maze

2,400

2,200

2,400

SAND CAVE LOOP

2,200

2,200

2,000

2,000

2,000

1,800

1,800

Knobby Rock

KNOBBY ROCK LOOP

Watts Creek

1,800

trail's end

1,600

1,600

1,600

WATT'S CREEK TRAIL

1,400

1,600

1,400

High Fork Branch

CAMP BLANTON RD

1,400

P

Watts Creek

1,400

Camp Blanton

WEBB RD

1,400

1,600

1,400

CARR GLASS RD

1,200

CONLEY

119 LOOP

Fourmile Branch

1,200

1,400

840

1,400

INDIAN RIDGE RD

1,200

© The Countryman Press

ELEVATION PROFILE

| 2,400 ft |
| 2,150 ft |
| 1,900 ft |
| 1,650 ft |
| 1,400 ft |
| 1,150 ft |

Sand Cave

Trailhead

Trailhead

1   2   3   4   5 miles

KNOBBY ROCK IN BLANTON FOREST

rock piles in this flat, open area are evidence that this area was once farmed.

Turn left on the yellow blazed Knobby Rock Trail, and soon begin a steady climb. Cross one more wooden bridge and begin some steep pitches. Some large hemlock trees here are the largest trees hikers will see along the loop.

At 1.4 miles, reach the westernmost of two closely spaced junctions of the Knobby Rock and Sand Cave Trails. Keep left at this junction to hike the full loop. After descending down a wooden ladder and passing through a split rock, the fun really begins. The trail climbs steadily alongside a massive thickness of sandstone inclined along the trail. There are small rockhouses, smaller overhangs, and a wealth of features to explore in the sandstone.

At 1.8 miles, pass one small rock-house before entering into Sand Cave (36.87508N & 83.37009W). Sand Cave is smaller than its namesake at Cumberland Gap, but probably formed in the same manner as a soft, poorly consolidated sandstone eroded away below a thick well-consolidated layer that was strong enough to form the roof of the cave. Unfortunately, spray paint vandalism mars the cave. Beyond Sand Cave is the even more spectacular Maze. Kudos to the trail builders here, as your route winds up, under, and around the huge sandstone blocks that have shed from the leading edge of the sandstone layer.

Take your time exploring this magical spot before emerging from the Maze at a wooden bridge over Watts Creek. From Watts Creek, the trail leaves the ridge and descends to the signed eastern junction of the Sand Cave and Knobby Rock Trails (36.86972N & 83.37166W) at 2.7 miles. The west side junction that you passed earlier is only 200 feet to your right.

Keep left at the sign and continue south to reach Knobby Rock (36.86867N & 83.37131W) at 2.8 miles. Knobby (or Knotty, as it called by some of the local hikers) Rock is an unusual outcrop of a bed of tilted sandstone. This particular bed, instead of being smooth and flat, has a surface covered in rounded knobs up to a couple of feet across. No vegetation has managed to take hold on Knobby Rock, so you can also enjoy year-round vistas here.

Continue to descend past Knobby Rock on a well-graded trail to reach the east side junction of the Knobby Rock and Watts Creek Trails at 3.6 miles (36.86216N & 83.3733W). To the right, the west side junction is only 100 feet away. Instead, turn left and follow the yellow blazed Watts Creek Trail. This gentle section is a favorite of family groups, but it can be troublesome to hike if the water in Watts Creek is high. The Watts Creek Trail abruptly ends just short of another small creek crossing at 4.1 miles (36.86588N & 83.36675W).

Retrace the Watts Creek Trail back to the trailhead to complete the hike in 5.3 miles.

In eastern Kentucky, coal is king and logging is a way of life. But in the early 1900s, Grover and Oxie Blanton found their own little patch of heaven on the forested slope of Pine Mountain. Grover and his family kept this land undisturbed until the turn of the century. In the 1990s, Marc Evans, on behalf of the Kentucky State Nature Preserves Commission, identified Blanton Forest as the largest remaining old growth forest in the state of Kentucky. The 2,350-acre, old-growth track contained maple, poplar, hemlock, beech, and magnolias hundreds of years old, with trunks up to four feet across and up to 120 feet high. Working together with the Blanton Forest Trust, the state was able to begin acquiring the property and opened the forest and trail system in 2001. The preserve has now grown to protect 3,100 acres along Pine Mountain and is open to foot traffic only during daylight hours.

OTHER HIKING OPTIONS

1. Short and Sweet. The easiest hike at Blanton Forest is out and back to the end of Watts Creek Trail, for a total of 2.4 miles.
2. You could also shorten the loop by 1.3 miles by skipping Sand Cave and the Maze, but who would want to do that?

3

Prospector—Geology—Overlook Loop

TOTAL DISTANCE: A 3.7-mile loop on hiking trails with a trio of side trips to overlooks. Part of the loop follows a self-guided interpretive trail. Guides to the trail are available at the park visitor center.

HIKING TIME: About 2.5 hours

DIFFICULTY: Moderate

LOCATION: Breaks Interstate Park, 7 miles east of Elkhorn City

MAPS: USGS Elkhorn City and Breaks Interstate Park Trail Map

Breaks Interstate Park is a unique, cooperative park managed jointly by both the states of Kentucky and Virginia. The park was established in 1954, and it protects "The Breaks," the gorge created where the Russell Fork River cuts through the mighty sandstones of Pine Mountain. The 4,500-acre park surrounds a five-mile long canyon that is up to 1600 feet deep. This deep gorge carved by the river has been called the "Grand Canyon of the South," and it is impressive by any standard. Twenty-five miles of hiking and mountain bike trails, which make an almost infinite array of loop hikes possible, grace the park.

GETTING THERE

From the junction of KY 80 and KY 197 in Elkhorn City, drive south on KY 80. At 7 miles, turn right on the VA 702, which is the park entry road. Go straight at the junction with VA 732, then past the visitor center and main lodge, for 0.9 mile to the parking area for the picnic shelter (37.28564N & 82.29983W).

THE TRAIL

Since there will be many trail intersections on this hike, it's a good idea to orient yourself on the trail map before you get started. All you need to do is take the Loop Trail to the Prospector Trail to the Laurel Branch Trail to the Geology Trail to the Overlook Trail and finally back to the trailhead. But it's really not that hard. The trail blazes are color-coded, and since all of the trails have something to offer, it really doesn't matter exactly which route you take.

Walk to the far end of the picnic shelter, and start by hiking on the green-blazed Loop Trail through thickets of laurel and rhododendron that yield spectacular blooms by July each

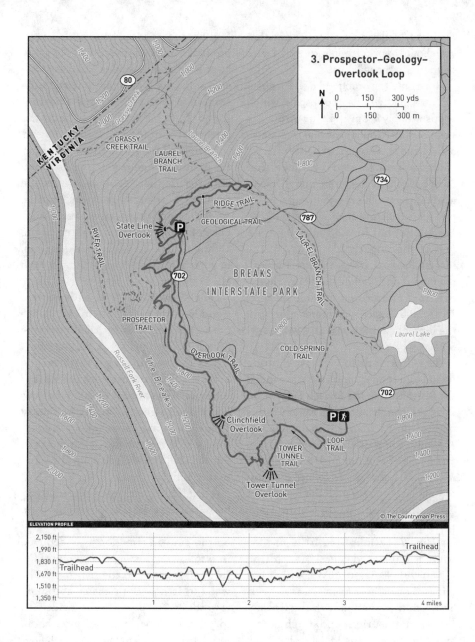

3. Prospector–Geology–Overlook Loop

N ↑

| 0 | 150 | 300 yds |
| 0 | 150 | 300 m |

BREAKS INTERSTATE PARK

ELEVATION PROFILE

year. In 0.4 mile, reach a junction with the yellow-blazed Tower Tunnel Trail (37.28529N & 82.30303W). The right branch leads back to the road, while the left branch (found just a bit farther down the trail) leads 0.1 mile to the first of many "can't miss" overlooks above the Russell Fork. From the fenced over-look, visible across the river, rising from the lush forests, are the bare stone out-crops of the Towers and Chimney Rock. Return to the Loop-Tower Tunnel trail junction, which also marks the start of the orange-blazed Prospector Trail. Here, a sign warns you that the Prospec-tor Trail demands a 3-mile loop, while the River Trail requires 4 miles and that you should expect to average only 1 mile per hour on those loops.

Turn onto the orange-blazed Prospector Trail, badly in need of repair, which drops steeply from the rim through a band of cliffs. You'll pass one rockhouse and zigzag through rock shelters. These shelters were formed by rocks that have broken off the cliffs, but still lean against them. The rugged bluffs above provide a constant reminder of the hard sandstone that forms Pine Mountain and of the remarkable ability of the Russell Fork to carve a channel through the mountain. Even in early May, rhododendrons and azaleas may bloom here. At 1.5 miles, reach the intersection with the blue-blazed River Trail (37.29015N & 82.30949W).

The first edition of this guide included a longer loop that descended the River Trail to the Russell Fork. However, the condition of the River Trail is now too poor to merit recommendation. A combination of steep, rocky terrain and a lack of maintenance have left the River Trail both hard to follow and hard to walk on. Keep right on the Prospector Trail, which continues to feature spectacular walking along the base of the bluff line. At 1.9 miles, reach the junction with the red-blazed Laurel Branch Trail (37.29478N & 82.30578W), which has climbed up steeply from Grassy Creek. To reach the junction with the Geological Trail, turn right and climb alongside and sometimes in Laurel Branch itself. Enjoy views of the "Notches," the rock formations that tower above you, before reaching the junction where you should take a right turn onto the Geological Trail at 2.0 miles (37.2947N & 82.30471W).

The Geological Trail and the Ridge Trail (the next trail to intersect Laurel Branch) together form the park's interpretive loop trail. An interpretive guide keyed to the red wooden posts is available at the visitor center. Curiously, the combined loop is called the Chestnut Ridge Trail. Whether you have the interpretive guide or not, be prepared to spend some extra time exploring the giant overhangs and turrets, along with the smaller scale features of the rock, such as cross beds and fossils. As expected, this trail traverses the base of a band of cliffs soaking in the sights of rock fins, chimneys, turrets, towers, and deep cracks choked with chockstones.

The Geological Trail ends after a wooden staircase at 2.4 miles, at the paved parking area for the State Line Overlook (37.29313N & 82.30798W). Cross the parking area to reach the overlook. From the overlook the roaring Russell Fork is almost 1,000 feet below. You can also see the mouth of Grassy Creek, Stateline Tunnel along the railroad track, reclaimed coal mines, and Potters Flat, a rare piece of level ground in this jumbled terrain.

Next, follow the green-blazed Overlook Trail from the south end of the parking area at 2.6 miles. Be careful to stay on the canyon rim; don't get seduced into following a steep "curiosity trail" through a crack in the cap rock. The walking is now both easier and more rewarding. You'll pass a short side trail to Pinnacle Rock marked by a chain link fence, and then you'll reach the 0.1-mile spur trail to Clinchfield Overlook at 3.2 miles (37.28642N & 82.30476W). Descend a series of wooden stairs down to the fenced overlook for the final spectacular views of the Breaks.

Return to the Overlook Trail, and continue to follow the green blazes back to the parking area at Picnic Shelter 2.

STATELINE OVERLOOK IN BREAKS INTERSTATE PARK

After crossing the Tunnel Overlook Trail, the Overlook Trail closely follows the park road to Shelter 2 at 3.7 miles.

In addition to prime time hiking, Breaks Interstate offers other outdoor excitement. The Russell Fork River includes a twelve-mile run with rapids rated up to Class 4. The run depends on dam releases from the John Flannagan Dam, which normally occur only on weekends in October. Contact the park for a list of approved outfitters. There is also an eight-mile mountain bike trail system that circles a beaver pond and the cottage area. There is no backcountry camping allowed in the park. Park amenities include lodges, cabins, cottages, a restaurant, a lake for fishing and boating, and a waterpark. Most of the park facilities are in Virginia and only the little used Center Creek Trail is in Kentucky.

OTHER HIKING OPTIONS

1. Short and Sweet. From State Line Overlook, combine the Geological and Ridge Trails and follow the interpretive guide. Together these trails are called the Chestnut Ridge Nature Trail and the loop is 0.9 mile long.

2. Other loop hikes can be made using the Overlook Trail and either the Cold Spring or Laurel Branch Trails.

3. The eastern end of the 120-mile Pine Mountain Trail is near Breaks Interstate Park at Potter's Flat, near Elkhorn City. The eastern trailhead of the Birch Knob Section is located near the Police Office in Elkhorn City. See Hike #4 for more information on the Pine Mountain Trail.

4. In 2006, Breaks dedicated an 8-mile system of mountain bike trails on the north side of Laurel Lake.

Pine Mountain Trail—US 23 to Bryant Gap

TOTAL DISTANCE: A 7.6-mile round-trip hike that uses some paved and gravel roads. The side trip to Skyview Rockshelter will add another 0.4 mile.

HIKING TIME: About 4 hours

DIFFICULTY: Difficult

LOCATION: Birch Knob Section, Pine Mountain Trail about 3 miles south of Jenkins

MAPS: USGS Jenkins East and Jenkins West and Pine Mountain Trail State Park Birch Knob Section Trail Guide and Maps

The Pine Mountain Trail east of Pound Gap represents the first step in an ambitious project to build 120 miles of hiking trail along the crest of Pine Mountain, from Breaks Interstate Park to Pine Mountain State Resort Park and then south to Cumberland Gap National Historical Park. Between US 23 and Bryant Gap lie spectacular crest line views into Virginia and Kentucky, and the remarkable Skyview Caves.

GETTING THERE

From the intersection of US 23 and US 119 west of Jenkins, drive south on US 23 over the Virginia Line at Pound Gap. The Pine Mountain Trail crosses US 23 just south of the Gap. There is no official trailhead at US 23, but parking is possible, after getting permission at service stations on US 23 near the crossing or at the intersection with VA 667 on the south side of the road. The Pine Mountain Trail reaches US 23 at the upper (Marathon) service station on the Southbound side (37.15413N & 82.63162W), crosses the highway, and follows the road shoulder to where a remarkably steep paved road to Stateline Apostolic Church joins US 23 above the (Valero) travel station on the northbound side. There is no trailhead parking at this location.

THE TRAIL

To start the hike from US 23, walk the steep paved side road to Stateline Apostolic Church (37.15566N & 82.6293W). Look for the Pine Mountain Trail's trademark yellow blazes on the guardrail as you make the steep climb up the road. The views from the open roadway stretch far across Virginia's Jefferson

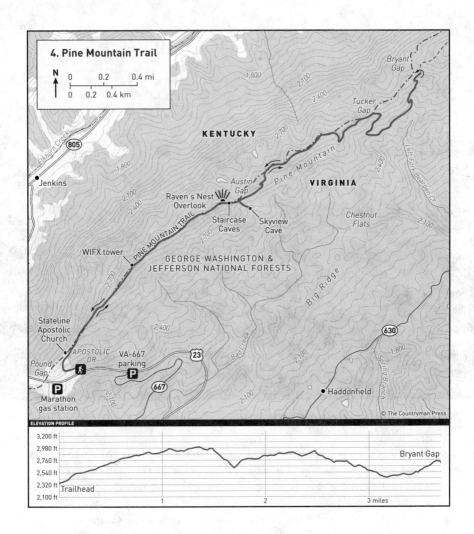

4. Pine Mountain Trail

KENTUCKY

VIRGINIA

Bryant Gap

Tucker Gap

Pine Mountain

Jenkins

Austin Gap

Raven's Nest Overlook

Staircase Caves

Skyview Cave

Chestnut Flats

PINE MOUNTAIN TRAIL

WIFX tower

GEORGE WASHINGTON & JEFFERSON NATIONAL FORESTS

Big Ridge

Stateline Apostolic Church

APOSTOLIC DR

VA-667 parking

Pound Gap

Marathon gas station

Bad Creek

Haddonfield

Spring Branch

© The Countryman Press

ELEVATION PROFILE

Trailhead

Bryant Gap

3,200 ft
2,980 ft
2,760 ft
2,540 ft
2,320 ft
2,100 ft

1   2   3 miles

National Forest. At 0.2 mile (37.15726N & 82.6303W), leave the paved road at a turn near the ridgetop for a two-track gravel service road. Continue to climb along the crest of the mountain. You'll pass the broadcast tower for WIFX (37.16467N & 82.62298W) at 0.9 mile before reaching an impressive array of satellite dishes at the end of the gravel road at 1.0 mile.

Beyond the satellite dishes, the trail becomes a narrow footpath. You'll continue along the crest of Pine Mountain, which here marks the boundary between Kentucky and Virginia and is also the north boundary of the Jefferson National Forest. Watch for the remains of a low stone wall. The wall is a remnant of Civil War–era breastworks from a battle at Pound Gap. One of the officers commanding this struggle was James Garfield, later to become President of the United States. At 1.3 miles is a fine overlook on the Kentucky

VIEW SOUTH INTO VIRGINIA FROM THE PINE MOUNTAIN TRAIL

side where Jenkins, and the many coal mines that surround it, are visible. The forest along the crest is mostly second growth. Pine and oak trees are perhaps the most common trees, but rhododendron, mountain laurel, holly, hemlock, and red maple can also be found here. Young sprouts of sassafras and American chestnut flourish in the dirt along the side of the trail. The trail follows the crest of the mountain so closely that often it must traverse across barren slopes of exposed rock.

At 1.6 miles, reach the Raven's Nest Overlook on the Kentucky side (37.1697N & 82.61369W). After enjoying the sky-high vistas, begin a steady descent on switchbacks past some shallow rock overhangs toward Austin

Gap. In the middle of the steep hillside, there is a side trail to Staircase Caves (37.1697N & 82.61299W) on the right. The side trail leads to the two main caves. One leads back 40 feet into the hillside. Next, the side trail continues downhill to another cave below the first two. At 1.7 miles, reach a sign at Austin Gap (37.16986N & 82.61191W). At the gap, rough, unmaintained side trails lead south into Virginia and north onto private property in Kentucky.

At 1.8 miles, reach a side trail that leads right, down 500 feet steeply to Skyview Caves. As you walk down the steep rhododendron-covered slope, it is hard to imagine a cave in this location, with its sweeping view of the horizon. In fact, the cave contains a huge natural arch, over one hundred feet long, one hundred feet across, and 30-40 feet high. The roof lies at the same steep angle, as does all the bedrock at Pine Mountain. The Skyview is a small hole near the center of the roof that seems to be a smokestack for this idyllic campsite. Few, if any, arches on Pine Mountain reach the size of Skyview, and few arches anywhere have such a private window into the heavens.

After Austin Gap, the Pine Mountain Trail leaves the crest to follow a gentle route on the south slope with several excellent vistas south into Virginia. At 2.0 miles, reach "Hurley's Knife," a long knife edge on this outcrop of the hard sandstone that caps the crest of Pine Mountain. At 2.6 miles, the trail turns sharply off the crest. The trail reaches signed Tucker Gap at 3.0 miles (37.17726N & 82.59671W). Just west of Tucker Gap, an unmarked trail leads north down onto private property in Kentucky. Just a few feet above the sign is a small overhang tucked into the rhododendrons that would be a perfect rest stop, especially on a rainy day.

At Tucker Gap, the Pine Mountain Trail makes a sharp switchback and heads west into Virginia on trail built in 2001. At 3.1 miles, turn left onto a trail that leads along the contour. Follow along the slope until the trail makes another sharp switchback to the left at 3.5 miles. This switchback occurs just short of a small drainage that hides "Moonshiner's Mansion." The mansion is a shallow cave where relics of this traditional industry can still be found. As the trail climbs toward the Bryant Gap, it passes alongside other rocky overhangs. You'll see the remains of old washtubs and broken glass that may also date back to the time of the moonshiners. It is easy to imagine people on lookouts, hiding in the thick growth at the edge of the rocky summits, anxious for any signs of the revenuers approaching.

The trail reaches the sign for Bryant Gap at 3.8 miles, where an old road crosses the crest. Bryant Gap is the end of this hike. At this point, most hikers will retrace their route back to Pound Gap. Beyond this point, if you choose to continue, the Pine Mountain Trail follows the old road to the left to reach Cable Gap at 4.5 miles. The trail continues along the old road, high above a huge limestone quarry, to a point about one mile past Mullins Pond, at which point it again follows a new footpath.

It doesn't take a trained geologist to know that Pine Mountain is a unique piece of Kentucky geology. While most rocks in the state occur in relatively level layers, those at Pine Mountain are tilted high into the sky. Around 230 million years ago, during a massive mountain-building event, a large rectangular slice of the earth's crust broke loose and was pushed to the northwest. This block slid over rocks of the same age that remained in place. When this episode of mountain building was complete, and erosion began taking its turn at sculpting the landscape, the thick, erosion-resistant sandstones of the Lee Formation remained in place, forming the crest of Pine Mountain.

When complete, the Pine Mountain Trail will be one of the premier hiking trails in the region. It will link state parks at Breaks, Kingdom Come, and Pine Mountain with Cumberland Gap National Historical Park. The trail will also visit the Blanton Forest and Bad Branch State Nature Preserves, and it will include the awesome overlooks at High Rock in Bad Branch. The trail was originally envisioned to include the 38-mile Little Shepherd Trail, a gravel road that serves as KY 1679 between US 119 near Whitesburg and US 421 near Harlan. Pending funding, the Pine Mountain Trail may be routed onto footpaths parallel to the Little Shepherd Trail. Two sections of the Pine Mountain State Scenic Trail have been completed. The 28-mile Birch Knob Section extends from US 23 at the start of this hike east to US 119 in Elkhorn City, near Breaks Interstate Park. The 15-mile Highland Section goes west from US 23.

The Pine Mountain Trail is a key link in an even more ambitious effort to connect trails in the Cumberland Mountains with the world-famous 2,000 mile long Appalachian Trail. The north end of the Pine Mountain Trail lies close enough to the Appalachian Trail across the Jefferson National Forest that a connection is possible. At the south end, the trail will someday connect with the north end of Tennessee's planned Cumberland Trail State Park at the tri-state marker in Cumberland Gap National Historical Park, and it could become part of the longer Great Eastern Trail.

OTHER HIKING OPTIONS

1. Short and Sweet. If you are dropped off at the end of the paved road, a round-trip hike to Skyview Caves and back is 3.2 miles.
2. The Pine Mountain Trail continues 28 miles east to Elkhorn City. Mullins Pond near VA 631 is 11.7 miles from US 23.
3. The east end of the Pine Mountain Trail is at the Police Station on the east side of Elkhorn City on KY 80. The trail starts by following gravel Carson Island Road, but it may not be blazed until it begins to climb Pine Mountain near Big Island Branch.
4. For updates on the most recently completed trail sections, contact the Pine Mountain Trail Conference.

5

Bad Branch Trail

TOTAL DISTANCE: A 7.4-mile semi-loop open to foot travel only

HIKING TIME: About 5 hours

DIFFICULTY: Moderate/Difficult

LOCATION: Bad Branch State Nature Preserve, 9 miles south of Whitesburg, and 18 miles east of Cumberland

MAPS: USGS Whitesburg and Bad Branch State Nature Preserve

The 2,639-acre Bad Branch State Nature Preserve is the second-largest of the state's preserves that is not associated with a state park. The preserve protects the watershed of Bad Branch, from the crest of Pine Mountain to its confluence with the Poor Fork of the Cumberland River. For hikers, Bad Branch is among the most accessible and rewarding of the preserves to visit. Both Bad Branch Falls and the sweeping summit views from High Rock are enough to lure any hiker out on the trail. The trail is open to foot travel only and dogs are not allowed in the preserve.

GETTING THERE

From the junction of KY 15 and US 119 in Whitesburg, drive south for 7.4 miles on US 119 over Pine Mountain. Turn left onto KY 932 and drive east 1.7 miles to the signed trailhead parking for the Bad Branch State Nature Preserve on the left side of the road (37.06761N & 82.77186W).

THE TRAIL

The trail begins in back of the signboard by the parking area and follows orange paint blazes. The flat area in back of the trailhead is an old home site, marked by the blooms of daffodils in early spring. An old shed, the remains of a tail-finned car, and other artifacts still remain. The first mile to the side trail to Bad Branch Falls is a gentle but steady climb. You'll cross Bad Branch twice on small wood bridges. Here, the trail's low elevation and proximity to the branch provide a lush environment much different from the high, dry conditions found on top of Pine Mountain. The nature preserve contains one of the largest concentrations of rare and uncommon plant species found in the state, but you don't

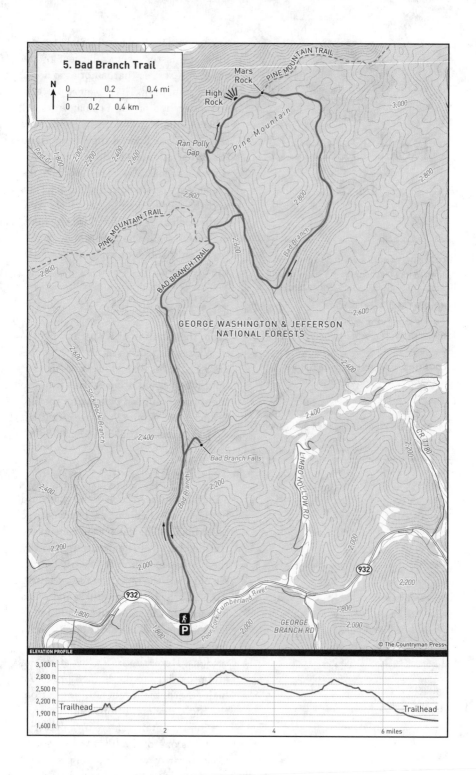

5. Bad Branch Trail

N

| 0 | 0.2 | 0.4 mi |
| 0 | 0.2 | 0.4 km |

Mars Rock

High Rock

PINE MOUNTAIN TRAIL

Ran Polly Gap

Pine Mountain

Perd Cr.

2,000
2,200
2,400
2,600
2,800
3,000
2,800

PINE MOUNTAIN TRAIL

BAD BRANCH TRAIL

2,600

Bad Branch

2,800

2,600

GEORGE WASHINGTON & JEFFERSON
NATIONAL FORESTS

2,400

Slick Rock Branch

2,600
2,400

Bad Branch Falls

Bad Branch

2,400
2,200

2,200

2,000

LIMBO HOLLOW RD.

CR 1180

2,400

2,200

2,000

932

1,800

932

2,200

Poor Fork Cumberland River

GEORGE BRANCH RD.

1,800

2,000

2,000

© The Countryman Press

ELEVATION PROFILE

3,100 ft			
2,800 ft			
2,500 ft			
2,200 ft			
1,900 ft	Trailhead		Trailhead
1,600 ft			

2   4   6 miles

have to be an ace botanist to enjoy the show. Chickweed is among the common flowers found here; some other favorites include showy orchis.

At 0.9 mile is the signed junction for the side trail leading right to Bad Branch Falls (37.07816N & 82.77205W). The side trail drops to a normally easy crossing of Bad Branch, then it climbs above the falls before emerging onto an overlook at the fall's base in 0.15 mile (37.07879N & 82.77046W). Here is a 60-foot drop down a massive cliff, fed into a plunge pool choked with immense boulders. The water's spray is cool and refreshing in summer, and it forms spectacular ice displays in the depths of winter. The small viewing area has an air of privacy appropriate for this secluded waterfall.

To continue to High Rock, return to the first junction, and continue climbing alongside a side stream. The cool mountain stream and steep, shaded gorge combine to create an environment closer to that of northerly or higher-elevation regions. Hemlock, tulip poplar, birch, basswood, buckeye, and beech are the most common varieties of trees. In spring, you also might recognize flowering dogwood or umbrella magnolia by their distinctive blossoms. Cross the stream, then pass through a thick grove of rhododendrons that shelters some rare painted trilliums.

All flowers of the trillium family are easy to recognize; their three petals, three leaves, and three sepals (the outer leaf-like part of the flower) give them away. Painted trilliums take this symmetry one step farther by adding a maroon triangle of "paint" to the base of the three petals. This flower is normally found further north, but its love of cool moist habitats also brings it to some spruce or fir forests in the southern mountains.

At 2.3 miles, reach the junction with the Pine Mountain Trail (37.09249N & 82.76982W). The Pine Mountain Trail here goes left along the crest of the mountain 3.2 miles to US 119. Our route goes right, and it will follow the same route as the yellow-blazed Pine Mountain Trail to Mars Rock. Next, the trail crests the small divide that marks the start of the Nature Conservancy's portion of the preserve. Drop down the divide and reenter the main Bad Branch drainage. Just beyond the crest is the huge Baker Rock, hanging over the trail.

At 2.6 miles, reach a signed junction with the High Rock loop portion of the trail (37.09362N & 82.76723W). To follow the loop clockwise, turn left on the trail, which here follows a dirt road, perhaps abandoned during 1940s-era logging, and begin climbing again. Soon the road becomes fainter, the forest more open, and slabs of sandstone are visible below the pines. Reach the crest of Pine Mountain at a sign for Ran Polly Gap. The upper portion of the trail climbs on top of a single inclined layer of pebbly sandstone. Geologists use the term "dip slope" for areas like this where the lay of the land follows a single angled rock layer.

At 3.3 miles, rejoin the crest of Pine Mountain and the spectacular views of High Rock. Below is Whitesburg, the North Fork of the Kentucky River, and rich coal country. The southern pine beetle has destroyed many stands of pine in the view shed. Long high ridges such as Pine Mountain are also a perfect habitat for raptors, and Bad Branch is home to Kentucky's only known nesting pair of common ravens.

Once you've finished lunch and completed your bird count, continue along the mountaintop, still soaking in the views. Closer at hand, you might

BAD BRANCH FALLS

VISTA FROM HIGH ROCK IN BAD BRANCH PRESERVE

spot a pink lady's slipper, or even an early blooming flame azalea. At 3.5 miles, reach Mars Rock (37.10215N & 82.76539W), where the Pine Mountain Trail continues east 1.2 miles to Lost John Gap and eventually to US 23 at the start of Hike #4. The Bad Branch Loop splits right here and drops south off the crest onto another faint old road, which follows along another side branch with two easy crossings. You'll soon reach the confluence with Bad Branch at a wood post at 4.8 miles (37.0893N & 82.76399W). Rockhop another small branch and look carefully for the remains of an old abandoned car on the right side of the trail. Climb up the old road to close the loop at 5.1 miles. From this point, retrace your steps up and over the divide, past the side trail to the falls, and back to the parking area at 7.4 miles.

If you loved the trail atop High Rock—who wouldn't?—consider hiking more of the Pine Mountain Trail (see also Hike #4). The Pine Mountain Trail is planned to cover 120 miles of the mountaintop from Breaks Interstate Park to Pine Mountain State Park. In addition to state nature preserves such as Bad Branch and Blanton Forest, the trail will also pass through Kingdom Come State Park and parts of the Jefferson National Forest. As of summer 2016, the Highland Section between US 119 and US 23 and the Birch Knob Section between US 23 and Elkhorn City are complete.

OTHER HIKING OPTIONS

1. Short and Sweet. The hike just to the falls and back is 2.6 miles round trip. There are no other trails at the Preserve.

2. An alternative access to the Bad Branch Loop is the Pine Mountain Trail, which leads 3.2 miles east from a large signed parking area at the crest of Pine Mountain on US 119.

3. Kingdom Come State Park near Cumberland, Kentucky contains 14 miles of hiking trails near the crest of Pine Mountain.

6

Sand Cave and White Rocks

TOTAL DISTANCE: An 8.7-mile semi-loop on trails shared with horses

HIKING TIME: About 5 hours

DIFFICULTY: Moderate/Difficult

LOCATION: Cumberland Gap National Historical Park, 13 miles east of Cumberland Gap, TN

MAPS: USGS Ewing, Cumberland Gap National Historical Park Trail System, and Outragegis Mapping, Cumberland Gap National Historical Park

GETTING THERE

From the Cumberland Gap National Historical Park Visitor Center just south of Middlesboro, drive 2.1 miles south on US 25E through the tunnel under Cumberland Mountain. Take the first exit south of the tunnel and turn left onto US 58. Drive 14.3 miles east to the small town of Ewing, VA, and turn left onto narrow VA 724. Drive 0.9 mile north (with excellent views ahead of the cliffs at White Rocks), and go left at a fork for another 0.1 mile to reach the Civic Park Trailhead and its beautiful gazebo (36.65212N & 83.43545W). The right fork road leads to the horse trailhead, which you may use for your descent route.

THE TRAIL

The joys of hiking are many and varied. They include both the big payoffs you get at the end of a hike from sweeping mountain top vistas, as well as the smaller rewards from things you see along the trail. The hike to Sand Cave and White Rocks offers hikers both a high impact payoff from the White Rocks overlook, and a more intimate, close-up visit to unique Sand Cave.

From the park gate, walk up the park road past the covered picnic shelter to another cable gate and trail sign that marks the boundary with Cumberland Gap National Historical Park. The footpath is wide and easy to follow. Just be careful not to step in the abundant poison ivy. You'll cross one small stream and pass a faint side trail leading left before reaching a T-junction with a horse trail at 0.6 mile (36.65765N & 83.43537W).

The combined horse and hiking trail turns left at the junction and soon begins climbing more steadily on a series of

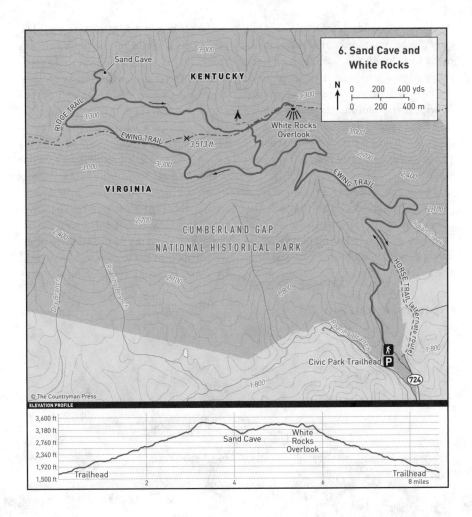

6. Sand Cave and White Rocks

N
0   200   400 yds
0   200   400 m

Sand Cave

KENTUCKY

White Rocks
Overlook

3,513 ft.

RIDGE TRAIL

EWING TRAIL

VIRGINIA

CUMBERLAND GAP
NATIONAL HISTORICAL PARK

EWING TRAIL

Indian Creek

Dry Branch

Roaring Branch

HORSE TRAIL alternate route

Roaring Branch

Civic Park Trailhead

724

© The Countryman Press

ELEVATION PROFILE

3,600 ft
3,180 ft
2,760 ft
2,340 ft
1,920 ft
1,500 ft

Sand Cave

White
Rocks
Overlook

Trailhead

Trailhead

2   4   6   8 miles

wide switchbacks. At around two miles, a major turn to the right leaves you staring at the sheer cliffs below the White Rocks overlooks. At 2.6 miles, reach a junction (36.66293N & 83.4458W) where a foot-only White Rocks Trail leads directly to White Rocks on the right. You'll come down this trail, so continue left toward Sand Cave.

The Ewing Trail will continue past the now-abandoned spur trail which led left to the former site of the White Rocks Lookout Tower. The trail continues toward Sand Cave on a sunny slope where chickweed continues to bloom even into the late spring. At 3.8 miles, reach a junction (36.66602N & 83.46112W) with the Ridge Trail, which leads 4.5 miles west to Hensley Settlement. Go right on the Ridge Trail to 4.0 miles, where a hitching rack for horses marks the start of the side trail to the Sand Cave (36.66747N & 83.4591W).

The 0.25-mile side trail splits just before reaching Sand Cave. The easier lower fork leads to a small waterfall, and the upper fork takes a rougher route to the top of the great sand dune that fills the cave. Sand Cave is remarkable for both its size and beauty. Though a hundred people could easily lounge inside, only on the most popular weekends are other visitors likely. If you're lucky, the noisy pigeons who nest in the roof of the cave will be your only companions. Lounge in the cool sand if you've arrived on a hot summer day, or enjoy the chain of icicles that line the roof of the cave, if you've arrived after a long winter cold spell.

The beauty of Sand Cave comes from the large beach-like dune that fills the cave. Unlike the jumble of fallen roof boulders and shade-loving plants on the floors of most Cumberland caves, here you're treated to cool, clean sand speck-

led with bright white quartz pebbles. Most caves are formed from hard rock layers that structure the cave roof as well as from softer layers that erode away to create the cave opening. Typically, in the Cumberlands, the hard layers are massive sandstones, while the softer layers are usually more easily eroded shales or very thin-bedded sandstones. What makes Sand Cave unique is that its soft layer is thick sandstone dotted with small pebbles of white quartz. The sandstone is poorly cemented, which means that its sand grains do not stick together well. This causes the rock to erode grain by grain, forming the dune on the cave

A FROSTY VIEW FROM WHITE ROCKS

HIKERS EXPLORING SAND CAVE

floor, rather than falling apart in huge boulders.

Return to the horse rail at 4.5 miles, and turn left on a wide contour trail toward White Rocks. Along this stretch, watch above for a huge outcrop of pebbly sandstone, and watch below for a wildflower display that includes numerous purple spurred violets. After passing a faint trail to the right, which is the remains of the unmarked trail to the fire tower site, reach a signed four-way junction at 5.2 miles (36.66577N & 83.44653W).

To the left at this junction, a side trail leads left 0.1 mile to the White Rocks backcountry campsite, located above the confluence of two small springs. The campsite has three tent sites within it, each large enough for two small tents.

In spring, water can be found below the confluence, about a five-minute walk below the lowest campsite. Later in the year, water will be more difficult to find. Campers might plan on getting water at the small waterfall at Sand Cave.

From the 5.2-mile junction, continue straight through the four-way junction along the ridgetop trail to White Rocks. You'll pass another hitching rack that marks the limit of horse traffic before starting the steep climb to the overlook at 5.45 miles. Be careful around the exposed cliffs, as you enjoy the views south into Virginia across the Tennessee Valley, and along the crest of Cumberland Mountain. When your eyes have had their fill, and your feet have had their rest, return to the four-way junction at 5.7 miles. At the junction, turn left (if you're coming from White Rocks) and take the signed foot trail on a steep descent down toward Ewing.

Reach the main Ewing Trail at 6.1 miles and close the loop portion of this hike. If you want, you can retrace your route back to the trailhead, or for variety, at 8.1 miles, continue straight ahead on the horse trail. After splitting from the foot trail, the horse trail leads south to a gate with a trail sign and a side road leading east. Go right at the next junction onto a gravel road. Continue downhill on the gravel road until reaching the paved road to the trailhead and Civic Park. Turn right briefly on the paved road to close your loop at 8.7 miles.

To use the White Rocks backcountry campsite, you must obtain a free backcountry camping permit from the Cumberland Gap Visitor Center before starting an overnight trip.

OTHER HIKING OPTIONS

Short and Sweet. The 1.7-mile Fitness Trail loop is one of the park's most popular trails. It begins at the far end of the visitor center parking area as a wide bark chip path; many of the species of trees on the trail are identified. After about a mile, it reaches a lovely stream across from one of the park shops and the Bartlett Park Picnic Area. Trail's end is on the Pinnacle Road side of the parking area.

Sugar Run and Harlan Road

TOTAL DISTANCE: A 6.5-mile loop hike to Pinnacle Overlook on foot trail. The Sugar Run Trail is open to horses, but there is little evidence of their use.

HIKING TIME: About 4 hours

DIFFICULTY: Moderate

LOCATION: Cumberland Gap National Historical Park, 3 miles east of Middlesboro

MAPS: USGS Middlesboro North and Middlesboro South, Cumberland Gap National Historical Park Trail System, and Outragegis Mapping, Cumberland Gap National Historical Park

GETTING THERE

From the Cumberland Gap National Historical Park Visitor Center just south of Middlesboro, drive east on KY 988 toward Pinnacle Overlook. At 1.3 miles, keep right on KY 988, where the road to the overlook splits left, and immediately pass the Thomas Walker Trailhead. Reach the small pullout for the Sugar Run Trailhead at 3.2 miles (36.63286N & 83.67512W). There is additional parking just beyond this point at the Old Homeplace Interpretive Site and, in another 0.9 mile, at the Sugar Run Picnic Area.

THE TRAIL

The Sugar Run and Harlan Road loop hike is another fine example of the efforts of the National Park Service to expand the hiking opportunities at Cumberland Gap. This hike combines the historic Harlan Road with the Civil War–era fortifications at Fort McCook, and then with the spectacular vistas from Pinnacle Overlook.

From the trailhead, walk south for 0.1 mile to a fork by an interpretive sign where the Sugar Run Trail goes left and the Harlan Road Trail goes right (36.63123N & 83.67582W). Our loop will go counterclockwise, so follow the Harlan Road Trail to the right. Even one hundred years after its last period of heavy use, the dugout road is still apparent, climbing steadily but gently through the hardwood forest. Two much fainter side roads will enter from the left side before the trail reaches a small gap in the mountain at 1.5 miles.

Beyond the small gap, the trail levels off a bit, and it is easier to imagine that this road might have been the gentlest and easiest of the three Civil War–era routes to Cumberland Gap. At 1.8 miles,

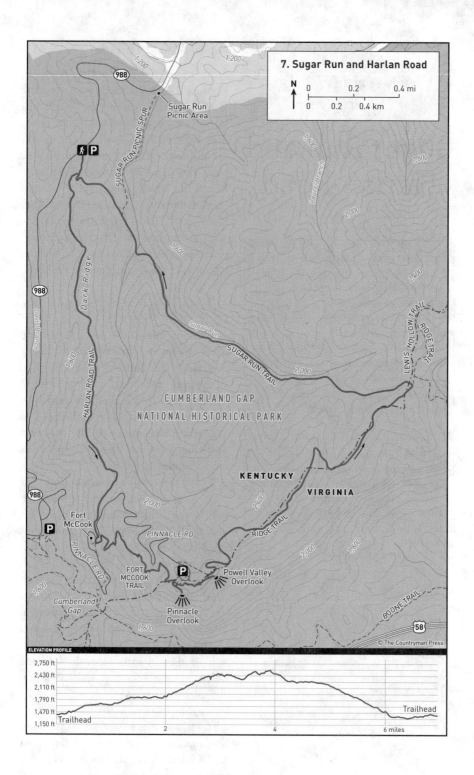

7. Sugar Run and Harlan Road

N

0   0.2   0.4 mi

0   0.2   0.4 km

1,200

988

Sugar Run
Picnic Area

SUGAR RUN PICNIC SPUR

988

Davis Branch

Dark Ridge

HARLAN ROAD TRAIL

1,600

Sugar Run

SUGAR RUN TRAIL

2,000

1,600

1,600

Laurel Branch

1,600

2,000

2,400

2,400

CUMBERLAND GAP
NATIONAL HISTORICAL PARK

LEWIS HOLLOW TRAIL

RIDGE TRAIL

988

Fort
McCook

PINNACLE RD

PINNACLE RD

KENTUCKY

VIRGINIA

2,000

2,400

RIDGE TRAIL

2,000

1,600

FORT
MCCOOK
TRAIL

Powell Valley
Overlook

BOONE TRAIL

Cumberland
Gap

1,600

Pinnacle
Overlook

1,600

58

© The Countryman Press

ELEVATION PROFILE

2,750 ft
2,430 ft
2,110 ft
1,790 ft
1,470 ft
1,150 ft

Trailhead

Trailhead

2   4   6 miles

THE TOWN OF CUMBERLAND GAP BELOW PINNACLE OVERLOOK

reach the intersection with the Pinnacle Road, which leads left and uphill to Pinnacle Overlook (36.60966N & 83.67403W). Go right and downhill on Pinnacle Road about one hundred yards to the parking area at Fort McCook. The fort is a worthy side trip just to see a Civil War Artillery Battery and the hilltop vista.

From the parking area (36.60843N & 83.67413W) you will now follow the Fort McCook Trail. The trail begins as a narrow footpath but soon merges with one of the seemingly innumerable old road grades that converge on the Pinnacle. At 2.5 miles, reach the apex of your climbing at the edge of the parking area for Pinnacle Overlook (36.6063N & 83.6673W). Here a throng of other visitors will break the solitude of the woods, but the added company will be worth it for the spectacular scenery.

From the parking area, follow the paved trail out to Pinnacle Overlook. Directly below the Pinnacle lies the small town of Cumberland Gap, Tennessee, and the Daniel Boone Trailhead. Middlesboro, Kentucky is visible to the north as well as Fern Lake, the park visitor center, the mouth of the US 25 Tunnel, and Cumberland Gap itself. Continue to follow the paved path around the Pinnacle to take advantage of other overlooks and another Civil War–era cannon battery before reaching a junction with the Ridge Trail at 2.9 miles at the end of the asphalt trail (36.60634N & 83.66506W).

For hikers, the Ridge Trail is the backbone of the park. Connecting the Pinnacle to Ewing, Virginia, it runs the length of Cumberland Mountain, connecting trails in the Gap, the Pinnacle, Wilderness Road Campground, and Hensley Settlement to the easternmost trail at Sand Cave and White Rocks. Once used for jeep patrols, the trail remains wide, relatively gentle, and easy to follow. In about a quarter mile, come to a register box for backcountry hikers. This western end of the Ridge Trail traverses a mature hardwood forest with just a few scattered pines. At 4.6 miles reach a junction with the Sugar Run Trail (36.61841N & 83.64855W). Both Sugar Run and the Ridge Trail to the east, from this point, are open to horses. The intersection of the Ridge Trail and the Lewis Hollow Trail, which leads south to the Wilderness Road Campground, is only one hundred feet further on, just out of sight.

Sugar Run is one of the park's older trails, and like many of them, it began life as an old road. Within the first half mile, pass a storm-damaged area with many downed trees, probably the result of the same storm that damaged and closed the Shillalah Creek Trail in 2015. There are several crossings of the shallow creek before the trail turns north and passes by some prominent cliffs and then traverses above a narrow gorge. Beyond the gorge, the grade lessens and reaches an intersection with a spur trail to the Sugar Run Picnic Area at 6.1 miles (36.62838N & 36.62838W). The spur leads 0.6 mile to the far end of the picnic area. Presumably, this is the route horses can use to access the Sugar Run Trail, but the spur seems little-used by either humans or horses.

From the spur junction, it is a gentle climb to reach the split in the Harlan Road and Sugar Run Trails at 6.4 miles, where you close the loop and then reach the Harlan Road Trailhead at 6.5 miles.

Perhaps no place has changed as much as has Cumberland Gap since the first edition of this guide was published. In addition to a much-expanded trail system and other upgrades, the Gap of today would be unrecognizable to visitors from much of the 1900s. The first modern highway built over the Gap was 2.3 miles of US 25E, completed in 1916. Even then, the narrow, steep highway was no one's ideal of a scenic roadway. The dangers of travel over the Gap earned it the nickname "Massacre Mountain." Even after a modernization in 1960, the accident rate for this stretch remained six times the national average.

By the 1980s, plans were formulated to build a tunnel through the mountain below the Gap. A pilot tunnel was bored in 1985, and construction began in June 1991 on the massive twin bore system now in place. In July 1992, the Kentucky and Tennessee ends of the tunnels met in the middle; by October 1996, the new highway tunnels were open. The final cost for the tunnels was $280 million, which included a 4,600-foot-long tunnel through 4,100 feet of bedrock, five miles of new four-lane highway, and two new interchanges.

By 2002, through the vision of NPS planners, the old route of US 25 had been reclaimed as a wagon road, looking as much as possible like the Gap familiar to the Native Americans and pioneers who visited the Gap in the 1700s. Fittingly, the park used much of the crushed rock excavated from the tunnel to bring the contours of the Gap back to something resembling its original topography.

OTHER HIKING OPTIONS

1. Short and Sweet. Both Pinnacle Overlook and Fort McCook are easily accessible from the Pinnacle Road.

2. This hike replaces the 10.6 mile round-trip hike to Hensley Settlement on the Shilalah Creek Trail, which is also open to bicycles and official vehicles, including the Park's van tours. The Shilalah Creek Trail was damaged by flooding and closed in July 2015, and it remained closed throughout the duration of the update of this guide. Check with the park visitor center on the status of this trail. The hike to Shillalah Falls and back is a 1.4-mile round trip on the Shilalah Creek Trail. If the trail is open, hikers unable to reach Hensley Settlement on foot should consider the NPS van tour.

3. Cumberland Gap will someday be a pivotal point in the region's long-distance trail system. It is the proposed northern end of the Cumberland Trail State Park, a trail that will extend across the Cumberland Mountains and across the entire length of Tennessee, as well as being the southern end of the proposed Pine Mountain Trail that will lead across the crest of Pine Mountain to Breaks Interstate Park.

Cumberland Gap

8

TOTAL DISTANCE: A 3.0-mile loop hike to Cumberland Gap and a side trip to the Tri-State Marker on foot trail

HIKING TIME: About 2 hours

DIFFICULTY: Easy

LOCATION: Cumberland Gap National Historical Park, 1 mile south of Middlesboro

MAPS: USGS Middlesboro South, Cumberland Gap National Historical Park Trail System, and Outragegis Mapping, Cumberland Gap National Historical Park

GETTING THERE

From the Cumberland Gap National Historic Park Visitors Center just south of Middlesboro, drive east on KY 988 toward Pinnacle Overlook. At 1.3 miles, keep right on KY 988 where the road to the overlook splits left and immediately reach the huge Thomas Walker Trailhead (36.60978N & 83.67837W). Both the Object Lesson Road Trail and the Wilderness Road Trail leave from the far end of the parking area next to some interpretive signs.

THE TRAIL

The modern transformation of Cumberland Gap from a busy US Highway corridor to a quiet interpretive monument has been remarkable. The Park Service has worked hard to recreate the spirit and historical significance of Cumberland Gap. Two trails on the Kentucky side offer glimpses into two different transportation eras, and a side trip to the Tri-State Marker offers the chance for mere mortals to be in three places at once.

This family-friendly loop hike begins by following the Object Lesson Road (OLR) Trail. This curiously named route is soon explained; the road was a 1907 US Department of Agriculture project intended to demonstrate the benefits of smooth, well-graded roads in rural areas. The "object of the lesson" was to demonstrate the convenience and value of road-building using "modern" techniques. US Highway 25 replaced the demonstration road, which was to be the last road built over Cumberland Gap. The wide corridor of the now-reclaimed highway is still apparent, but it will become less so as the surrounding forest gradually reclaims the old highway cut. The OLR trail is still a wide tree-shaded corridor. At 0.4

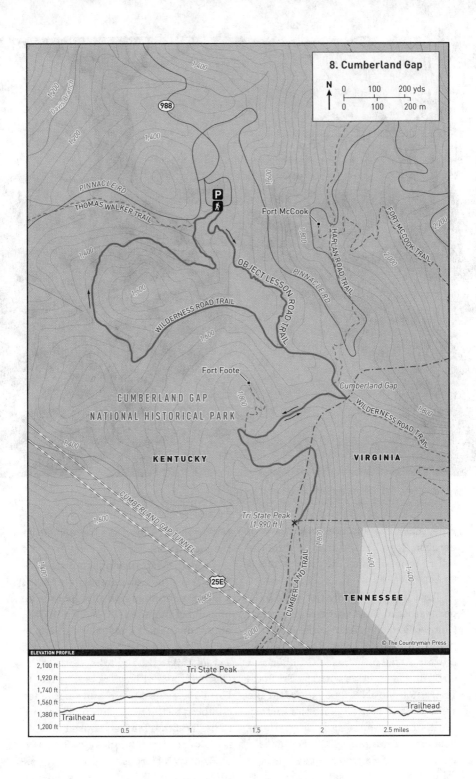

8. Cumberland Gap

N

| 0 | 100 | 200 yds |
| 0 | 100 | 200 m |

988

Davis Branch

1,200

1,400

1,200

1,400

PINNACLE RD

THOMAS WALKER TRAIL

1,400

P

1,600

Fort McCook

HARLAN ROAD TRAIL

FORT McCOOK TRAIL

2,200

OBJECT LESSON ROAD TRAIL

PINNACLE RD

1,800

2,000

WILDERNESS ROAD TRAIL

1,400

1,400

Fort Foote

1,800

Cumberland Gap

WILDERNESS ROAD TRAIL

1,800

CUMBERLAND GAP
NATIONAL HISTORICAL PARK

KENTUCKY

VIRGINIA

1,400

CUMBERLAND GAP TUNNEL

1,600

Tri State Peak
(1,990 ft.)

CUMBERLAND TRAIL

1,800

1,600

1,400

TENNESSEE

1,600

25E

1,800

2,000

© The Countryman Press

ELEVATION PROFILE

2,100 ft		Tri State Peak			
1,920 ft					
1,740 ft					
1,560 ft					Trailhead
1,380 ft Trailhead					
1,200 ft	0.5	1	1.5	2	2.5 miles

PINNACLE OVERLOOK AT CUMBERLAND GAP NATIONAL HISTORICAL PARK

mile, reach the junction with the Wilderness Road Trail, which will be the return route of this hike (36.60532N & 83.67577W).

Turn left and follow the wide Wilderness Road Trail as it climbs toward Cumberland Gap. At 0.5 mile, pass the junction of the Harlan Road Trail on the left. At 0.6 mile, reach Cumberland Gap and the junction with the Tri-State Trail (36.60409N & 83.67365W). Take some time to contemplate the history of this unique spot and the restlessness of the human spirit. For untold generations, this was the key passage for hunters, traders, settlers, and warriors on their laborious travels across the mountains.

From the Gap, turn right onto the Tri-State Trail. The trail immediately passes a large monument and then passes an unusual crater, the relic of a Civil War–era detonation of a magazine of explosives. Cross under a powerline and pass a spur trail to the right that leads to the Civil War site of Fort Foote. The trip to Fort Foote adds 0.3 mile and some steep climbing to the hike. Continue upward to the Tri-State Marker, housed under a large gazebo at 1.2 miles (36.6008N & 83.67534W). Here is the unique opportunity to stand in Kentucky, Tennessee, and Virginia, all at the same time. Beside relief from the summer sun, the site offers views to the north into Kentucky.

To the west of the Tri-State Marker, the white-blazed Cumberland Trail leads two miles to what is currently a dead end. However, the NPS is working with Tennessee's Cumberland Trail State Park and the Cumberland Trail Conference to complete the trail through the Cumberland Mountains to Chattanooga, Tennessee. Many sections of the trail are now complete, with other new sections opening every year. When the Cumberland Trail is complete, and if the trail system in Cumberland Gap National Historical Park can be connected to Kentucky's Pine Mountain Trail, Cumberland Gap will have significance for long-distance hikers rivaling that of its historic legacy.

From the Tri-State Marker, return to the junction of the Object Lesson and Wilderness Road Trails at 2.0 miles. This time turn left to follow the Wilderness Road Trail. The trail immediately passes Indian Rock on the right and follows a gradual downhill through mature forest. At 2.4 miles, an interpretive sign alerts hikers to one of the sections of the original bed that remains intact, without disturbance from more modern road construction. This over 200-year-old path was only recently opened back up to hikers as part of the reclamation of the Gap area following the removal of old US Highway 25. Just after a small wooden bridge, reach the intersection with the Thomas Walker Trail at 2.9 miles (36.60859N & 83.67876W). The Thomas Walker Trail leads left 0.7 mile to the visitor center. Keep right to follow the combined trails to close the loop at the Thomas Walker Parking Area at 3.0 miles.

Cumberland Gap was an important transportation route well into prehistoric times. The Gap was likely used by animals and the Native Americans who hunted them long before the first explorations of white settlers. The Gap was a crucial part of the Warrior's Path, connecting the lands east of the mountains to the continental interior. Dr. Thomas Walker first described and mapped the Gap in 1750, but it remained little-used until the 1760s, when Daniel Boone and other long hunters began to hunt the lands west of the Gap. The route was blazed by Boone and other woodsman in the mid-1770s and was eventually used by over 100,000 people migrating west. In the 1790s, a wagon toll road, the Wilderness Road, was built by the state of Kentucky and remained the primary passage through the mountain until the 1810s.

By 1840, the road had been abandoned, but the Gap was still considered strategic by both sides in the Civil War. The Confederates occupied the Gap first, but control was to change hands three times during the war, each time without a battle being fought. The Gap itself was the loser in this war. To fortify and defend the Gap, a variety of gun placements and defensive structures were built, and in order to hinder potential attacks on the Gap, all the surrounding trees were cut down into a horrific pile of jumbled dead timber.

The advent of tourist travel by car triggered the next stage in the evolution of Cumberland Gap. In 1918 the modern "Object Lesson Road" was built for automobiles. The road was continuously improved and became part of US 25 in 1926. As part of the reclamation of US 25 following the construction of the Cumberland Gap Tunnel, NPS researchers were able to use a variety of historical sources to verify the original alignment of the Wilderness Road and other historical routes through the Gap. By 2002 reclamation was complete and the Gap's forests had been replanted to be consistent with its historical setting.

The history of Cumberland Gap is far too rich to be detailed in this guide. For a fuller appreciation of the historic importance of this place visit the park's visitor center, watch the park movie, or participate in a ranger-led event.

OTHER HIKING OPTIONS

1. Short and Sweet. You can reach Cumberland Gap from the Thomas Walker Trailhead and return in 0.8 mile on the Object Lesson Road Trail, or make just the loop with the Wilderness Road Trail in 1.4 miles.

2. The Park Fitness Trail leaves from the back of the visitor center and makes a pleasant 1.7 mile loop.

3. The Wilderness Road Trail continues south over Cumberland Gap into Tennessee and reaches the town of Cumberland Gap in 0.6 mile and the Daniel Boone Parking Lot in 0.9 mile. There is an extensive trail network on the Tennessee side of the park centered around the Wilderness Road Campground.

9

Chained Rock Trail

TOTAL DISTANCE: A 3.4-mile one-way hike on the Laurel Cove, Chained Rock, Timber Ridge, and Rock Hotel Trails. This hike requires a 2-mile car shuttle or road walk, or it can easily be reversed by strong hikers.

HIKING TIME: About 2 hours

DIFFICULTY: Easy/Moderate

LOCATION: Pine Mountain State Resort Park, 3 miles south of Pineville

MAPS: USGS Pineville and Middlesboro North and Pine Mountain Visitor's Guide

The hiking trails in Pine Mountain State Resort Park form two systems centered around the Herndon Evans Lodge, and around Laurel Cove Amphitheater. But only the Laurel Cove Amphitheater trails on the east side of the park give hikers a taste of what the park is really about. Here you can climb Pine Mountain nearly from its bottom to its top, rewarding yourself with two of the finest views in all of southeast Kentucky. And nowhere else can you see a rock that had to be chained in place to protect a town.

GETTING THERE

From the junction of US 25E and KY 119 about one mile south of Pineville, drive south on US 25E for 0.3 mile to a paved road on the north side of the park's golf course. Coming north from Middlesboro, this same junction is 0.5 mile north of the intersection of US 25E and KY 190, which is the main entrance to the park. Drive west on this road, past the golf course, for 1.1 miles to reach the sometimes-gated entrance to Laurel Cove Amphitheater (36.74164N & 83.7071W).

THE TRAIL

This hike starts off with a tour through Laurel Cove Amphitheater which is used for the annual Mountain Laurel Festival. This rustic setting features seating on chairs, on benches, and on wood planks with rock bases. Walk through the Amphitheater on a concrete path, then descend to a picnic shelter. Across tiny Laurel Creek from the shelter is a trailhead sign for the Laurel Cove Trail (36.74348N & 83.70589W).

Most of the climb to the crest of Pine Mountain will be through a dry pine-oak forest. For better or worse, it's a

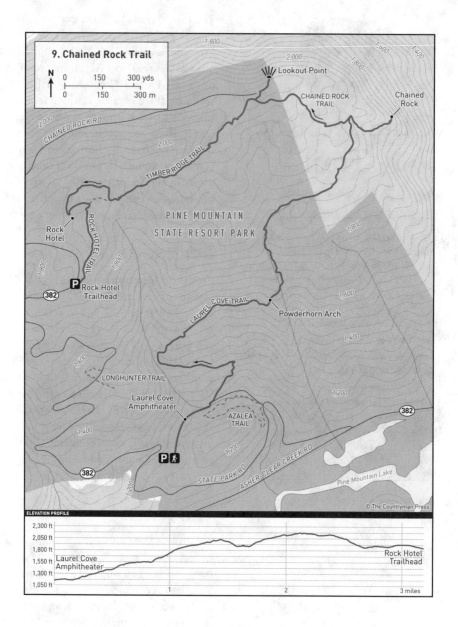

9. Chained Rock Trail

N

| 0 | 150 | 300 yds |
| 0 | 150 | 300 m |

Lookout Point

CHAINED ROCK TRAIL

Chained Rock

CHAINED ROCK RD

2,000

TIMBER RIDGE TRAIL

PINE MOUNTAIN STATE RESORT PARK

Rock Hotel

ROCK HOTEL TRAIL

382 P Rock Hotel Trailhead

LAUREL COVE TRAIL

Powderhorn Arch

LONGHUNTER TRAIL

Laurel Cove Amphitheater

AZALEA TRAIL

382

P

STATE PARK RD

ASHER CLEAR CREEK RD

Pine Mountain Lake

382

© The Countryman Press

ELEVATION PROFILE

| 2,300 ft |
| 2,050 ft |
| 1,800 ft |
| 1,550 ft |
| 1,300 ft |
| 1,050 ft |

Laurel Cove Amphitheater

Rock Hotel Trailhead

1   2   3 miles

good place to examine the workings of the southern pine beetle. The bark of several pines along the trail has been stripped off, giving an up-close view of the tunnels carved by the beetle in the soft living tissue of the tree. One of the other common trees along the trail is sassafras, best recognized by the mitten-shaped leaves, which can have one, two, or three lobes. At 1.1 miles, the trail passes beneath Powderhorn Arch (36.74721N & 83.70319W). Arches are rare in the steeply tilted rocks of Pine Mountain, and they are more common in the flat-lying sandstone layers of rocks in areas like the Big South Fork or Red

POWDERHORN ARCH

River Gorge. This rare treasure is only about 20 feet long, eight feet wide, and eight feet high.

Climb up a steep section with great examples of rock work constructed by both the Civilian Conservation Corps (CCC) and Mother Nature. Next, a short side trail leads left to a bare slab of sandstone, but there are no views. Beyond, the trail hugs a small stream and ascends on an intricate series of rock steps up a steep gully made to seem even narrower by a dense growth of rhododendrons. At 1.8 miles, reach the well-worn junction with the Chained Rock Trail beside a small rockhouse (36.75346N & 83.69966W). From the intersection onward, the Chained Rock Trail descends steeply, then it goes down a set of stone steps with railings to a spot where the chain is visible at 1.9 miles (36.75341N & 83.69778W).

Once at the chain you'll be torn between examining it, and enjoying the views from the rocks around it. The chain itself is 101 feet long, weighs 3,000 pounds, and spans a 75-foot gap. Each link is four inches wide, six inches long, and weighs 4 1/2 pounds. If you look carefully you can see pieces of a comparatively dinky older chain still in place. The town of Pineville lies below, obviously in the path of any wayward boulders that might escape from the mountain. Below also is the mighty Cumberland River making the only cut through Pine Mountain for over one hundred miles. In late spring and early summer, the thick rhododendron blooms around the overlook add to the spectacle.

The story of the chained rock is a unique combination of civic pride and civic sense of humor. A menacing-looking boulder had always loomed above the city of Pineville, but residents had joked that they were safe from it because the rock was chained in place. Then, in the early 1930s, some tourists asked why the chain could not be seen from town. This gave some enterprising citizens the idea to install a real chain to replace a smaller one that had once been in place but had fallen into disrepair. The Pineville Kiwanis Club obtained a huge chain formerly used on a steam shovel at a rock quarry in Hagen, VA. The chain was shipped to town, hauled up the mountain by mules, and secured in place with considerable effort. With the chain in place, visible from the town below, Pineville had what it needed: protection from the falling rock and the tourist attraction it wanted. Supposedly, the story of the chained rock was reported in over 6,000 newspapers across the country.

All has gone well on top of the mountain until recent years, when the chain, and the rock that it holds, have been the subject of threats from "geology rights" advocates who want to "Free the Pine Mountain Rock." These groups believe it is wrong to enslave the rock, and that chaining it to the mountain violates the rock's right to erode as nature intended. Whether the advocates will be success-ful in removing the chain and freeing the rock remains to be seen.

Return to the Laurel Cove-Chained Rock junction at 2.1 miles, and continue straight ahead on the Chained Rock Trail. The trail here is wide and heavily used. Reach another signed trail junction at 2.4 miles (36.75413N & 83.70384W). The sign indicates that the Timber Ridge Trail continues on ahead. To the right, a trail climbs 0.1 mile to the parking area at Lookout Point, a worthy side trip for another view of the valley to the north of Pine Mountain.

Take the Timber Ridge Trail and enjoy some easy ridgetop walking. You can ignore a side trail to the right, which leads to an overgrown overlook. Be careful to watch for blazes on rocks in an open area filled by blueberry and laurel. At 3.0 miles, reach a junction with the yellow-blazed side trail leading right to the Rock Hotel (36.75063N & 83.71033W). Take this side trail down along a small stream lined with hemlock and rhododendron, and reach the Rock Hotel after a small climb at 3.2 miles (36.74998N & 83.71201W). This deep rockhouse stretches for one hundred feet along the bluff line, and is up to thirty feet high, obviously large enough to hold a hotel full of people.

Continue on the side trail until you rejoin the Rock Hotel Trail only a hundred yards from where you left the Timber Ridge Trail. Continue on the trail until you reach the main park road at 3.4 miles near a pullout large enough to hold only 2-3 cars (36.7477N & 83.71184W). If you weren't able to shuttle a car to this point, you have two options for your return. Obviously, you can retrace your route back to Laurel Cove Amphitheater. If you ignore the side trips to Chained Rock and Rock Hotel this will be a 2.8-mile journey.

If you turn left, and walk down the road, you will have 2.6 miles of little-traveled pavement ahead of you. If you walk down the road, the Longhunter Trail located at the Upper Picnic Area is a worthy side trip (36.74469N & 83.71058W). This 0.2-mile trail explores a high cliff band containing a small arch before circling underneath the CCC-era bridge affording an unusual perspective on the beautiful construction of the bridge.

While no backcountry camping is allowed in the Pine Mountain State Park, there is a 36-site campground open April through October. The campground lacks electric hookups, but it does have showers, so it is perfect for those looking to camp in tents. The park also features a lodge, a restaurant, cottages, and a golf course.

Two areas within the park are preserved as part of the Kentucky State Nature Preserves system. The small Hemlock Garden area behind Herndon Evans Lodge protects a small old growth forest of huge hemlock, beech, and tulip poplars. The larger area on the south slopes of Pine Mountain protects the habitats of two plants rare in the Commonwealth and includes the trails from below the Chained Rock to above Laurel Cove.

OTHER HIKING OPTIONS

1. Short and Sweet. If you start from Lookout Point, the Chained Rock is about a 1.0-mile round-trip hike.

2. The 0.2-mile Longhunter Trail features a small arch and a unique view of an historic CCC-era bridge.

3. The Azalea Trail is a scenic 0.5-mile loop hike near the start of the Laurel Cove Trail. Both are located off the road to the Chained Rock.

4. The other trails at Pine Mountain State Resort Park all start from Herndon Evans Lodge located off KY 190, four miles from US 25E. Hemlock Garden is a 1.1-mile semi-loop trail that passes by an CCC-era picnic shelter, and goes through some old growth forest with hemlock and tulip poplars reaching over 100 feet tall. Honeymoon Falls is a 1.5 mile semi-loop to a wet weather falls. The Living Stairway and Fern Garden Trails are nested loops 0.5 and 1.4 miles long. The new 1.5-mile Ridge Runner Trails connect to both the Fern Garden and Honeymoon Falls Trails. The other new trail at Pine Mountain is the 1.5-mile Clear Hollow Trail which connects routes 190 and 191 south of the lodge area.

II.

DANIEL BOONE COUNTRY— SOUTH

10

Blue Heron Loop

TOTAL DISTANCE: The loop is 6.4 miles around. Horses use a small part of the trail.

HIKING TIME: About 3.5 hours

DIFFICULTY: Moderate

LOCATION: Big South Fork National River and Recreation Area, about 10 miles south of Whitley City

MAPS: USGS Barthell and National Geographic/Trails Illustrated Big South Fork National River and Recreation Area

Blue Heron Loop contains all that is great about hiking in the Big South Fork country in a single hiking trail. You'll see spectacular geology up close in the narrow passage through Crack-in-the-Rock, enjoy spacious views over the Big South Fork from overlooks both next to the river and from high above it, and relive history in a restored coal mining camp.

GETTING THERE

From the junction of US 27 and KY 92, drive west on KY 92 through Stearns for 1.1 miles. Turn south on KY 1651 for 1.1 miles to Revlo, then turn right onto KY 742. Drive 6.8 miles on KY 742 (the Blue Heron or Mine 18 Road) to the Blue Heron Visitor Center and park (36.66983N & 84.54757W). A fun alternate way to reach Blue Heron is to ride the Big South Fork Scenic Railroad that operates seasonally from Stearns.

THE TRAIL

Even in a land where coal is king, many visitors are surprised to learn that the Blue Heron area isn't named for a bird. Blue Heron was the miners' name for a special type of coal mined at one of the many mining communities that dotted the Big South Fork in pre-park times. The community prospered when the mines were new and the digging relatively easy. But the good times didn't last. Usually, the coal companies were diligent about drilling out their coal so they'd know how thick their seams were, and how far they stretched. But at Blue Heron, the miners didn't drill enough holes to make an accurate estimate. The mines proved a disappointment to both the company and its workers. You'll see

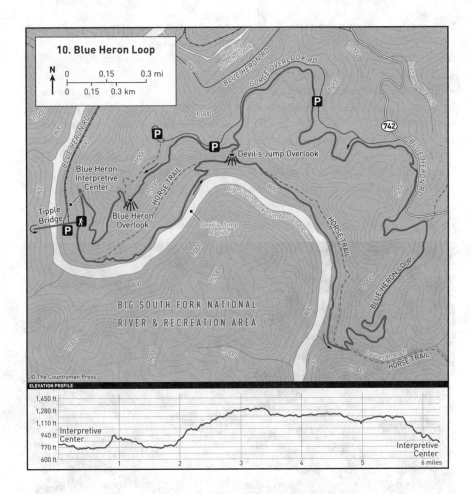

10. Blue Heron Loop

N

| 0 | 0.15 | 0.3 mi |
| 0 | 0.15 | 0.3 km |

BLUE HERON RD

Roaring Punch Creek

GORGE OVERLOOK RD

Yaccaro Branch

742

BLUE HERON RD

Devil's Jump Overlook

Blue Heron Interpretive Center

HORSE TRAIL

Tipple Bridge

Blue Heron Overlook

Big South Fork Cumberland River

Devil's Jump Rapids

HORSE TRAIL

BLUE HERON LOOP

BIG SOUTH FORK NATIONAL
RIVER & RECREATION AREA

Laurel Branch

HORSE TRAIL

© The Countryman Press

ELEVATION PROFILE

1,450 ft						
1,280 ft						
1,110 ft						
940 ft	Interpretive Center					
770 ft						Interpretive Center
600 ft	1	2	3	4	5	6 miles

plenty of remains of the mining era as you walk the loop, but be sure to leave enough time also to wander the interpretive displays and explore the Blue Heron tipple at the visitor center by the trailhead.

From far end of the visitor center, follow the trail leading upstream along the river to walk the loop in a counterclockwise direction. In 200 feet, a horse trail will split left. The horse trail offers a flatter and more direct, but also muddier, 1.9-mile route to the far end of the loop. At 0.6 mile, reach a side trail leading right to an overlook above Devil's Jump

Rapid, one of the most feared rapids on this stretch of the river. There is a small campsite opposite the side trail. Soon after passing the rapid, the loop enters a grassy area that is actually a reclaimed waste pile from the coal mines. After climbing two switchbacks, look for a set of stairs leading up the steep hillside to a right turn onto the horse trail leading to Bear Creek at 0.9 mile.

The horse trail follows a mining tram route, so enjoy some level walking with views of the river. Look closely here, and you'll see some thin, exposed coal seams and small pieces of the soft black rock scattered across the trail. Make a right turn off the horse trail at 1.2 miles (36.67347N & 84.53477W), descend gradually back to the river, and then pass a large well-used campsite above the river in a grove of pines. There's another well-used campsite near the mouth of Laurel Creek at 2.1 miles, where there is also a four-way trail junction with the horse trail (36.66376N & 84.52892W). The horse trail leads left to Blue Heron, and right to cross Laurel Branch, where the Lee Hollow Loop leads south to the Bear Creek Horse Camp.

At the mouth of Laurel Creek, the Blue Heron loop turns left, crosses the horse trail, and begins a long climb up switchbacks and stairs toward the rim of the canyon. At the base of the rim is a long, narrow rockhouse. Reach the rim at 3.0 miles where side paths lead right to KY 742 and the Blue Heron Campground

THE BIG SOUTH FORK NEAR BLUE HERON

in 0.6 mile (including the Blue Heron CG Road) (36.6698N & 84.5232W).

Follow the trail alongside KY 742 and then along the road to Devil's Jump Overlook, at one point climbing a set of stairs to walk alongside the road. At 3.5 miles, begin a steady descent. Reach a junction with a short spur trail leading to a trailhead on the Blue Heron Overlook Road at 4.6 miles. Pass one more trailhead at 5.0 miles before reaching

a side trail left at 5.1 miles to an overlook above Devil's Jump Rapid. The rapid and the narrows above it are even more intimidating from this aerial view than from our earlier, close-up encounters. At 5.6 miles, Blue Heron Overlook has benches and a wood canopy above the Blue Heron Tipple (36.67167N & 84.544W).

The Blue Heron Overlook marks the start of the trail's descent to the river. At 5.8 miles, reach an elaborate set of stairs and walkways through the giant boulders of Crack-in-the-rock. The narrow, shadowed passage lends the trail here an air of mystery and suspense, as hikers try to guess just where the path will lead. Crack-in-the-rock is a set of huge boulders that have split from the main rim of the Big South Fork gorge. The rock split along vertical fractures, and many of the blocks have come to rest leaning back against other blocks to form small arches.

The trail continues to descend and reaches the Blue Heron Visitor Center at 6.4 miles at the end of the loop. The visitor center contains an elaborate set of displays depicting the history of the coal and timber operations in the area, as well as the lives of the people that lived there. Here you can listen to the personal stories of life in the mining communities told in the original voices of the miners and their families.

The highlight of anyone's visit to Blue Heron will be a walk across the Tipple Bridge. The tipple was an elaborate operation that sorted the raw coal transported from the mines by size and quality for shipment to customers. Coal was brought in by rail on the tracks over the river, dumped into the top of the tipple, sorted and cleaned, then loaded into rail cars at the bottom of the tipple. The Park Service restored the tipple and bridge after taking over management of the area. A walk across the bridge gives an unprecedented view of the Big South Fork, and it is a useful connector to the Kentucky Trail on the west bank of the river.

As you enjoy the Big South Fork, be thankful that the area ever became a park. After the ravages of coal mining and clear cutting of timber, the land around the river was unable to support even the few people who chose to remain after the mines closed and the timber camps were shut down.

The US Army Corps of Engineers began looking at dam sites along the river to control flooding and to produce hydroelectric power for the region. A dam was first proposed at Devil's Jump as early as 1933. During the 1950s and 1960s, the dam was authorized by the US Senate, but not by the US House of Representatives. However, by this time, others began to realize the unique recreation value of the river and the steep gorge surrounding it. With the region's only national park in the Great Smoky Mountains badly congested, and since it was receiving more visits than any other national park, it was easy to see the benefits of converting the Big South Fork to a park instead of a reservoir.

By the early 1970s, the battle between developers and conservationists was settled by a bill establishing the Big South Fork National River and Recreation Area. The Army Corps of Engineers managed the 125,000-acre area until 1991, at which time it was turned over to the National Park Service. Only 114,000 acres of the park have been purchased. Several land parcels along the edge of the park still remain private land.

OTHER HIKING OPTIONS

1. Short and Sweet. The walk around the displays at Blue Heron and over the Tipple Bridge is less than 1 mile.
2. Additional short hikes nearby are the trails to unusual Split Bow Arch (0.6 mile semi-loop) and to the spectacular Bear Creek Overlook (0.5 mile out and back). Both trails leave from the same trailhead south of KY 742.
3. Across the Tipple Bridge is the Kentucky Trail, which leads south 1.6 miles to Dick Gap and 3.4 miles to Big Spring Falls. To the north, the Kentucky Trail leads 2.6 miles to Nancy Graves School Site and connects with the Koger-Yamacraw Loop.

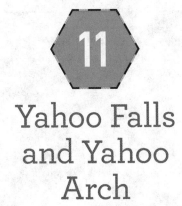

Yahoo Falls and Yahoo Arch

TOTAL DISTANCE: The entire 9.7-mile loop combines the Big South Fork Yahoo Falls Trails plus the Daniel Boone National Forest Yahoo Arch, Negro Creek, and Sheltowee Trace Trails. The shortest route to Yahoo Falls, Kentucky's highest waterfall, is 0.4-mile round-trip. Progressively longer hikes lead to Yahoo Arch, to Markers Arch, and to a loop using part of the STT.

HIKING TIME: About 5 hours for the full loop

DIFFICULTY: Moderate

GENERAL LOCATION: Big South Fork National River and Recreation Area (BSFNRRA) and Stearns Ranger District, about 5 miles northwest of Whitley City

MAPS: USGS Barthell and Nevelsville, and National Geographic/Trails Illustrated Big South Fork National River and Recreation Area

If you like to have a lot of options when you hike, the Yahoo Falls area will be perfect for you. Depending on your energy level, and the time available, you can walk anywhere between one half mile and ten miles here. Each extra mile adds another treat, so there's little incentive to stop and turn back before the loop is complete. The full loop has two road crossings, so if you can arrange a shuttle or car drop off, almost any length of hike is possible.

GETTING THERE

Two miles north of Whitley City, leave US 27 and turn west onto KY 700. In 2.8 miles, cross an alternate trailhead for Yahoo Arch Trail (DBNF 602). At 4.0 miles, turn right onto a gravel road with a sign reading "1.5 miles to Yahoo Falls Picnic Area" (36.76184N & 84.52795W). Reach the day use only picnic area shortly after entering the BSFNRRA. The trailhead is at the far end of the picnic area near a signboard and restrooms (36.77373N & 84.52419W). If you plan to camp overnight, you must continue straight on KY 700 for another 1.6 miles and park at Alum Ford boat launch and campground (36.76514N & 84.54535W).

THE TRAIL

Before you start the hike, take a good look at the Yahoo Falls trail map on the signboard at the trailhead. It looks complicated, doesn't it? Well, don't worry. Even though the real trail system is every bit as confusing as the map, finding your way to the falls and back really isn't that hard. The main thing to remember is that the BSFNRRA divides the trails into three loops, the Topside (yellow blazes), Cliffside (green blazes),

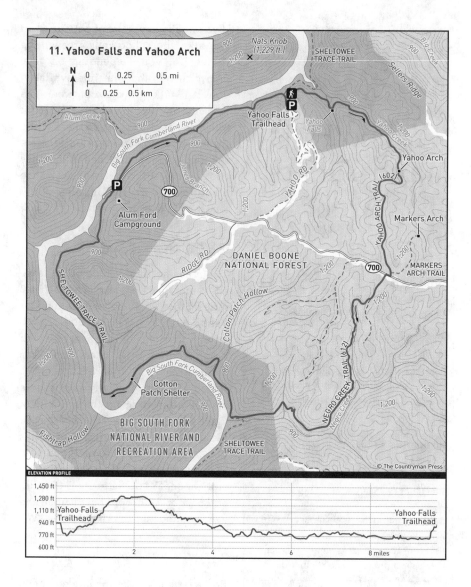

11. Yahoo Falls and Yahoo Arch

ELEVATION PROFILE

and Cascade (blue blazes). These loops overlap in several places. For example, the section of trail that leaves from the trailhead is part of all three loops. Lying below all three loops, and closest to the Cumberland River, is the Sheltowee Trace Trail.

This loop will describe the shortest route to Yahoo Falls and Yahoo Arch. Hikers who have only time to explore the Yahoo Falls area should at least continue around the Blue Loop to Roaring Rocks Cataract.

From the trailhead, pass a short side trail on the left leading to an overlook. Take the next left turn, which leads downhill on a long set of narrow metal stairs along a green-blazed trail. Pass by the next junction, where a trail at your left leads to the STT. Beyond this junction, enter the huge natural amphitheater that holds Yahoo Falls (36.77232N & 84.51957W) at 0.4 mile. The Falls pours over the lip of a mammoth rockhouse in a narrow ribbon of glistening water. Here, water freefalls 113 feet from the lip to crash into a tiny plunge pool. The creek that feeds the falls is a small one. It's the setting of the falls, not the power of its water, that make this a special place. The opening of this magnificent rockhouse stretches for several hundred feet in a broad semi-circle.

On the far side of the Yahoo Falls, pass two branches of the blue–blazed Cascade Trail. Follow the yellow blazes uphill to a signed junction with the Yahoo Arch Spur Trail. Turn left onto the spur trail to Yahoo Arch (DBNF 602) (36.77236N & 84.51754W) at 0.6 mile. As you approach the arch, watch the bluffs for a good lesson on how arches are formed. The first stage is the sheer solid cliffs formed from massive sandstone. As weaker layers below the sandstone are eroded, part of the base of the cliffs gives way, and shallow overhangs are formed. As overhangs become deeper, those with thin roofs may collapse, forming an arch. At the back of the Yahoo Arch, you can see the fallen blocks of sandstone that once formed the roof of the rockhouse at Yahoo Arch. Yahoo Arch is larger than most in the region, with a 70' by 50' span and a height of nearly 20 feet. If you look closely at the far side, notice that it is really a double arch, if you count a small opening on the left.

Leave Yahoo Arch at 1.4 miles (36.76656N & 84.51091W), and climb stone steps to gain the top of a broad ridge where you may encounter fallen pines killed in 2001/2002 by the southern pine beetle. In late spring and summer, bluets, fire pinks, and robin's plantain, along with scattered white blazes, decorate the old roadway that the trail follows. At 2.3 miles, just before the crossing of KY 700, reach a signed junction with the Markers Arch Trail (DBNF 603) (36.7569N & 84.51202W). Arch lovers should take a side trip down to this small arch (36.76033N & 84.50877W), which adds 0.8 mile round-trip to the hike. Like Yahoo Arch, Markers Arch also resembles the remains of a collapsed rockhouse. The thin span is 12 feet tall and 25 feet long.

Back at KY 700, walk 200 feet right up the road to gated DBNF Road 6003. This is the starting point for the Negro Creek Trail (DBNF 612). Follow the road for 0.2 mile past an old burned area to the right of the trail. At a powerline, look for an arrow on a pole that points toward stairs carved into a short rock face. The footpath, now marked with white diamond blazes, winds around the head of Negro Creek, then follows it on the slope above. About a mile from KY 700, there is an informal campsite to the right of the trail. As the trail approaches the Sheltowee Trace Trail, make several crossings of old two-track dirt roads in quick succession.

Intersect the Sheltowee Trace Trail at 4.6 miles at a well-signed junction (36.74355N & 84.53138W). A large, popular campsite here, next to the river, has a sandy beach, ideal for a lunch break or an overnight stay. If you decide to spend the night, the best source of water for this campsite is just south on the Sheltowee Trace, where the trail crosses Negro Creek on a wooden bridge. On the rest of this hike, you'll never stray far from the river until the final climb back to the Yahoo Falls Picnic Area. Although powerboats use

YAHOO FALLS

this section of the river, which is now part of Lake Cumberland, the walk is usually quiet and peaceful. There's a signed bridge over Cotton Patch Creek at 5.0 miles, where the trail looks down into a giant's jigsaw puzzle of house-sized boulders wedged into the narrow creek bed. In spring, the forest floor is covered by the bright yellow buds and variegated leaves of the yellow trillium, May apple, and purple violets. At 5.8 miles, a faint side trail leads left to the Cotton Patch Shelter (84.53138N & 84.54364W). No water, except for that from the river, is available here. Just beyond the shelter, a huge chimney marks an old homestead.

Cross one more creek before walking through the Alum Ford Primitive Campground and reaching another crossing of KY 700 at 7.9 miles (36.76514N & 84.54535W). The small, primitive campground offers tent sites, with picnic tables, a boat launch, and latrines. Follow KY 700 to the right for 200 feet before turning left at a sign indicating that Yahoo Falls is 2 miles away. You'll pass two "pour over" waterfalls along small creeks before reaching a junction with the green-blazed Cliffside Trail at Yahoo Falls at 9.3 miles (36.7735N & 84.52556W) alongside a mammoth-sized block of sandstone. Unless you yearn for another view of Yahoo Falls, turn right and begin a steady climb. The bluffs here are so steep that the park has installed metal ladders to help hikers get up the roughest sections. Near the top, ignore the spur trails leading right to picnic sites. The trail rejoins the picnic area at 9.7 miles, just beyond a final fenced overlook.

OTHER HIKING OPTIONS

1. Short and Sweet. The dense network of short trails surrounding Yahoo Falls is confusing to many hikers, but it provides numerous vantage points for viewing the falls and Roaring Rock Cataract. Round-trip to Yahoo Falls only is 0.5 mile.

2. A round-trip hike to Yahoo Arch is 3.0 miles. Adding Markers Arch increases the total to 5.6 miles. Alternatively, Markers Arch can be reached from KY 700 on a 0.8-mile round-trip hike.

3. Yahoo Falls is also a convenient starting point for longer trips on the Sheltowee Trace Trail. South of the loop, the STT leads 3.0 miles to Yamacraw Bridge on KY 92. North of the loop, the STT leads out of the BSFNRRA 6.8 miles to cross US 27 north of Stearns.

Kentucky Trail, Ledbetter Trailhead to Troublesome Creek

TOTAL DISTANCE: A 9.4 mile out-and-back hike. A short cut via the Hill Cemetery Road on the return leg makes for an 8.8-mile semi-loop. Horses share some of these trails.

HIKING TIME: About 5 hours

DIFFICULTY: Moderate/Difficult

LOCATION: Big South Fork National River and Recreation Area, about 16 miles southwest of Stearns

MAPS: USGS Barthell and Oneida North, and National Geographic/Trails Illustrated Big South Fork National River and Recreation Area

The Kentucky Trail is a 27-mile alternate route to the Sheltowee Trace Trail between the Peters Mountain Trailhead and Yamacraw Bridge. The section between Ledbetter Trailhead and Troublesome Creek travels some of the park's most remote backcountry and makes a fine day hike or overnight trip. Here the trail traverses the banks of both the Big South Fork and Troublesome Creek in an area where the inner gorge of the river is especially narrow.

GETTING THERE

From the junction of KY 1363 and KY 92, at the west end of the Yamacraw Bridge over the Big South Fork, turn south onto KY 1363. Drive 2.3 miles and turn left onto Beach Grove (also called Devil's Branch) Road. In 1.3 miles, go straight on the paved road at a 4-way intersection where the Sheltowee Trace Trail crosses the road. Keep on the main road for 2.7 miles to a junction just beyond Beach Grove Church. Go right at this junction for 0.9 mile, and then turn left onto gravel Ledbetter Road. The trailhead is 1.6 miles down this road on the left side of the road, with parking a short distance farther on the right. (36.63914N & 84.56157W).

THE TRAIL

From the Ledbetter Trailhead, follow the Kentucky Trail south along the dirt road. At 0.2 mile, the road forks (36.63589N & 84.56243W). The lesser-used fork that splits right to Hill Cemetery is a horse trail that can be used as an alternate return route from Oil Well Branch. At 0.6 mile, the trail leaves the road on a foot trail branching to the right. A sign indicates that the trail ahead is closed to vehicles and horses.

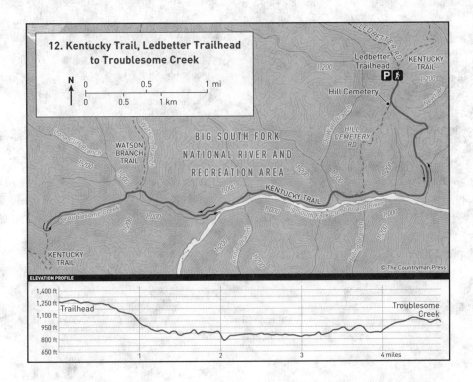

12. Kentucky Trail, Ledbetter Trailhead to Troublesome Creek

BIG SOUTH FORK NATIONAL RIVER AND RECREATION AREA

ELEVATION PROFILE

Descend from the plateau through craggy cliff bands covered by thick dark hemlock forest.

You will reach the Big South Fork River at a junction in 1.5 miles, just after crossing two short foot bridges (36.62519N & 84.55887W). To the left is an unmaintained old route that continues down the inner gorge. Turn right and follow the powerful river upstream, which is compressed into several small rapids by huge boulders that clog the river bed. A small, sandy beach offers an invitation to swim. At 2.1 miles, a steep graveled road joins the route on the right (36.62519N & 84.56869W). This is the bottom end of the horse trail down Hill Cemetery Road that splits from the Kentucky Trail at the 0.2-mile point. Next to this junction is a large campsite on the riverbank.

Just beyond the junction, at Oil Well Branch, is the first of two bridges built in 2001 by volunteers from the Student Conservation Association (SCA). Look for a sign on the left noting a short path leading to the Beatty Oil Well, which was drilled in 1818. The well was finally plugged recently by the NPS as part of a larger effort to plug abandoned oil and gas wells in the BSF.

According to Dreaver et al., the Beatty Well was the first commercial oil well drilled in the country. The discovery was an accident, however; the hole was drilled in the hope of finding brine to make salt. The flowing well along the riverbank became the site of the first commercial oil spill in the country. It wasn't long before residents downstream began to complain about the crude oil in the river.

FOOTBRIDGE OVER DIFFICULTY CREEK

The next mile and a half of trail continue to follow the narrow gorge alongside the Big South Fork. Huge boulders that have broken loose from the cliffs above line the route, and large, cone-shaped piles of smaller debris (called talus) cover the base of some cliffs. Much of the area north of the river was burned in the 1999 Watson Fire. In some areas, the fire burned extremely hot, destroying all life in its path, while in other areas, the fire was smaller, and most trees survived with only a blackening of their base to mark the fire's passage.

At 2.9 miles is the second of the 2001 SCA bridges near where the trail leaves the Big South Fork (84.56869N & 84.59107W). Just beyond the bridge is a large campsite between the trail and the river. At 3.5 miles, leave the main road on the right to briefly follow a foot trail before rejoining the main road and proceeding up Troublesome Creek. If you stay on the main road here, ignore a less-used branch that fords Troublesome Creek, and continue south along the trail along the bank of the Big South Fork.

Pass a campsite and make a rock-hop crossing of Watson Fork to reach a signed junction at 4.1 miles (36.62614N & 84.60176W). Here the old road branches right to lead to the Divide Road in 2.7 miles. The right fork is shown on the most recent Trails Illustrated map for the park as the Watson Branch Trail, but on my visit in 2014, the trail had not been signed or blazed. However, it is an old road (once considered as a potential route for the Sheltowee Trace), and it is easy to follow for experienced hikers.

The Kentucky Trail takes the left fork where a sign indicates that Difficulty Creek is 3 miles. Make another potentially wet rock hop crossing of Lone Cliff Creek. Continue along the north bank of Troublesome Creek, enjoying views of

the small creek and dense groves of rhododendrons. Reach the footbridge over Troublesome Creek at 4.7 miles, which marks the end of this hike (36.62179N & 84.61402W). Beyond Troublesome Creek, the Kentucky Trail climbs up and over the divide to Difficulty Creek. The west end of the Kentucky Trail is 7.7 miles away via Cat Ridge Road, the Laurel Hill Trail, and the Laurel Ridge Road.

You could return to the Ledbetter Trailhead by retracing your steps, or by taking the shorter, and less scenic, Hill Cemetery Road. Hill Cemetery Road is 1.1 miles long. This shortcut saves 0.6 mile on the return. This road climbs very steeply from the bottom of the gorge through an area heavily damaged by the Watson Fire. The road was surfaced with a layer of gravel, probably to enable access by the equipment used to plug the Beatty oil well. Once on the rim of the gorge, the road is gated and is usable by 4WD vehicles. It passes a low rockhouse with a classically arched roof. Just before joining the Ledbetter Road, pass Hill Cemetery, which was used by both the Hill and Watson families.

The wild heart of the Big South Fork is drained by three creeks named No Business, Difficulty, and Troublesome. Christened back in pre-Chamber of Commerce days, these creeks tell the story of the hard times and bleak prospects faced by the first pioneers who moved to the area. Poor soils and steep slopes made farming marginal, while working in the coal mines or on the timber crews offered hard work, low wages, and little job security. It is no wonder now that people have abandoned what few settlements there were.

Back before pioneer times the Big South Fork was rich in game. Elk, deer, and black bear roamed the woods. But the early settlers killed off much of the game, and loss of habitat spelled the end for some species. Black bears were absent from the region since at least the early 1900s. But by the 1980s, bears were moving back into the Daniel Boone National Forest north of the park, and park managers expected that soon some bears would enter the park itself.

A study commissioned from the BSF-NRRA by the University of Tennessee determined that the Big South Fork contained excellent bear habitat, and it was large enough to support a viable population of bears. After a round of sometimes contentious public hearings, an experimental release of bears relocated from Great Smoky Mountain National Park was begun in 1996. Twelve adult females were transplanted to the Big South Fork in two stages. Some summer released bears immediately fled the area, traveling as far as Knoxville and Chattanooga. Researchers had better luck with their second crop, pregnant females moved while hibernating in their winter dens.

The release has been a success so far. By 2001 the population had risen to 30 bears and they are now frequently seen in the park. The current estimate is that almost 300 bears live in the park with the majority of those on the Tennessee side. Hikers in the backcountry and particularly those camping overnight, should follow the food storage guidelines and backcountry suggestions from the park.

OTHER HIKING OPTIONS

1. Short and Sweet. The hike from the trailhead to the river and back via Hill Cemetery Road is 3.4 miles.
2. The Kentucky Trail leads 7.7 miles west from Troublesome Creek, and 14.8 miles north from Ledbetter Trailhead past Blue Heron and Wilson Ridge to Yamacraw Bridge. The Sheltowee Trace-Kentucky Trail Loop between Peters Mountain Trailhead and Yamacraw Bridge is 42.6 miles.

Koger— Yamacraw Loop

TOTAL DISTANCE: This 11.1-mile semi-loop includes a short side trip to Koger Arch. Two short sections of this loop follow gravel roads.

HIKING TIME: About 6 hours

DIFFICULTY: Difficult

LOCATION: Big South Fork National River and Recreation Area and Stearns Ranger District, about 5 miles west of Stearns

MAPS: USGS Barthell and National Geographic/Trails Illustrated Big South Fork National River and Recreation Area

The Koger-Yamacraw Loop combines the north end of the Kentucky Trail with the Sheltowee Trace Trail. These scenic trails are little used, but they offer a visit to Koger Arch as well as streamside hiking along both Rock Creek and the Big South Fork. The loop does require two fords of Rock Creek, which can be dangerous in high water; six potentially wet crossings of Grassy Fork; and two short sections of little-traveled gravel road on Wilson Ridge.

GETTING THERE

To reach the Yamacraw Bridge Trailhead from Stearns, drive 5.4 miles west on KY 92 and park in the gravel lot at the northeast corner of the bridge over the Big South Fork (36.72531N & 84.54306W).

THE TRAIL

From the trailhead, walk west on the Sheltowee Trace Trail across Yamacraw Bridge to KY 1363. At the far end of the bridge, turn left off of KY 1363 onto a river access dirt road. Where the road makes a turn to the left, the Sheltowee Trace continues straight ahead into the woods. The Sheltowee Trace here is infrequently blazed, but you will find a few of the STT white turtle blazes to guide you. Here, the trail is wedged into a thin strip of land between the river and KY 1363. Pass a small beach at 0.7 mile, and then follow an overgrown two-track dirt road. Watch carefully for poison ivy here.

At 0.9 mile, the trail passes under a mammoth railroad bridge across the Big South Fork. The coal trains have long ago quit rumbling towards Stearns, so the bridge is now inactive. At 1.2 miles, the trail reaches a powerline cut that may be choked with vegetation and nearly

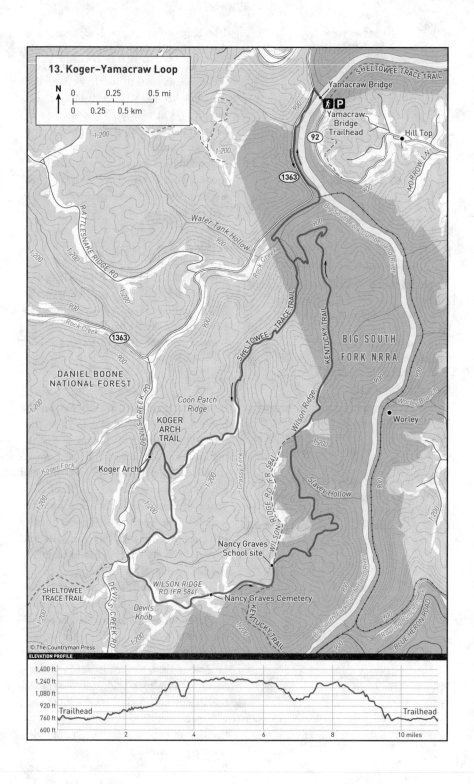

13. Koger–Yamacraw Loop

ELEVATION PROFILE

impassable in summer. Just beyond is a signed junction with the bypass route of the Sheltowee Trace around the Rock Creek Ford, which may be needed if water levels are high. The bypass route climbs the bank to KY 1363 and then follows the Devils Creek (or Beach Grove) Road 2.4 miles up to Wilson Ridge where it rejoins the STT via the Koger Arch Trail. To continue on the main route, turn left at the junction and reach the signed ford across Rock Creek at 1.4 miles (36.71368N & 84.54856W). Normally, this wide stream is less than knee-deep and the rocky bottom is easy walking, but remember that the ford can be dangerous in high water.

Go straight across Rock Creek and climb the bank of the creek. Next, cross Grassy Fork and look for a blaze on the far bank. There is a campsite located here. From this point, the trail begins a long trip up the valley of Grassy Fork, one of the highlights of the loop. At 1.6 miles, the Kentucky Trail, your return route, enters on the left (36.7117N & 84.54678W). The STT heads steadily up the valley on the bed of an old coal road. Farther up the valley, the trail begins four potentially wet crossings of Grassy Fork and its tributaries. You'll pass a six-foot high cascade, huge boulders shed from the sandstone cliffs, and a lush fern garden in the upper valley. At 2.5 miles, the portal of an abandoned coal mine has been broken open. This old mine, like most others, is partly flooded and is likely to be very unstable. It's hard to overemphasize the danger that wandering into old mines presents. Opposite the old mine is a potential campsite.

After two more crossings of Grassy Fork, the trail leaves the valley floor by following a small branch to the right. It eventually reaches a power line cut at 2.9 miles. This cut can be overgrown and difficult to penetrate in summer. Switch back underneath the road before crossing the powerline again on an old roadway. At 3.3 miles, turn right off the roadway onto an overgrown, unmarked foot trail where the roadway is blocked by a large brush pile (36.6937N & 84.55933W). Reach an old road (DBNF 6120) and signed trail junction on a ridgetop at 3.5 miles (36.69456N & 84.561W).

From this junction, the Koger Arch Trail (DBNF 633) leads right to Koger Arch in 0.2 mile. To take the side trip, just cross the road 50 feet to your right and descend a series of switchbacks to reach the arch at 3.7 miles. The DBNF lists this arch as 18 feet high and 91 feet long. This massive arch can be an oasis of cold air on a hot summer day and a welcome resting place after a difficult climb. Native flowers appreciate the cold air, also, and you might spot red columbine blooming underneath the arch. The Devils Creek Road Trailhead is another 0.2 mile down the Koger Arch Trail and the bypass route for the Rock Creek Ford enters the main route here also.

Return to the signed junction at 3.9 miles, and continue to follow the old dirt road and STT to the south. If you have battled the thick growth of summer in the powerline cuts, now is the time to reap your rewards. Much of this old road is lined with a feast of blackberries for hikers whose timing is right. Follow the road until it comes to a 4-way junction at 4.7 miles (36.68626N & 84.56527W).

At this junction, the paved Devils Creek/Beech Grove Road goes right down to Rock Creek and straight towards the Ledbetter Trailhead. The Sheltowee Trace Trail to the south follows the paved road straight for 0.1 mile before branching off to the right onto another dirt DBNF Road 6127. Our route leaves the STT and makes a sharp left to follow the Wilson Ridge Road. This

KOGER ARCH

stretch of road is little traveled but is necessary in order to connect the STT and Kentucky Trails. At 5.4 miles, pass the modern Nancy Graves Cemetery. Leave the road at 6.0 miles, opposite a wide parking area on the left. This is the site of Nancy Graves School, which burned "long ago" according to a local resident. From the school site (36.68535N & 84.54887W), bushwhack straight into the woods for 50 feet until you intersect the Kentucky Trail, which will be marked by the green squares and white on red arrowheads of the BSF. If you come out in exactly the right place, you should see a trail sign for the school site. From this point Blue Heron is 3.6 miles to your right on the Kentucky Trail and the junction with the Sheltowee Trace is 2.8 miles to the left.

Turn left onto the Kentucky Trail, which follows the rim of Wilson Ridge. Take a look at a small rockhouse and a vista across the gorge. This is also a good spot to look for yellow trillium during the spring wildflower bloom. The trail comes

to a rebuilt wooden bridge at 6.9 miles. Pass a few more small rockhouses and cross under a powerline before rejoining the Wilson Ridge Road at a fork at 7.5 miles (36.69737N & 84.54574W).

Take the left fork onto the gravel road and keep left at the junction with the Wilson Ridge Cemetery Road. At 8.5 miles, beside a solitary home on the left side, Wilson Ridge Road turns from gravel to dirt. Continue straight, and cross under the junction of a major powerline with a smaller one. At 8.9 miles, turn left off the crest of the ridge at an unsigned split in the road. The trail soon switches back sharply to the left off the old road onto an intricately constructed section of trail featuring delicate rock steps. You'll cross a bridge over Grassy Fork before rejoining the Sheltowee Trace and closing the loop at 9.6 miles. Turn right onto the Sheltowee Trace and retrace your route across the Rock Creek ford, reaching the trailhead at 11.1 miles.

This unofficial loop uses trails managed by both the Big South Fork NRRA and the Stearns Ranger District of the DBNF. From Yamacraw Bridge to Rock Creek, the route is part of the Big South Fork. The remainder of the STT is in the National Forest. The Kentucky Trail is also in the BSF until it reaches the Wilson Creek Road, which is the boundary of the area.

OTHER HIKING OPTIONS

1. Short and Sweet. Koger Arch can be reached in 1.0 mile from the junction of the Sheltowee Trace and the Devils Creek/Beach Grove Road. There is an alternate trailhead on the Devils Creek/Beech Grove Road 0.8 mile from KY 1363, but there is no parking along the road. The 0.4-mile trail is marked with white diamond blazes and reaches the arch in 0.2 mile.

2. To the north from Yamacraw bridge the Sheltowee Trace Trail leads 1.4 miles to an intersection with the Lick Creek Trail (DBNF 631), and 2.9 miles to the Negro Creek Trail (DBNF 612). Princess Falls is located 0.2 mile along the Lick Creek Trail, and at 1.2 miles is the beginning of the 0.6-mile side trail to Lick Creek Falls (DBNF l631A).

3. If water levels in Rock Creek are too high, the loop can be accessed from Blue Heron via the Kentucky Trail at the end of the Tipple Bridge. This access adds four miles to the loop as the distance from the Tipple Bridge is much longer than that from the Yamacraw Highway Bridge. Also, the crossing of Lin Hollow Creek on the Kentucky Trail and the six crossings of Grassy Fork on the Sheltowee Trace are potentially wet in high water.

14

Gobblers Arch and Mark Branch Falls

TOTAL DISTANCE: A 6.1-mile loop for hikers that uses a short section of forest service road. The loop combines the Sheltowee Trace Trail with the Gobblers Arch Trail (DBNF 636), and with small portions of DBNF Road 6105 and DBNF Road 569, the Divide Road. The Sheltowee Trace Trail can be very wet at high water.

HIKING TIME: About 3.5 hours

DIFFICULTY: Moderate/Difficult

LOCATION: Stearns Ranger District, about 20 miles west of Stearns

MAPS: USGS Bell Farm and Barthell SW and Trails Illustrated Big South Fork National River and Recreation Area

The area around the Big South Fork is nowhere near crowded, by the standards of areas such as Red River Gorge or Great Smoky Mountains National Park. But still it is nice to know of a few backcountry hideaways, where any hiker can reach a beautiful spot with solitude almost assured. Gobblers Arch and Mark Branch Falls have the scenery that would draw a crowd in almost any park. But being a long way from anywhere protects them from being overrun. Chances are you'll hear the lonesome call of the coyote more than you'll see the faces of other hikers. If you are willing to drive long miles on lonely gravel roads, this loop is for you.

GETTING THERE

From the junction of KY 92 and KY 1363 on the west side of the Yamacraw Bridge over the Big South Fork, drive west on KY 1363 for 11.2 miles. Here the road splits between Bell Farm Horse Camp and Hemlock Grove Picnic Area. Follow the gravel road (DBNF 139) on the left, past the horse camp, for 4.5 miles to a T-junction. Straight ahead at the junction is the Peters Mountain Trailhead (36.62346N & 84.68929W). The gravel road leading right is the Divide Road (DBNF 569), which will take you to Pickett State Park in Tennessee in 10.6 miles. The gravel road leading left is the Laurel Ridge Road (DBNF 575), as well as being the northbound Sheltowee Trace Trail, which follows the road for 1.6 miles. The southbound Sheltowee Trace starts from the corner of the Divide Road and DBNF Road 139. The Peters Mountain trailhead now features a latrine. Only the concrete footings remain from a fire tower that once stood here.

An alternate way to reach the loop during low water would be to drive to the Hemlock Grove Picnic Area and

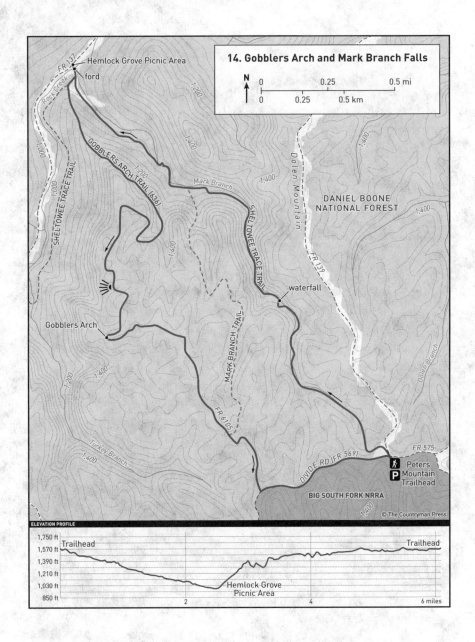

14. Gobblers Arch and Mark Branch Falls

ELEVATION PROFILE

ford Rock Creek to join the loop near the junction of the Sheltowee Trace and Gobblers Arch Trails.

THE TRAIL

This hike is unusual in that it starts at the high end, rather than from the bot-

tom. So make sure to take your time, and reserve plenty of energy for the climb back to the plateau from Rock Creek. Also, be aware that the Sheltowee Trace features many crossing of Marks Branch, and that these crossings can be wet and cold when the water is up. From the Peters Mountain Trailhead, begin hik-

WATERFALL ALONG MARK BRANCH

ing north on the Sheltowee Trace Trail towards the trail's south end in Pickett State Park, blazed with the trail's familiar white turtle emblem and the white diamonds typical of the DBNF trails. The forest here is typical of the dry plateau supporting a variety of pines, hemlock, red maple, and sassafras. The trail soon dips beneath the first set of cliff bands. Traveling alongside a series of shallow overhangs in the sandstone cliffs, watch for fascinating iron concretions threaded through the rock.

The trail next drops into the very narrow valley of Mark Branch. Soon you can see where forest service trail crews have cut an almost unbelievable amount of downed timber from the trail. It almost seems as if Mother Nature changed her mind about having a valley here and decided to fill it in with fallen trees. The forest service has done a commendable job of keeping this route clear.

As you descend further down the valley, hemlock and rhododendron become the dominant trees. At 0.6 mile is a small campsite opposite a rockhouse that might be useful for long-distance hikers on the Sheltowee Trace Trail. Just beyond, watch for a large cave in the cliffs on the opposite side of the creek. At 0.9 mile, reach the base of a 30-foot waterfall, where Mark Branch pours over the rim of a resistant bed of sandstone into a tiny plunge pool at the center of a spacious rock amphitheatre. Through most of the year, this is a modest column of water, but after heavy storms, water gushes over the lip and the pool.

Beyond the falls, the trail is less used and can be wet or muddy. There often is simply not enough room in the narrow valley floor to get the trail away from the creek, so this section can be wet in high water. But consider these obstacles a chance for close-up views of the mammoth boulders and blowdowns that choke the valley floor. Eventually the valley opens up somewhat, and the trail becomes fern-lined and friendlier.

At 1.6 miles is the unsigned junction with the Mark Branch Trail (DBNF Trail 635) (36.63816N & 84.70362W). This trail is a useful bypass route for northbound hikers who might find the previous section of the Sheltowee Trace Trail closed due to heavy rain or storm damage. Mark Branch can be used to reach the Gobblers Arch Trail in 1.3 miles and the Peters Mountain Trailhead in 2.3 miles, but these shortcuts do not go past Gobblers Arch.

Below the junction with Mark Branch is another section of Kentucky canyoneering where the trail and creek are compressed into the bottom of a shear narrow canyon. The trail will soon exit the canyon on the west side, but this turn may not always be well marked. Near the confluence of Mark Branch and Rock Creek at 2.2 miles, look for a signed junction with the Sheltowee Trace Trail in a small meadow by a large cedar and a tumbled rock cairn (36.64412N & 84.71131W). In summer, look for the prominent orange heads of butterfly milkweed amid the meadow's vibrant growth. An unmarked route leads straight from the junction to a ford over Rock Creek, where Mark Branch joins the path. This unsigned route leads to Hemlock Grove Picnic Area, an alternate starting point for this hike. Horses sometimes use this ford as the start of the trip to Gobblers Arch.

To continue on the loop, follow the Sheltowee Trace Trail, which turns left up the bank of Rock Creek to reach the junction with the Gobblers Arch Trail (DBNF 636) at 2.3 miles. If you miss this turn, you'll follow the STT along Rock Creek for five miles, passing the Great

Meadows Campground, before reaching a signed junction with the Parker Mountain Trail. Turn left onto the Gobblers Arch Trail, leaving the STT, and begin a steep climb. Watch out for poison ivy on the lower section of this trail. After the trail moves away from the nose of the ridge, pass to the left of an imposing chimney rock. Next is a shaded rockhouse where fire pinks flourish well into the summer. Continue along the bluff line until reaching a small draw, where the trail exits on a switchback to the right. Rejoin the ridge crest where there is a small overlook above Rock Creek with "winter views." At 3.7 miles is a signed side trail to a better overlook above the creek. Beyond the overlook, the trail follows the base of a twenty-foot high band of cliffs.

At 4.3 miles, reach Gobblers Arch (36.63024N & 84.70916W). The arch is about 10 feet high, 50 feet wide, and 15 feet across. It appears more like a wide tunnel through a narrow ridge of sandstone than it does a classic arch. Though others may have camped here before you, the Daniel Boone National Forest prohibits camping in arches and rockhouses. Walk through the arch, and climb switchbacks to reach the top of it.

At 4.5 miles, join DBNF Road 6105 at the road's end. Turn right on the road, and follow past an old turnaround beyond which the road is somewhat more used. At 5.1 miles is a signed junction with the Mark Branch Trail leading back down to join the STT near Mark Branch (36.62506N & 84.70071W). At 5.6 miles reach the Divide Road (DBNF 569) (36.62217N & 84.69852W) and follow it to the left to return to the Peters Mountain Trailhead at 6.1 miles.

OTHER HIKING OPTIONS

1. Short and Sweet. Via DBNF Road 6105, it is a 2.6-mile round trip to Gobblers Arch.
2. From the Gobblers Arch Trail, the Sheltowee Trace Trail leads 14.9 miles south to Pickett State Park. The Rock Creek Loop in the Tennessee portion of the BSF and the Hidden Passage Loop in Tennessee's Pickett State Park are two excellent loops that use parts of the STT.
3. Backpackers can make a 27 mile, three day loop by combining the Rock Creek Loop, STT, Laurel Hill, Kentucky, and John Muir Trails.
4. The 0.4-mile Buffalo Arch (DBNF 634A) and 2.4-mile Parker Mountain (DBNF 634) Trails are both in the Stearns Ranger District just west of this loop. The spectacular winged buttress of Buffalo Arch is one of the largest arches in the DBNF and can be reached with only a 0.8-mile hike.

Natural Arch Scenic Area

TOTAL DISTANCE: A 6.8-mile semi-loop on the Natural Arch and Buffalo Canyon Trails that uses a short stretch of a gravel road. No horses or mountain bikes are allowed.

HIKING TIME: About 3.5 hours

DIFFICULTY: Easy/Moderate

LOCATION: Stearns Ranger District, 7 miles northwest of Whitley City

MAPS: USGS Nevelsville and DBNF Natural Arch Scenic Area

The Natural Arch Scenic Area protects 945 acres of the Stearns Ranger District centered around spectacular Natural Arch. This mammoth structure rivals Natural Bridge in the state park near Red River Gorge for the most impressive sandstone span in the Cumberland region. While most visitors stay on the one-mile Natural Arch Trail, a longer and more rewarding hike on the Buffalo Canyon Trail circles the Scenic Area. This six-mile loop passes through a superb wildflower area, lingers along Cooper Creek, and returns past lesser-known Chimney Arch.

GETTING THERE

From the junction of US 27 and KY 927 seven miles north of Whitley City, drive west for 1.8 miles on KY 927. Parking for the Scenic Area is on the right side of the road on DBNF 867, and includes a picnic area and restrooms (36.84108N & 84.51213W). Natural Arch is a self-service fee area. In 2015, the fee was $3.

THE TRAIL

The toughest part of the hike around Natural Arch can be tearing yourself away from the parking area. At the far end of the parking area is the classic postcard view of the arch. This view of Natural Arch is alone worth the drive, even if you don't do any hiking at all. But of course you'll want to visit the arch up close, so head east around the picnic area along the paved path. You'll pass several other overlooks above the arch before starting to descend a series of stone steps. Keep an eye out for nature's smaller wonders as well; false Solomon's seal, yellow krigia, aster, bird's foot violet, and robin's plantain bloom alongside the trail. At 0.3-mile, come to a trail junction and go

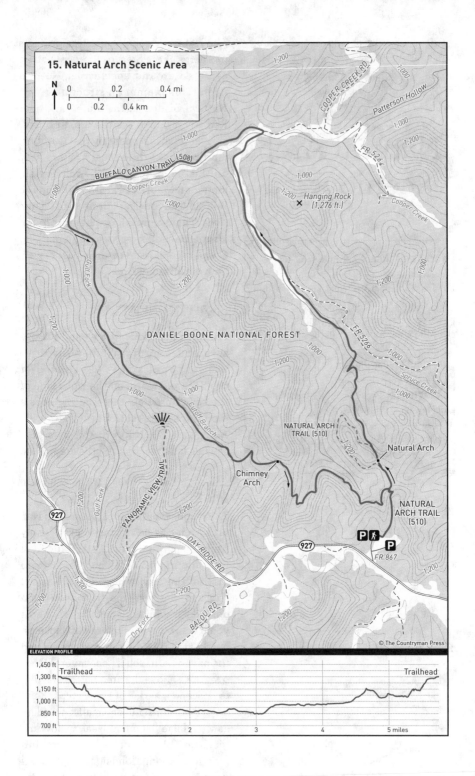

15. Natural Arch Scenic Area

N

| 0 | 0.2 | 0.4 mi |
| 0 | 0.2 | 0.4 km |

COOPER CREEK RD.

Patterson Hollow

FR 5264

Cooper Creek

BUFFALO CANYON TRAIL (508)

Cooper Creek

Hanging Rock
(1,276 ft.)

×

DANIEL BOONE NATIONAL FOREST

Gulf Fork

FR 5266

Cooper Creek

Spruce Creek

PANORAMIC VIEW TRAIL

Cutoff Branch

NATURAL ARCH
TRAIL (510)

Natural Arch

Chimney
Arch

NATURAL
ARCH TRAIL
(510)

Gulf Fork

927

DAY RIDGE RD.

927

FR 867

BALOU RD.

Dry Fork

© The Countryman Press

ELEVATION PROFILE

1,450 ft	Trailhead				Trailhead
1,300 ft					
1,150 ft					
1,000 ft					
850 ft					
700 ft		1	2	3	4	5 miles

right (36.84407N & 84.51094W). The left fork is the Buffalo Canyon Trail DBNF 508, which is your return route.

At 0.4 mile, reach the start of the loop section of trail 510 (36.84517N & 84.51189W). Here the Natural Arch Trail splits just before reaching the arch. Go right at this junction, and climb up to the underside of Natural Arch. The arch was formed by what is called headward erosion of a long narrow ridge. This simply means that the hard massive and resistant sandstone that forms the span of the arch began as a long, narrow ridge. The ridge was attacked by erosion from two opposing sides. Rain and wind were able to erode the softer underlying rocks more easily than those that form the span of the arch. Eventually, some of the softer rocks below the top of the ridge are worn through, creating a small opening in the ridge. As the opening enlarged, some of the unsupported rock of the span fell away, creating the typical curved shape of the arch.

Natural Arch is 50 feet high and 90 feet across. It is the largest in Kentucky, south of the Red River Gorge. Note that the arch is formed from a thick sandstone bed (you can see the individual sand grains in the rock), with many white quartz pebbles embedded in it. This rock is part of the Lee Formation from the Pennsylvanian period, and is over 300 million years old, older even than the time of the dinosaurs. Rock this old deserves special respect, so make sure not to leave any evidence of your passage. Better yet, pick up any trash less careful visitors might have left behind.

You can circle the arch on the Natural Arch Trail, adding an extra 0.6 mile to the loop, or simply enjoy an up-close view of this breathtaking feature. To continue from the arch on the Buffalo Canyon Trail, go to the left side of the arch and follow the trail in the shadow of a large overhang. You'll follow the white diamond-shaped blazes to the far end of the Trail 510 loop at 0.6 mile and bear right at this unsigned junction (36.8462N & 84.51232W). The trail next heads down a sunny slope, which can be a wildflower bonanza in the spring. Keep your flower book handy and see if you can spot common varieties such as chickweed, rue anemone, hepatica, foamflower, violets, bellwort, or maybe even a pink lady's slipper.

Though you're hiking mostly under hemlock trees, you next cross a branch of Spruce Creek on an impressive wooden bridge at 1.2 miles. The wildflower show isn't quite over, though. Spring hikers still have the chance to add yellow trillium, phlox, spring beauty, fire pink, and betony to your list for the day. At 1.7 miles, the trail turns left onto little-traveled gravel DBNF Road 5266 (36.85597N & 84.51859W). A few minutes after passing the Young family farm, leave the road immediately after it makes the usually shallow ford of Cooper Creek (36.86452N & 84.52047W). Turn left onto a rough two-track road that follows along Cooper Creek at 2.5 miles.

You'll see the Young farm again through the trees as you walk along Cooper Creek. Make another usually easy crossing before reaching an overused campsite next to an inviting swimming hole at 3.6 miles (36.85906N & 84.53522W). This is the midpoint of the hike and a great spot to stop for lunch.

Beyond the campsite, the Buffalo Canyon Trail continues to follow the white diamonds along the Gulf Fork of Cooper Creek. You'll next have several normally dry crossings of Cutoff Branch before reaching Chimney Arch at 5.4 miles (36.84537N & 84.51943W). Chim-

NATURAL ARCH

ney Arch lacks the classic symmetry of most natural arches. Instead of gently sloping to the ground, the left side of the arch is nearly vertical, controlled by a pre-existing crack in the rock.

Beyond Chimney Arch, cross the upper reaches of a branch of Spruce Creek, then pass a low rockhouse on your right. Higher up in the same cliff band, you can later spot a tree that seemingly grows straight out of the cliffs. Close the loop at the junction with the Natural Arch Trail at 6.4 miles, and retrace your route to the parking area at 6.8 miles.

Like many parts of the Daniel Boone National Forest, the Natural Arch Scenic Area contains many pine trees that have been killed by the southern pine beetle.

Hikers should be aware that dead trees and branches could remain a hazard, particularly in high winds.

OTHER HIKING OPTIONS

1. Short and Sweet. The hike just to Natural Arch and back on Trail 510 is a one-mile round trip, or you can take the paved path from the parking lot 0.1 mile to another spectacular overlook.
2. Farther west on KY 927, the Panoramic View Trail (DBNF 528) leads 0.6 mile to an overlook offering good views of the cliffs rimming Gulf Bottom.
3. The former Gulf Bottom Trail (DBNF 509) system no longer exists.

16

Blue Bend Trail

The Blue Bend loop was established in 1996 and is still the newest trail at Cumberland Falls State Resort Park. It traverses the Cumberland Falls State Nature Preserve before descending to the Cumberland River and joining the Sheltowee Trace Trail. The nature preserve section is a paradise for birders and wildflower lovers, while the STT offers prime river views and leads past scenic rockhouses.

GETTING THERE

From I-75, get on US 25W near either Corbin or Williamsburg. Drive west to intersect KY 90. The Cumberland Falls State Park Office is 7.5 miles west on KY 90. Continue another 0.8 mile, across the Cumberland River, to reach the trailhead for Blue Bend and Eagle Falls (36.83687N & 84.3455W). You can stop at the park visitor center near the falls for a trail map and information.

THE TRAIL

This hike begins directly across KY 90 from the popular Eagle Falls Trail. A hike around Blue Bend is the opposite of Eagle Falls in more ways than one. The other cars parked at the trailhead likely belong to hikers out on the Eagle Falls Trail. Expect to have Blue Bend to yourself. Instead of hearing the roar of falling water, on this trail your background music will be the sound of singing birds. And lastly, you'll stroll along a quiet stretch of the Cumberland River, instead of beside the noisy falls and shoals of the lower river.

The Blue Bend Trail begins by following a long-abandoned dirt road across a low gate. Just beyond the gate look for some stone steps and the trace of an old road to your left. The steps and road are all that remain from Mr. Mart Campbell's Cumberland Falls Hotel. The hotel

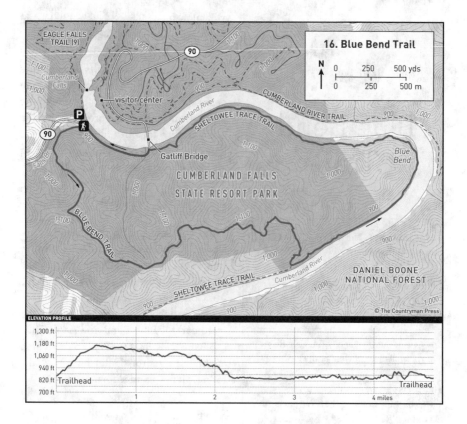

16. Blue Bend Trail

ELEVATION PROFILE

was built across the river from the better known Brunson Inn in the 1920's. The hotel burned down in 1947, just after the property was acquired by the state, and was not rebuilt. A beautifully situated pair of outhouses and an old stone and mortar outbuilding nearby may post-date the hotel.

Follow the blue blazes, and climb steadily past slopes where bluets and white violet flourish in spring. Clusters of tiny bluets are one of spring's special delights. The four small petals of this delicate plant are arranged like compass points around a yellow eye. At 0.5 mile, reach a T-junction with another old road on the ridgetop (36.83175N & 84.3459W). Turn left onto this road and follow it through an open forest of Virginia pines, holly, sweet gum, and a few dogwoods. Some of the common songbirds that you may see, or hear, along the trail include Carolina chickadee, tufted titmouse, juncos, sparrows, or goldfinches. Both the red bellied and downy woodpeckers are also found in the park. At 1.0 mile is a second gate (36.82826N & 84.34122W). This one marks the boundary of the Cumberland Falls State Park Nature Preserve. The preserve protects 1,300 acres of the park west of the Cumberland River, home to several species of rare plants and animals.

The trail continues along the ridge top, and it keeps right at the next fork in the road. By fall, flowers are less common, but you might spot the bright red blooms of cardinal flower here. At 1.5 miles, there is a sign that tells you the Sheltowee Trace is only 0.6 mile away (36.83019N & 84.33426W). There is another sign where another faint old roadway enters on the left, stating that the Trace is only 0.4 mile farther. Here, the trail leaves the ridgetop to descend steadily on a worn two-track road. You'll know the Cumberland River, and the Sheltowee Trace, are just ahead when you pass a low, sandy-floored rockhouse on the right.

The junction of the Blue Bend and Sheltowee Trace Trails at 2.1 miles is marked by a sign indicating that KY 90 and Gatliff Bridge are 2.2 miles to your left (36.82814N & 84.32854W). To the right, red blazes mark the boundary between the State Park and the Daniel Boone National Forest. Though unsigned, the Sheltowee Trace also goes right along the Cumberland River toward Sycamore Shoals to reach KY 700 in 3.6 miles, eventually leading to the Big South Fork National River and Recreation Area. There is a campsite under a pair of huge beech trees only 300 feet to the right. The portion of the Cumberland River that flows through the park has been designated a Kentucky Wild River.

The Blue Bend Trail goes left at the junction and follows the STT back to KY 90. This quiet river walk is a paradise for wildflower lovers in spring. The diverse forest of the plateau has been replaced by the dark evergreens hemlock and rhododendron. The prolific blooms of the May apple love the same moist, shady habitat as does the hiker's bane, poison ivy. May apple is one of the few flowers more easily recognized by the leaves than by the flowers. This low plant looks like a small green umbrella open on the forest floor. Plants with two leaves

support a single white flower on a short stalk growing below the leaves. Ripe fruit of the May apple can be made into jelly. Though modern biotech researchers have found some compounds from the plant useful in the treatment of cancer, the plant can be poisonous. Robin's plantain, purple violets, chickweed, white trillium, sessile trillium, and crested dwarf iris are some of the other flowers blooming later in the spring.

At the tip of Blue Bend, the trail narrows and passes a large rockhouse opposite a sandy beach along the river. The route then pulls away from the river to explore the base of a band of cliffs. You'll round Blue Bend below the base of a high cliff. At 3.2 miles, a dilapidated roadway enters on the left. The trail continues along the hillside in a dark forest dominated by hemlock and rhododendron. At 4.2 miles, the trail crosses a small creek, then it climbs steeply up the far bank. Just beyond is a sign indicating that Cumberland Falls is 0.5 mile ahead and KY 700 is 5 miles behind. Reach Gatliff Bridge at 4.5 miles (36.83511N & 84.33985W), and turn left and walk 0.2 mile along the road back to the trailhead.

The Cumberland River below the falls is a popular whitewater run during high river flows. Contact the park for a list of outfitters currently offering river trips.

The rocks that form the Cumberland Falls are the oldest rocks of the Pennsylvanian period, famous in Kentucky for the thick coal beds deposited during that time. Geologists call the sandstone and pebble conglomerates that form the falls, and the gorge around it, the Lee Formation. The layers below the Lee Formation are the easily eroded Pennington Shale and the more resistant Chester Limestone, both of which were deposited in the earlier Mississippian period.

CUMBERLAND FALLS

OTHER HIKING OPTIONS

1. Short and Sweet. If your time is limited, try an out-and-back hike on the STT along the river.
2. From Blue Bend, the Sheltowee Trace continues south toward the Big South Fork and Pickett State Park. It is 3.6 miles south to the next road intersection at KY 700, but this hike requires either a long return hike or a shuttle between the trailheads.

17

Eagle Falls Trail

TOTAL DISTANCE: The hike is a 2.2-mile semi-loop, including a side trip to Eagle Falls, and it is open to hikers only.

HIKING TIME: About 1.5 hours

DIFFICULTY: Easy

LOCATION: Cumberland Falls State Resort Park, 16 miles southwest of Corbin

MAPS: USGS Cumberland Falls and Cumberland Falls State Park Visitor's Guide

If you have time for only one hike at Cumberland Falls, this is the trail to take. A short, easy walk will lead to dramatic views of Cumberland Falls. The trail then enters a loop, from which a steep side trail with stairs leads to the slender water column of Eagle Falls. Few trails anywhere are as well designed for viewing two completely different waterfalls as is this one. The waterfalls and wildflowers make this trail a perfect place to introduce youngsters to the outdoors.

GETTING THERE

From I-75, take US 25W near either Corbin or Williamsburg. Drive west to intersect KY 90. The Cumberland Falls State Park Office is 7.5 miles west on KY 90. Continue another 0.8 mile, across the Cumberland River, to reach the trailhead for Blue Bend and Eagle Falls (36.83687N & 84.3455W). You can stop at the park visitor center near the falls for a trail map and information.

THE TRAIL

The Eagle Falls Trail begins at a gravel trailhead on KY 90, just across the Gatliff Bridge, and opposite the trailhead for the Blue Bend Trail. The start of the trail is relatively easy, and it is the most scenic. It is also a favorite with wildflower watchers, who come to see robin's plantain, and bluets, along with purple and white violets. If you have children with you, do your best to keep them on the trail and away from the poison ivy that also flourishes here. The trail follows a line of bluffs close to the edge of the Cumberland River. You'll pass one rockhouse and then climb a set of stone steps before reaching the trail's highlight, a

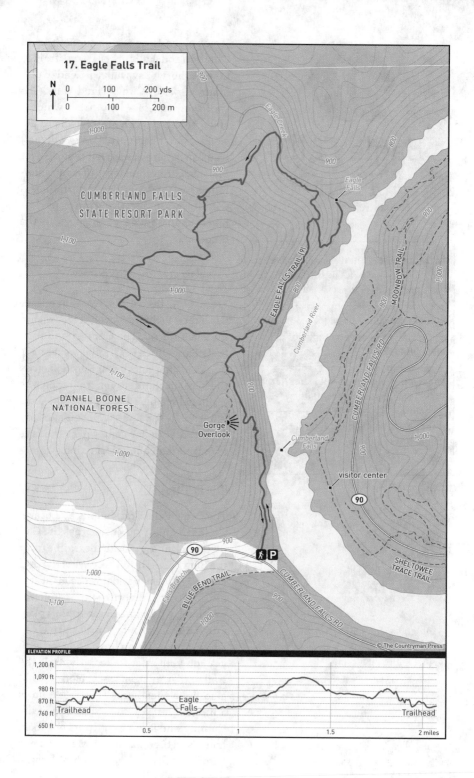

17. Eagle Falls Trail

N

| 0 | 100 | 200 yds |
| 0 | 100 | 200 m |

CUMBERLAND FALLS
STATE RESORT PARK

Eagle Creek

900

1,000

Eagle
Falls

800

900

MOONBOW TRAIL

EAGLE FALLS TRAIL (9)

Cumberland River

800

1,100

1,000

CUMBERLAND FALLS RD

1,000

DANIEL BOONE
NATIONAL FOREST

Gorge
Overlook

Cumberland
Falls

900

1,100

1,000

visitor center

90

900

90

SHELTOWEE
TRACE TRAIL

Falls Branch

BLUE BEND TRAIL

CUMBERLAND FALLS RD

1,000

1,100

900

© The Countryman Press

ELEVATION PROFILE

1,200 ft				
1,090 ft				
980 ft				
870 ft	Trailhead	Eagle		Trailhead
760 ft		Falls		
650 ft				

0.5   1   1.5   2 miles

spectacular overlook almost directly above the falls. Your view of the falls from the overlook will be relatively private. The powerful river separates you from the hordes across the river at the park visitor center. The shallow bluffs and rocky overhangs along the trail add to the sense of intimacy. Just watch your step! It is a short drop from the cliffs to the river and its swift current surging toward the falls.

The trail beyond the first overlook has some steep sections of stairs, but it is well worth the effort. In spring, the variety of flowers includes pussy toes, fire pink, little brown jugs, halberd-leaved violet, Solomon's seal, and yellow violet. You will also pass a side trail leading left uphill to an overlook and CCC-era picnic shelter at 0.3 mile (36.84032N & 84.34637W). At 0.4 mile (36.84089N & 84.34601W), there is a split where the loop part of Trail 9 begins. Turn right here to hike the loop clockwise and use the shortest route to Eagle Falls.

Beyond the loop junction are deep rock overhangs and wide open fenced overlooks perched high above roaring Cumberland Falls. Here is another great photo spot, with the falls and lower river gorge displayed. Below the falls you may see rafts, kayaks, or canoes beginning a scenic float trip downriver from this point.

At 0.6 mile, a steep side trail leads 0.2 mile right down to the river and to the base of Eagle Falls (36.84347N & 84.34422W). You'll descend wood stairs, then newer metal stairs. The falls lies at the head of an intimate alcove of steep sandstone, perfect for a picnic. In contrast to the Niagara-like power of Cumberland Falls, here a small stream pours over a thick rock shelf in a narrow column of water. It's a great spot to stop for lunch and enjoy both the river and falls.

When you are ready to complete the loop, hike back to the junction with the main trail at 1.0 mile. The rest of the loop continues with a climb alongside Eagle Creek and leads past a small rockhouse. The loop is a bit tougher than the hike to the falls. The path is marked by yellow plastic diamonds and is easy to follow. Here, however, are even more wildflowers, including some common ones, such as wild geranium, spurred violet, chickweed, foamflower, buttercup, cinquefoil, squaw root, and crested dwarf iris; and some rarer ones, like jack-in-the-pulpit and yellow lady's slipper. The unusual jack-in-the-pulpit is best recognized by its distinctive mottled foliage. A green hooded pulpit covers the "jack," which stands within it. The pulpit is often vertically striped, but it can also be mottled. The actual flowers are tiny, and cluster at the foot of the jack.

Once you've closed the loop at 1.8 miles, retrace your steps back to the trailhead at 2.2 miles. On your return, you might also take the 0.1-mile side trail leading to the overlook and shelter constructed by the Civilian Conservation Corps in the 1930s.

In recent years, black bears have become regular visitors to Cumberland Falls State Park. When hiking and camping in black bear country, you'll need to take a few simple precautions to keep bears away from human food. Pay attention to the park's guidelines on interacting with bears, and most importantly, don't feed them or leave food anywhere that is accessible to them.

Cumberland Falls is a State Resort Park, and so it has a full array of amenities. The park has a campground which is open seasonally, woodland rooms, cabins, and a full-service lodge, with a restaurant offering one of the

VIEW OF THE CUMBERLAND RIVER

best breakfast spreads in the region. Inside the lodge building is the Bob Blair Museum, containing displays on the cultural and natural history of the area. Fishing in the river is popular, as are guided horseback rides. The park also has an Olympic-sized pool, which is open in summer. Contact the park for a list of outfitters that guide river trips.

Cumberland Falls State Resort Park was created in 1931 with a grant from Senator T.C. DuPont, who grew up in Kentucky. The 1.776-acre park was one of the four original Kentucky state parks. The original park lodge was built in 1933 by the CCC and was named for the Senator. The first lodge burned in 1940, was rebuilt in 1941, and then it was expanded in 1951.

OTHER HIKING OPTIONS

1. Short and Sweet. You can hike out to the best of the overlooks and back in a round trip of less than one mile.

2. In addition to the hikes described in other chapters, Cumberland Falls has a number of short hiking trails perfect for exploring. From DuPont Lodge, Trails 3 and 6 lead down to the Cumberland River by the falls. Trail 4 is a self-guided interpretive trail that explores the contributions made by members of the Civilian Conservation Corps to the park in the 1930s. Trail 5 connects the camping and cabin areas to Trail 4. Trails 7 and 12 form a confusing network between KY 90 and the Sheltowee Trace Trail.

18

Cumberland River Trail

TOTAL DISTANCE: The loop is 7.1 miles around on the Cumberland River (Trail 2) and Sheltowee Trace Trails at Cumberland Falls State Resort Park, and in the Daniel Boone National Forest including a side trip to the restored Pinnacle Knob Fire Tower. The loop is open to hikers only.

HIKING TIME: About 4 hours

DIFFICULTY: Difficult

LOCATION: Cumberland Falls State Resort Park, 16 miles southwest of Corbin

MAPS: USGS Cumberland Falls and Cumberland Falls State Park Visitor's Guide

The Cumberland River Trail is the longest trail in the Cumberland Falls State Park area. Combined with the Sheltowee Trace Trail on the Daniel Boone National Forest, it is also the only trail with the opportunity for backpacking, but you must camp on the forest, not in the park. But don't choose this trail simply for its length. The Cumberland Trail visits many of the park highlights, including Cumberland Falls, rockhouses, overhangs, and a restored fire tower.

GETTING THERE

From I-75 take US 25W near either Corbin or Williamsburg. Drive west to intersect KY 90. The Cumberland Falls State Park Office is 7.5 miles west on KY 90. Continue 0.5 mile down to the river and park at the Cumberland Falls Visitors Parking Area (36.83845N & 84.34369W). You can stop at the park visitor center near the falls for a trail map and information.

THE TRAIL

This is the longest loop trail in the Cumberland Falls area, and it can be walked either as a backpacking trip or as a moderately long day hike. Overnighters should remember that there is no backcountry camping allowed in Cumberland Falls State Resort Park, so be sure to find a camping spot in the Daniel Boone National Forest.

If you've parked at the visitors area next to the falls, the best way to pick up the trail is to head for the strip of trees between the parking area and KY 90. Here you'll find the Sheltowee Trace Trail. Follow it upstream to the end of the parking area, then cross KY 90 at 0.2 mile where the Trace bears right to

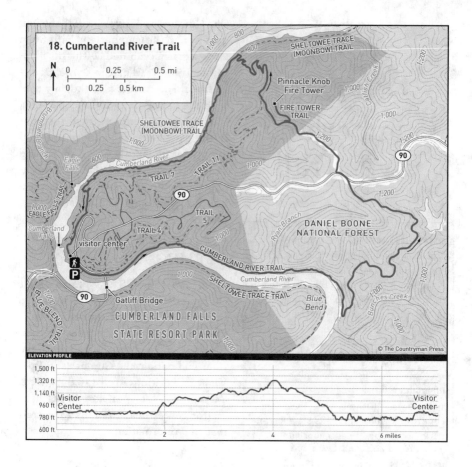

18. Cumberland River Trail

ELEVATION PROFILE

cross the highway bridge and walk along the road leading to a picnic area. Just as you enter the parking area, a side trail leads left at a sign that reads "to Trail 4." This short diversion leads to a huge rockhouse with a picnic table and a slender, wet-weather waterfall.

At the end of the picnic area at 0.5 mile (36.83845N & 84.33647W), leave the road for a narrow trail that will continue to follow the river. Springtime hikers should have their wildflower guides open and ready. This is one of the park's best trails for flower lovers. Bluets, little brown jugs and robin's plantain are among the most prolific in spring. Foam-

flower, crested dwarf iris, cinquefoil, and several types of violets also grow here. Later in the year, laurel and galax will bloom.

Beyond the junction with Trail 5 at 0.7 mile, Trail 2 receives much less use. After passing the concrete park boundary marker at 1.1 miles, you will come to a flat area that could be used for camping, now that you have left the park for the Daniel Boone National Forest. Continuing alongside the river, look for signs of hungry beavers who may have attacked some impressively large trees. Keep the flower books out: You may be able to add trillium, trout lily, chickweed, rue anemone, May apple, and wild geranium to your list.

At 1.8 miles (36.83371N & 84.31693W), across the river from Blue Bend, the trail intersects a dirt road and follows it to the left, uphill and away from the river. The trail, which has been well marked to this point, has fewer blazes until it re-enters Cumberland Falls State Park near Pinnacle Tower. In the cool, moist area beneath a rockhouse, check for the bright red flowers of columbine, a rare flower in this area. After gaining the ridge, the trail passes underneath a powerline at 2.8 miles. Next, bear right at a junction with a dirt road. From the junction, descend through an area rich in both pine and myrtle to reach a gate at the junction of KY 90 at 3.3 miles (36.8442N & 84.31644W). The trail resumes about 100 yards to your left across the highway at another gated dirt road. Small pull-off areas at both roads make this an alternate starting point for the loop.

Continue up the road and reach a second gate at 3.8 miles, which marks the state park boundary. Just beyond, at 3.9 miles, is a side trail leading right 0.2 mile to the Pinnacle Knob Fire Tower (36.84835N & 84.32257W). The tower was built by the US Forest Service in 1937 and was used for fire control until the 1970s, when it fell into disrepair. A renovation effort on the steel structure and the cabin was started in 2007 and completed in 2008. The cabin and catwalk are open during tours scheduled by Cumberland Falls State Park, but casual visitors can still enjoy an expansive view of the Cumberland River Gorge and the state park water tower from the upper levels of the stairs. From the tower, return to the junction with the main trail at 4.3 miles and turn right.

Just beyond the tower site trail, our route turns right off the old roadway. Next is the junction with Cumberland Falls Trail 11 at 4.5 miles (36.85021N & 84.32498W). A left turn onto Trail 11 provides a slightly shorter, but more hilly, route back to the park. After circling in back of the bluffs below the tower, Trail 2 soon starts to switchback downhill past a rockhouse toward the Cumberland River. At 5.2 miles, reach the signed junction with the Sheltowee Trace Trail (36.85352N & 84.32733W). To the right the STT leads 0.7 mile to a campsite, 1.1 miles to Dog Slaughter Falls Trail, and 1.3 miles to Dog Slaughter Falls.

Turn left on the Sheltowee Trace Trail, also called Trail 1, or the Moonbow Trail, here. This section of the river is a favorite of white-water enthusiasts. The steep, boulder-strewn river bed would seem at best a daunting obstacle for even skilled boaters. But this is a great stretch for hikers also. The trail winds up and down rock stairs, around rockhouses, and passes underneath an arch formed by a massive rock fall. Trillium, crested dwarf iris, and sun drops form a colorful floral carpet. At 5.9 miles is the first of two junctions with Trail 7. After the second junction, just as Eagle Falls comes into view across the river, take a sharp switchback left at 6.7 miles and walk uphill. In very high water, this is the first section of the Sheltowee Trace to flood, and it may be necessary in those conditions to bypass the STT and return to the trail via Trails 7 and 12.

If you miss this switchback, and many people do, you can follow casual trails along the riverbank to the end of the visitor center trails. Along the river's edge you may see an unusual deposit of black rock. This is a gravel bar formed from coal, which is unusual because coal is soft and easily broken up by the mixing action of a river. The presence of coal in the gravel bar indicates that there must be a layer of coal at river level, very close by.

Meanwhile, the Sheltowee Trace Trail reaches the first of two intersections with Trail 12, which are spaced 250 feet apart. The sign marking the first intersection indicates that KY 1277 is 10 miles back on the Sheltowee Trace Trail. Next, the trail merges with the paved walkways leading from the visitor center to overlooks below Cumberland Falls and back to the parking area at 7.1 miles. Summer hikers can enjoy a reward of cold drinks or ice cream before returning to the parking area.

Cumberland Falls is the only place in the western hemisphere where "moonbows" are found. Moonbows are just like rainbows, except that moonlight, rather than sunlight, forms them. Moonbows are rare because so many different things must take place at the same time for them to occur. Moonbows need strong light from a full moon, a clear sky, clear air, and the prodigious spray of water that only a powerful waterfall can make. Besides Cumberland Falls, only Africa's Victoria Falls on the Zambezei River produces similar moonbows. Be aware that the park is always more crowded close to the full moon.

Even without the moonbow, every visitor finds Cumberland Falls a wonder. Most waterfalls on the Cumberland Plateau occur when small streams pour over the edge of a rockhouse. At Cumberland Falls, a full-fledged river crashes 68 feet into a foaming, churn-

ROCK PASSAGE ON THE MOONBOW TRAIL

ing pit of white water. Most likely you'll hear the falls well before you see it. Normally the falls are over 100 feet wide, but the river has been recorded to flow as little as little as 4 cubic feet per second. Maximum-recorded flow on the river was almost 15,000 times stronger than that.

OTHER HIKING OPTIONS

1. Short and Sweet. A web of trails downstream from Cumberland Falls starts from the developed visitors area on the east side of the river. Exploring all the available overlooks and walking down to the sandy beach below the falls is less than one mile round trip.

2. The 0.2-mile trail to Moonshiners Arch (DBNF 418) starts 3.1 miles east of the entrance to DuPont Lodge at an unsigned turnout. The trail to this small arch is not well maintained.

3. The 10.5-mile hike on the Sheltowee Trace between Cumberland Falls and Laurel Lake is a popular hike, especially for backpackers. From the falls, it is two miles to Trail 2, 2.9 miles to the Dog Slaughter Falls Trail, 7.4 miles to Bark Camp Trail, and 10.7 miles to the Mouth of Laurel Boat Ramp. Backcountry shelters are found at Bark Camp and Star Creeks.

19

Bark Camp Trail

TOTAL DISTANCE: A hike to the Bark Camp Creek Shelter along the Cumberland River and back is a 5.4 mile round trip that is foot travel only.

HIKING TIME: About 3 hours

DIFFICULTY: Moderate

LOCATION: London Ranger District, 11 miles southwest of Corbin

MAPS: USGS Sawyer, DBNF Bark Camp Trail 413

The Bark Camp Trail (DBNF 413) is a pleasant hike along Bark Camp Creek. The stream passes numerous rockhouses and ends with an impressive series of cascades near the Cumberland River. There is a backcountry shelter on the Sheltowee Trace Trail near the trail's end. This is a great day hike or an easy overnight trip.

GETTING THERE

From US 25W 2.9 miles north of the junction with KY 90, take County Road 1193 west. In 4.5 miles, continue straight onto County Road 1277 where 1193 turns right. Drive 1.2 miles, then turn left onto gravel DBNF Road 193. Take the gravel road south for 1.9 miles and park at a small turnout where the road crosses Bark Camp Creek (36.90463N & 84.28118W). The trailhead can also be reached from KY 90 near Cumberland Falls in 8.8 miles by following gravel DBNF roads 195, 88, and 193.

THE TRAIL

Creekside walks are always a hiker favorite, no matter what the season. The rollicking splash of water rolling downstream provides a soothing serenade, even on a dreary winter day. In spring, the cool, wet areas along the bank are home to wildflowers rarely seen elsewhere in the forest. And when summer rears its steamy head, cool waters are ready to refresh. In fall, the stream is a magnet for fishermen seeking the rainbow trout stocked by the National Forest.

Bark Camp Creek isn't the only attraction along this trail. The route follows the base of high sandstone

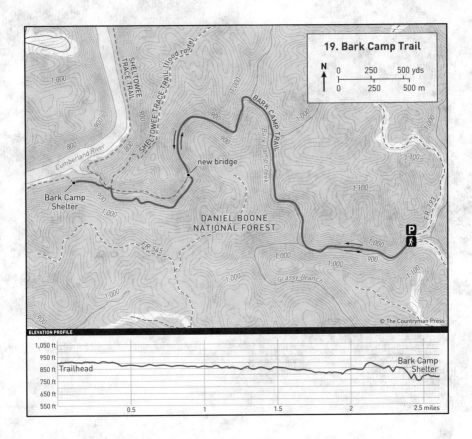

ELEVATION PROFILE

cliffs for much of its length. The cliffs, overhangs, and rockhouses, along with two seasonal waterfalls along the way, make this hike seem like a much shorter walk, and the attractions are plentiful enough to keep younger hikers entertained throughout.

Like the geologic formations, spring wildflowers are more plentiful toward either end of the trail. The more abundant flowers include bluets, little brown jugs, crested dwarf iris, and galax. Lucky hikers may also spot columbine, squaw root, pink lady's slipper, and the elusive jack-in-the-pulpit. The pink lady's slipper is a rare, slow-growing member of the orchid family. It grows only in a symbiotic relationship with a special fungus that helps the plant absorb nutrients from the soil. Once seeds of the pink lady's slipper germinate, the plant waits up to two years for the fungus to develop, and then it may wait several more years before flowering.

There are several overused campsites in the first mile of the trail. Less considerate hikers may have left behind some trash, so it's not a bad idea to pack a plastic bag to "carry out" what others have "carried in."

Rockhouses are important plant habitats in the forests of the Cumberland Plateau. Conditions here are cooler, wetter, and less sunny than elsewhere in the forest. At least four species of ferns

CASCADES ALONG BARK CAMP CREEK

and seven species of flowering plants, including members of the otherwise common buttercup family, are known to occur only in rockhouses in the eastern United States.

Just after the release of the first edition of this book, the trail bridge over Bark Camp Creek washed out. The old bridge's location near the mouth of the Cumberland River, just below the creek's cascades, made these washouts inevitable. In late 2015, the DBNF was completing construction of a replacement bridge well upstream at the 2.0-mile mark of the trail (36.90839N & 84.29875W). The new composite frame bridge uses natural abutments and sits high above the creek. Both sections of trail downstream from the bridge are now part of the Sheltowee Trace Trail. To reach the river and the Bark Camp Shelter, turn left to cross the bridge. A new section of trail now leads along the south bank of the creek. At 2.5 miles, the new section joins the old STT near the location of the old bridge, where the north abutment of the bridge can still be seen. At 2.7 miles, a short spur leads uphill to the Bark Camp Shelter (36.90798N & 84.30797W).

The shelter is an "Adirondack-type" structure similar in construction to those used on the Appalachian Trail. Because it is located on a stretch of river accessible to powerboats, the shelter suffers some excess wear and tear. However, it was recently refurbished, along with the reconstruction of the bridge and associated trail work. To the left and south on the STT, Dog Slaughter Creek is 5 miles away and Cumberland Falls is 8 miles away.

If you continued right on the STT at the new bridge, you would reach the high-water bypass trail (36.90762N & 84.30499W) for the STT in 0.4 mile; you would reach the Mouth of Laurel Boat Ramp in 3.7 miles if you were to stay on the main STT. The trail is mainly used by fishermen seeking the trout regularly stocked in the creek.

The Daniel Boone National Forest was originally named the Cumberland National Forest. The Cumberland region, in turn, got its name during the explorations of Dr. Thomas Walker in the 1700s; Walker named the Cumberland River for England's Duke of Cumberland. This apparently was not quite the honor it might seem; Walker felt that the winding river and the Duke were equally crooked.

The name Cumberland has come to describe the entire Cumberland Plateau and the mountains that surround it. A confusing array of recreation areas has taken the name as well. In addition to Cumberland Falls State Park and Cumberland Gap National Historical Park in Kentucky, there are Cumberland Mountain State Park and the South Cumberland Recreation Area in Tennessee, plus the Cumberland Trail State Park. And, of course there's the Big South Fork (of the Cumberland) River and National Recreation Area. President Lyndon Johnson saved us all from further confusion by signing an order in 1966 that changed the name of the national forest to honor Daniel Boone.

The forest consists of 692,000 acres that are federally owned and spread over a 2.1 million acre area. Lacing the forest are 423 miles of hiking trails. There are two wilderness areas, three Kentucky Wild Rivers, and a National Wild and Scenic River. The DBNF manages three lakes, twenty-two campgrounds, and twenty-three picnic areas. Other special areas in the forest include the Red River Gorge Geological Area, Natural Arch Scenic Area, and the Pioneer Weapons Wildlife Management Area.

OTHER HIKING OPTIONS

1. Short and Sweet. Hikers pressed for time could turn around after visiting the rockhouses along the first half mile of the trail.

2. The Sheltowee Trace Trail leads 3.7 miles from Bark Camp Creek to the Mouth of Laurel Boat Ramp.

3. The Dog Slaughter Falls Trail (DBNF 414) is located six miles to the south. It follows a stream-side route similar to that of the Cumberland River. Hikers could combine the Dog Slaughter and Bark Camp Trails into an 11.2-mile trip using a short car shuttle.

20

Beaver Creek Wilderness

TOTAL DISTANCE: A 1.9-mile semi-loop on the Three Forks Beaver Loop (DBNF 512) and Three Forks of Beaver (DBNF 512A) Trails, with an optional 1.4-mile off-trail side trip to campsites at three forks. Open to hikers only.

HIKING TIME: 1 hour for the loop plus another hour for the side trip

DIFFICULTY: Easy/Moderate

LOCATION: Stearns Ranger District, about 16 miles northeast of Whitley City

MAPS: USGS Hail. DBNF Beaver Creek Wilderness Trails. The 1990 DBNF Clifty Wilderness and Beaver Creek Wilderness Recreation Guide (R8-RG) contains a number of errors and should not be used.

Beaver Creek was the first wilderness area created in Kentucky. The area is rough, rugged, remote, and rarely visited by hikers who can easily be intimidated by the hostile terrain. However, the short hike out to the Three Forks of Beaver Creek Overlook is easy and well marked, ending with a remarkable view above the three forks. For backpackers, there is also an optional side trip down to campsites along the three forks. Summer hikers should be warned that this is prime chigger habitat.

GETTING THERE

From the junction on US 27 and KY 90 north of Whitley City, drive north on US 27 for 4.2 miles to the junction with paved DBNF Road 50. This road may be marked with a watchable wildlife sign, and signs for Three Forks Trailhead and Bowman Ridge. Follow Road 50 for 2.4 miles, then turn right onto gravel DBNF Road 51. Drive 0.7 mile on Road 51 to the Three Forks of Beaver Trailhead (36.90702N & 84.44837W). The trail starts at the far end of the trailhead, next to Road 51C, which is the return route.

THE TRAIL

Though much of the Beaver Creek Wilderness remains the roughest hiking in the state, the walk to the Three Forks of Beaver Creek Overlook is easy, pleasant, and rewarding. Be sure to take your camera along for the walk. This is a photo-worthy vista at any time of year.

From the trailhead, follow signed Trail 512, which is marked with white diamond blazes. The well-maintained trail will wander through a forest dominated by pine and oak trees that is typical of the dry ridgetops of this part of Kentucky. You'll also see red maple,

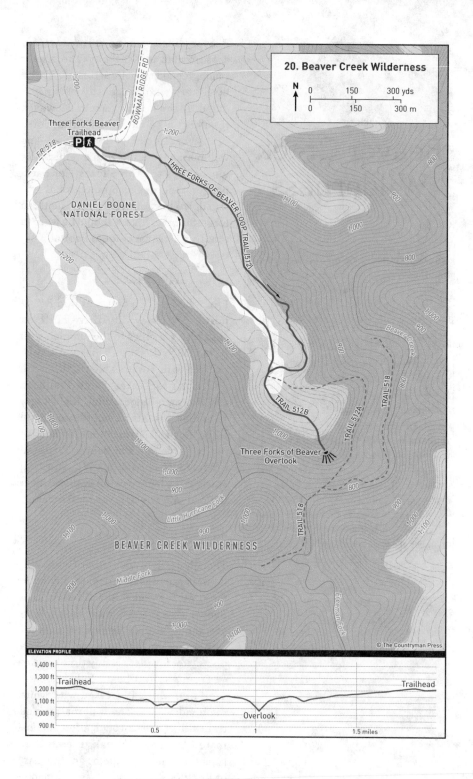

20. Beaver Creek Wilderness

N

| 0 | 150 | 300 yds |
| 0 | 150 | 300 m |

BOWMAN RIDGE RD

Three Forks Beaver
Trailhead

FR 518

1,200

DANIEL BOONE
NATIONAL FOREST

1,200

1,200

THREE FORKS OF BEAVER LOOP TRAIL 512J

1,200

1,100

1,000

800

900

800

Beaver Creek

1,050

900

006

TRAIL 518

800

TRAIL 512B

1,100

1,100

TRAIL 512A

Three Forks of Beaver
Overlook

1,000

1,000

800

900

1,100

1,000

900

Little Hurricane Fork

1,000

1,000

TRAIL 518

900

1,100

1,100

BEAVER CREEK WILDERNESS

1,000

Middle Fork

900

Freeman Fork

1,100

1,000

1,100

© The Countryman Press

ELEVATION PROFILE

| 1,400 ft |
| 1,300 ft | Trailhead |
| 1,200 ft |
| 1,100 ft |
| 1,000 ft |
| 900 ft |

Trailhead

Overlook

0.5 1 1.5 miles

sassafras, tulip poplar, Fraser magnolia, and hemlock trees.

The route turns away from the rim beside a pair of beech trees. The scraggly branches of Virginia pine are common here, as are the prickly leaves of holly in the understory. At 0.8 mile, come to an unsigned T-junction with a grassy former road (36.90035N & 84.44165W). The Three Forks Loop Trail (512) goes right and north along the road back to the trailhead. To follow the Three Forks of Beaver Trail (512A) to the overlook, turn left and south onto the road. The road splits in 50 feet. The right branch is the trail to the overlook and should be marked with a watchable wildlife sign.

The right branch quickly narrows and begins to tunnel through the laurel and blueberry flourishing beneath a canopy of pines. This combination of spring flowers and fall berries makes this a great hike in either season. At 1.0 mile, reach the fenced overlook (36.89818N & 84.43956W), above the three forks of Beaver Creek. The Freeman, Middle, and Hurricane Forks of Beaver Creek are all in view below. The streams have carved tall turrets into the narrow divides between them, and they have sculpted sheer cliffs to form the canyon walls.

From the overlook, retrace your route back to the T-junction. Because the boundary of the Beaver Creek Wilderness is drawn along the rim of the canyon, this hike has not yet entered the wilderness proper. If you would like to enter the wilderness, and you feel your route-finding skills are up to the task, an unblazed and unmaintained route (Three Forks Spur Trail 512B) to the three forks also begins near the T-junction. This 1.4-mile round-trip route begins on the south part of the grassy road. Instead of taking the right branch of the road toward the overlook, keep left and descend on a rough former roadbed. This route gets narrow and overgrown not far from the rim. A few old waterbars remain, indicating that this may once have been a maintained trail. The wilderness boundary is well signed.

Once into the wilderness, the trail drops steeply through the cliffs that guard the inner canyon. In summer, this is the most overgrown part of the trail, but when the leaves are down, it is the prettiest, with views of cliffs and rock overhangs on both sides. You'll pass a huge overhanging boulder that could serve as an emergency shelter just as you get your first view of Hurricane Fork. Reach the confluence of the Middle and Hurricane forks near a possible campsite in a grove of hemlock trees (36.89675N & 84.44005W). The route continues past a crossing of the Hurricane Fork and follows the Middle Fork upstream a short distance to a larger campsite, the confluence with the Freeman Fork, which is 0.7 mile from the T-junction. A few old "i" shaped blazes lead across the Freeman Fork, but there is only a faint trace of a route beyond them. A similarly rough path that may be the remains of trail 518 also continues downstream. There are several nice campsites located in the spacious creek bottoms at this confluence. From the confluence, retrace your route back to the T-junction.

To complete the Three Forks Loop from the T-junction, turn right on the old road. Stay on the ridgetop to reach a cleared wildlife opening. Follow the trail straight across the opening, and continue on the road through the woods on the other side. Return to the trailhead at 1.9 miles. Because of the likelihood of encountering chiggers in the wildlife opening, summer hikers should return via the main trail.

The 4,791-acre Beaver Creek Wilderness was part of the Eastern Wilderness Act of 1975 that created 13 wilderness areas. The act protected some of the best-loved hiking areas in the mountains from New Hampshire to Alabama. The lack of an extensive trail system, poor upkeep of the existing

THREE FORKS OF BEAVER CREEK OVERLOOK

trails, and confusing maps of the area have kept Beaver Creek the least-used of any of these areas. However, these same qualities can attract wilderness users who don't like trails, who want the feeling of truly exploring the land they pass through, and who value solitude in the woods.

OTHER HIKING OPTIONS

1. Short and Sweet. The 1.9-mile round trip hike to the overlook is the only easy way to see the wilderness.

2. A second trail system enters the wilderness from the Bowman Ridge Trailhead located 1.7 miles farther on DBNF Road 51. The Bowman Ridge (DBNF 514) and Beaver Creek (DBNF 532) Trails begin together at this trailhead. The trails split in 0.2 mile. The Bowman Ridge Trail reaches a bridge over Beaver Creek at 0.9 mile and climbs the opposite rim to reach the Swain Ridge Trailhead on DBNF Road 52 at 1.9 miles. The Bowman Ridge Trail follows a road that was closed with the creation of the wilderness and still remains easy to follow. The 1990 DBNF Beaver Creek Wilderness Map shows a confusing variety of trails here. The Beaver Creek Trail (DBNF 532) follows an old logging road for the first 1.7 miles down to Beaver Creek at an overgrown clearing. There is no marked route, and virtually no footpath, for the next 1.3 miles until you reach a spacious campsite only 0.2 mile from the Beaver Creek Bridge and the Bowman Ridge Trail. Because of the difficulty in finding the start of the logging road out of the valley near the clearing, it is probably easier to descend Trail 532 and ascend 514 if you try to hike this loop.

3. Maps of the wilderness area show the Middle Ridge Trail (518) extending from DBNF Road 839 down the Middle Fork to Trail 514 at the

bridge over Beaver Creek. However, there has never been a hiking trail between these two points. There is however, an old road that leads from the trailhead on Road 839 down to the Middle Fork, where it disappears in an overgrown area. Since the publication of the 1990 Clifty Wilderness and Beaver Creek Wilderness Map by the DBNF, many hikers have been lured onto this route, only to find unending frustration trying to follow this nonexistent trail. Forest Service maps showed this connection, simply to indicate that it was possible to walk along the valley of Beaver Creek. In 2015, a little-used trail led off the main trail toward the wilderness boundary (36.86895N & 84.4832W).

21

Bee Rock Loop

TOTAL DISTANCE: A 3.9-mile loop on the Bee Rock Loop (DBNF 529) and Rockcastle Narrows (DBNF 503) Trails, which can be combined with a short walk on the road through the Bee Rock Campground.

HIKING TIME: About 2.5 hours

DIFFICULTY: Moderate

LOCATION: Stearns Ranger District, about 20 miles southwest of London

MAPS: USGS Ano and DBNF Bee Rock Trails

The Bee Rock Trails have the well-groomed feel of scenic front country trails. This loop gives hikers the chance to sample the best of hiking near the Rockcastle River, with towering overlooks, close-ups of cliffs, and views of the Rockcastle Narrows. For the second edition, I've revised the loop to include a visit to the Bee Rock Overlook.

GETTING THERE

From Exit 38 off I-75 on the south side of London, follow KY 192 west for 18.9 miles to DBNF Road 623. This road begins immediately after crossing the Rockcastle River and serves the Bee Rock West Campground. Drive 0.5 mile on the road, past the west end of the Bee Rock Loop Trail, to park near the footbridge across the river or in the small pullout at the trailhead on the left past Campsite 3 (37.02928N & 84.31853W).

THE TRAIL

The Bee Rock Loop features the rock'-n'roll scenery famous along the Cumberland Plateau. The loop first climbs past the shear sandstone rock of the Rockcastle Gorge to the Bee Rock Overlook, then it descends to follow the rolling waters of the Rockcastle River.

From the signed east end of the Bee Rock Loop Trail, follow the white diamond-shaped blazes north towards Bee Rock Overlook. While signs at the trailhead indicate that Trail 529 is open to both horses and mountain bikes, it is difficult to imagine that riders of either type would be able to negotiate, much less enjoy riding on, this trail. Ascend a narrow rock-choked gorge where a slender wet-weather waterfall pours off a massive

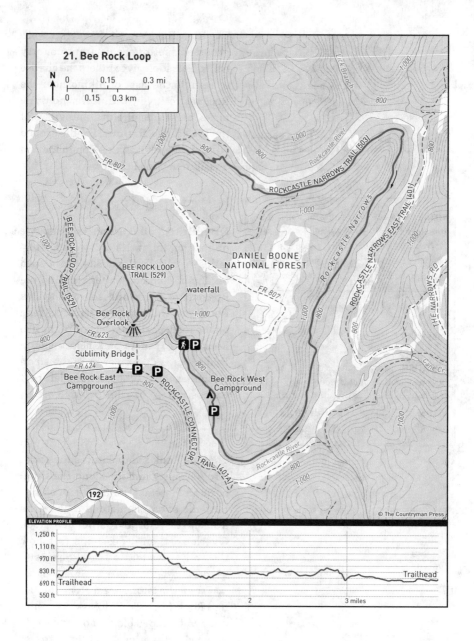

21. Bee Rock Loop

N

| 0 | 0.15 | 0.3 mi |
| 0 | 0.15 | 0.3 km |

FR 807

Lick Branch

1,000

800

Rockcastle River

ROCKCASTLE NARROWS TRAIL (503)

1,000

800

800

1,000

BEE ROCK LOOP TRAIL (529)

DANIEL BOONE
NATIONAL FOREST

Rockcastle Narrows

ROCKCASTLE NARROWS EAST TRAIL (401)

THE NARROWS RD

waterfall

FR 807

1,000

1,000

Bee Rock
Overlook

1,000

800

Cane Cr

FR 623

800

1,000

Sublimity Bridge

FR 624

Bee Rock East
Campground

P P

P

Bee Rock West
Campground

ROCKCASTLE CONNECTOR TRAIL (401A)

800

1,000

Rockcastle River

800

1,000

192

© The Countryman Press

ELEVATION PROFILE

| 1,250 ft |
| 1,110 ft |
| 970 ft |
| 830 ft |
| 690 ft | Trailhead |
| 550 ft |

Trailhead

1   2   3 miles

band of cliffs. After climbing steeply up the cliff band, the trail reaches an often-unsigned junction with the side trail to the Bee Rock Overlook at 0.4 mile (37.03083N & 84.32147W). The clifftop here was once blanketed with pine trees. However, the pines here were killed by an infestation of the southern pine beetle, causing the trail to be closed temporarily in 2003, when the dead trees began to topple. The forest here has still not recovered from the infestation and the underbrush can be thick on the ridgetop.

From the junction, the overlook is 0.1 mile to the left. The stone and wood

BEE ROCK OVERLOOK

fenced overlook has a tremendous view of the Bee Rock campgrounds, the KY 192 bridge over the Rockcastle River, and other cliffy areas along the Rockcastle Gorge. To continue on the loop, return to the junction and continue along the main trail at 0.6 mile. The trail passes the 1.0 milepost (you have one mile to reach the west end of the Bee Rock Loop Trail) before reaching a signed junction with the Rockcastle Narrows Trail (DBNF 503) at 0.9 mile, just after the trail joins long abandoned DBNF Road 5063 (37.03594N & 84.32351W). Though Trail 503 is listed as open to mountain bikes, only a short section along the river bottom east of the campground is suitable for riding.

Trail 503 turns right and continues along the contour until it reaches paved DBNF Road 807 at 1.1 miles (37.03747N & 84.3215W). Trail 503 is marked with white and orange diamond blazes. After crossing Road 807, descend steadily from the rim through a set of cliff bands, then wind alongside shallow rock overhangs covered with maidenhair ferns and rhododendrons. The trail clings precariously to the steep hillside. Some trail relocations on the descent have made the grade less steep, and the walking easier. At 1.3 miles, avoid an unmaintained social trail that branches left to reach Beach Narrows (37.03906N & 84.31938W).

Once you reach the riverside, the walking is nearly level and much easier, on a path that follows the trace of an old road. At 1.5 miles there is a sign pointing left to Beach Narrows along the social trail (37.03885N & 84.31594W). Two faint roads will join the route before a larger road intersects the trail at 1.8 miles, descending from the canyon rim (37.03707N & 84.31107W). The next mile of trail boasts some of the best early season wildflower watching in the state. Here you'll find spring beauties, trout lily, and bloodroot far earlier than on other nearby trails. This part of the narrows is perfectly sited to get enough early season sun to yield a prolific and diverse wildflower display.

A side trail next leads 300 feet down to the river at the Rockcastle Narrows. This all-day hangout spot gets up close to the class III white water of this Kentucky Wild River. The huge boulders shed from the plateau rim litter the narrow valley like pieces of a giant's puzzle set. If you look closely at some of the larger rocks in the river, you can spot the highwater marks left over from many years of spring floods.

Return to the main trail, and continue toward the campground. Just beyond the one-mile post, the cliffs to the right of the trail reach nearly one hundred feet above the river. You'll leave the old road to the right, then rejoin it near another side trail leading to the river. You'll reach the end of the trail at the end of the campground road at 3.6 miles. Walk back on the campground road, reaching the east end of the Bee Rock Loop Trail at 3.9 miles (37.02589N & 84.31646W).

The Rockcastle River has been designated a Kentucky Wild River. The 17-mile run from KY 80 to KY 192 at Bee Rock is rated class III-IV. Below Bee Rock, the Rockcastle River flows into the backwaters of Lake Cumberland.

The Bee Rock West Campground is open from April until October. Just across the river is the Bee Rock East Campground, which has a boat ramp and is open year round. Both campgrounds have some of the nicest sites in all of the national forest. The sites are spaced far apart, situated either next to the river or on private bluffs above it, and they have broad, smooth, level areas for tents. Several sites on the east bank are very private and can only be accessed by short side trails.

Bee Rock is a fee area. In 2015, the day use fee was $3, and overnight camping cost $8 for single campsites.

OTHER HIKING OPTIONS

1. Short and Sweet. The climb to the Bee Rock Overlook is a one mile round-trip.
2. The Bee Rock Loop Trail is 2.2 miles around and finishes on the west side of Sublimity Bridge on the campground entrance road.

Rockcastle Narrows

TOTAL DISTANCE: A 9.4-mile semi-loop on the Rockcastle Connector (DBNF 401A), Rockcastle Narrows (DBNF 401), and Sheltowee Trace (DBNF 100) Trails. The crossing of Cane Creek can be dangerous in high water. Though open to mountain bikes, these trails show no sign of use by bikes.

HIKING TIME: About 5 hours

DIFFICULTY: Difficult

LOCATION: London Ranger District, about 20 miles southwest of London

MAPS: USGS Ano and DBNF Bee Rock Trails

The Rockcastle Narrows hike begins across the river from the Bee Rock Loop. While the Bee Rock Loop has a friendly front country feel, the Rockcastle Narrows hike has a rougher, more backcountry feel. But the attractions along the trail are still first-rate. You'll see both the Rockcastle Narrows and Cane Creek, and you can make a short side trip to Vanhook Falls.

GETTING THERE

From Exit 38, off I-75 on the south side of London, follow KY 192 west for 18.8 miles to DBNF Road 624 on the east side of the Rockcastle River. Drive 0.4 mile through the Bee Rock Campground, and park either at the boat ramp or near the gate marking the start of the trail (37.02763N & 84.3206W). The Bee Rock area requires a $3 parking fee.

THE TRAIL

Begin by hiking along the Rockcastle Connector Trail (DBNF 401A), which starts out as an old road and is sporadically marked with white diamond blazes. Beyond a low hilltop capped with a concrete pad, the route turns into a footpath. The trail often ventures close enough to the river to offer some nice views of both its gentle and its more rollicking sections. You'll cross only one side stream, beside a house-sized boulder, before reaching the valley of Cane Creek at 1.6 miles, in an area where there are some possible campsites (37.02851N & 84.30432W).

Hike just far enough upstream to find Cane Creek choked with boulders shed from the plateau rim above. Close to the creek, the trail disappears from

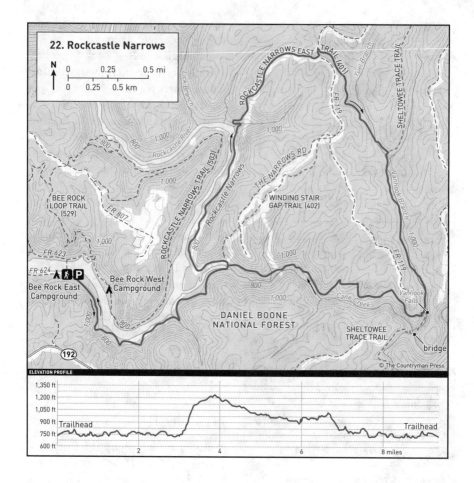

22. Rockcastle Narrows

periodic washouts, so you will need to work your way down the bank and try to make a dry crossing on the larger rocks. In spring, or in any high water, this crossing could be dangerous, and it should be avoided.

On the far bank of the creek, the trail is again difficult to find. In 2015, there was a blaze on the far side of the creek. Finding this spot is a great example of how useful GPS can be in the backcountry (37.0288N & 84.30349W). You should find a well-trodden trail here. Turn left to find a campsite near an old fire ring. This is the start of

the loop on the Rockcastle Narrows East Trail (DBNF 401). Take care to mark the place where you first intersect the trail. You will need to repeat this crossing on your return hike. To continue around the loop clockwise, go left. At 1.7 miles, you should find an unmarked trail entering on the right. This is the lower end of the Winding Stair Gap Trail (DBNF 402) (37.02912N & 84.30494W).

Past the junction with the Winding Stair Gap Trail, a short side trail leads left to a campsite near the confluence of Cane Creek and the Rockcastle

River. You next return to the river's edge and follow a pretty route through rhododendron and hemlock trees. At 2.4 miles, a side trail leads left to an overlook above a rocky set of narrows. Just beyond is another fine campsite. At 2.9 miles, cross a substantial side stream just above a small cascade. Beyond this crossing, look for a sharp right turn that marks the start of the climb away from the river (37.04105N & 84.30187W).

A few switchbacks along the climb lessen the grade somewhat, but the climb still remains steep. Near the plateau rim, the trail joins an overgrown logging road which enters from the left at 3.5 miles. Follow the logging road until you reach a stop sign at the junction with gravel DBNF Road 119 at 3.8 miles (37.04692N & 84.29296W). The stop sign doesn't protect you from much traffic. The road is gated closed about two miles north at its junction with DBNF Road 457. Turn left onto Road 119, and go about 250 feet; you'll see a sign pointing to a right turn off the road and down toward the valley of Vanhook Branch.

The Rockcastle Narrows East Trail descends along the right bank of Vanhook Branch. The trail here is wide, the forest open. You'll cross Vanhook Branch just before reaching the intersection with the Sheltowee Trace Trail (STT) and the north end of the Rockcastle Narrows East Trail, at 4.8 miles (37.03844N & 84.28539W). Turn right onto the STT, which continues a steady descent above the branch, but out of sight of it.

At 5.9 miles, the STT reaches the split with Trail 401 at a signed junction (37.02493N & 84.28091W). From this junction, the south end of the Rockcastle Narrows East Trail continues to the right. If you go left at the junction, and stay on the STT, you will reach Vanhook Falls in 0.1 mile, the bridge over Cane Creek in 0.25 mile, and the trailhead at the junction of KY 192 and 193 at 2.4 miles. The falls is a small water column that pours over the lip of a deep rockhouse. Both the falls and the bridge are scenic side trips.

Turn right and find the south end of the Rockcastle Narrows East Trail, which is signed, 150 feet up DBNF Road 119. A sign indicates that Winding Stair Gap Trail is 1 3/4 miles and Rockcastle River is 2 miles. Bear left at this point, avoiding an unsigned route that continues uphill to the right, likely to connect eventually with DBNF Road 119. The trail descends gradually alongside the Cane Creek midway between the creek and the cliffs above it. Few blazes mark this leg of the trail, so be careful not to miss a switchback to your left at 6.8 miles. Beyond the switchback, the trail crosses over the lip of a small waterfall. The trail moves closer to the creek as the valley narrows and high cliffs tower above.

At 7.8 miles, you should close the loop near the place where you first crossed Cane Creek. If you missed your crossing, you would intersect the unmarked, but blazed, lower end of the Winding Stair Gap Trail. Recross Cane Creek, and locate the Rockcastle Connector Trail on the other side. Retrace this trail to return to the trailhead at 9.4 miles.

The Rockcastle Narrows Loop traverses the heart of the 6,700-acre Cane Creek Wildlife Management Area. The DBNF first stocked Cane Creek with 20 whitetail deer in 1978, and the area is now an important habitat for these game animals.

BEE ROCK FROM SUBLIMITY BRIDGE

OTHER HIKING OPTIONS

1. Short and Sweet. A hike out and back on just the Rockcastle Connector Trail is 3.2 miles.

2. If water is high, the Sheltowee Trace Trail can be used to access the loop from the open portion of DBNF Road 119. This approach to the loop is 0.5 mile shorter, but it requires considerably more driving. Another access point is the STT, from the trailhead near the junction of KY 192 and 193.

3. The Winding Stair Gap Trail leads from the crossing of Cane Creek 1.2 miles to a point midway along the closed portion of DBNF Road 119. A return leg via Winding Stair Gap can be used to shorten the loop.

III.

DANIEL BOONE COUNTRY— NORTH

Indian Fort Mountain

23

TOTAL DISTANCE: A 3.3-mile semi-loop on trails for hikers only

HIKING TIME: About 2 hours

DIFFICULTY: Easy/Moderate

LOCATION: Berea College Forest, 3 miles east of Berea

MAPS: USGS Berea and Big Hill and Berea College Indian Fort Mountain Trails

---

The Berea College trail system is one of those pleasant surprises that hikers sometimes stumble across. Here is a place with beautiful trails leading to spectacular overlooks, situated just off the interstate by one of the Commonwealth's prettiest towns. The trail network at Indian Fort Mountain is a complex web that leads to five different overlooks on the mountain. The semi-loop described here combines the Indian Fort Overlook with a side loop to West Pinnacle. Part of the trail between Indian Fort Lookout and the West Pinnacle is steep enough to be difficult. The rest is easy walking.

GETTING THERE

From Exit 76 off I-75, drive east on KY 21. Keep right in 2.0 miles on KY 21, where the road splits at the Boone Tavern in the town of Berea. Pass the west trailhead for the Berea Trails, where KY 21 crosses KY 1617 at 4.0 miles. At 5.1 miles, reach the large parking area on the left side of the road for the Indian Fort Amphitheater (37.55426N & 84.24046W).

THE TRAIL

From the parking area, follow the paved path for 0.1 mile to Indian Fort Amphitheater. Here a trail sign indicates that the mountain was sacred to the prehistoric Hopewell Culture who lived in the area between 2,100 and 1,600 years ago. Beyond the trail is dirt, but wide and easy to follow. There are no blazes on the Berea Trails, but generally the trails easy to follow, as long as you pay attention to the many trail intersections. Much of the understory here is poison ivy, so be sure to stay on the trail. Climb steadily to reach a four-way signed junction at 0.6 mile

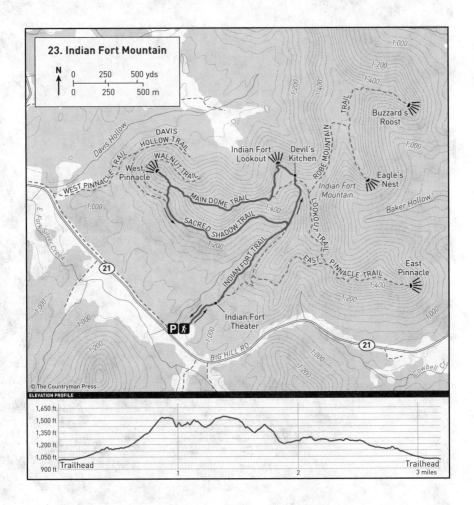

23. Indian Fort Mountain

N
0   250   500 yds
0   250   500 m

Davis Hollow

DAVIS HOLLOW TRAIL

WEST PINNACLE TRAIL

WALNUT TRAIL

West Pinnacle

Indian Fort Lookout

Devil's Kitchen

Buzzard's Roost

ROBE MOUNTAIN TRAIL

Eagle's Nest

Indian Fort Mountain

Baker Hollow

MAIN DOME TRAIL

SACRED SHADOW TRAIL

E. Fork Silver Creek

INDIAN FORT TRAIL

LOOKOUT TRAIL

EAST PINNACLE TRAIL

East Pinnacle

21

Indian Fort Theater

P

BIG HILL RD

21

Cowbell Cr

© The Countryman Press

ELEVATION PROFILE

1,650 ft
1,500 ft
1,350 ft
1,200 ft
1,050 ft
900 ft

Trailhead   Trailhead

1   2   3 miles

(37.56041N & 84.23283W). The trail to the right leads to East Pinnacle. The Sacred Shadow Trail to the left leads to West Pinnacle; this is your return route. Your route continues straight ahead on a narrower trail.

As you approach the crest of Indian Fort Mountain, several other trails will split off the main path. Just continue straight to reach another four-way intersection at the crest of the mountain (37.56331N & 84.2321W). The trail to the right leads to Robe Mountain, and the trail to the left leads to the West Pinna-

cle. Go straight, then bear left to reach a view above the roof of a deep rockhouse known as Devils Kitchen at 0.8 mile. There's no trail down into this opening, so you must be content with your view from above. Next pass "Jail House Rock," a wide crack in the rock rim that has been covered with iron bars. Finally, the overlook at Indian Fort comes into view at 1.0 mile.

From this vantage point, you can see west toward the town of Berea and West Pinnacle and north to Robe Mountain. Indian Fort Mountain lies at the edge

DEVIL'S KITCHEN

of the plateau country. To the west lies rolling farmland, the heart of the Bluegrass Country, while the land to the east is mostly rugged forests. In late spring, wild roses bloom at the overlook.

Though most hikers simply return to the trailhead from this point, adventurous hikers can reward themselves by visiting the other overlooks along the trail system. To reach the West Pinnacle, continue hiking along the rim to the west until you reach a signed junction at 1.2 miles (37.56237N & 84.23405W). Keep right at this junction toward West Pinnacle, and descend a steep, narrow, and well-worn route straight down the ridge

cap rock, regain the ridge crest. Don't be tempted to stop here. The real West Pinnacle is just a few minutes ahead. Stay on the trail and watch carefully for poison ivy growing alongside it. At 1.7 miles (37.56316N & 84.242W), note a side trail leading left off the ridge. This will be part of your return route.

At 1.8 miles, reach West Pinnacle, actually a pair of high capstones around which you can circle on the right side. You can enjoy some views through the trees from the overlook without getting to the top of the capstones, which most likely would require some rock climbing skills. Otherwise the view is partially obscured by trees. The capstones are formed from a hard pebbly sandstone layer overlying more easily eroded sandstone with cross-beds.

From West Pinnacle, return by retracing your route to 1.9 miles, to a point where a side trail leads south, off the crest. If you missed the side trail on your outbound leg, look for it at a line of short stubby, toadstool-like sandstone formations. At 2.0 miles, reach a junction (37.56203N & 84.24232W) where the signed Walnut Trail leads to the right. Just below, another old road by a post with no sign also leads to the right. This is the West Pinnacle Trail. Keep left on the Sacred Shadow Trail, which is now a wide old roadway and offers good views of the cliffs that guard the crest of Indian Fort Mountain. At 2.7 miles, intersect the main trail at a signed four-way junction to close the loop portion of the hike. To return to the trailhead, turn right and walk down past the amphitheater to reach the parking area at 3.3 miles.

Berea College was founded in 1855 by opponents of slavery, with the then-radical idea of equal education for men and women of all races. The college also

crest. This unlikely-looking route can be difficult for some hikers, but it levels off after reaching the base of a cliff band. With several unexpected turns, it may be hard to follow. The trail leads through a forest of pine, oak, maple, and sassafras, where fire pinks can also be found. About 50 feet before reaching a set out to provide work in lieu of tuition for as many as its students as possible. The founders were driven from the area during the Civil War, but returned afterward and continued to teach. From 1904 to 1950 Kentucky law prohibited interracial education, but the school became mixed again as soon as state law permitted.

Berea's popularity grew so much that in 1911 the school was forced to focus its efforts on students from the "neglected" region of Appalachia. After 1968 the College confined its efforts to undergraduate education, often receiving the highest awards for its academic programs. Berea still provides work-based full tuition scholarships to all students, and retains its commitment to serving Southern Appalachia.

The Berea College Forest protects 8,000 acres of woodlands east of the college and helps to protect the water source for the city of Berea. The forest was logged in the 1880's, but is now covered in mature second growth pine-oak on the drier ridgetops, and hardwood forest of basswood, oak, maple, walnut, ash, and hickory in the moister valleys. The forest is used for timber, recreation, education activities, and watershed management. It serves as a natural laboratory for the study of entomology, forestry, and water and timber management in the school's Forestry Department. In over 100 years as a working forest, it has produced 16 million board feet of saw timber.

The forest contains about eight miles of hiking trails. The forest also contains four water reservoirs and a treatment plant that, together, provide the surrounding area with nearly 800 million gallons of water per year. The 1,300-acre

Ownsley Fork watershed and 150-acre lake were purchased in 1970.

Much of the forest was logged around the turn of the last century. Other parts of the forest had been cleared, then over-farmed or over-grazed, subsequently becoming badly eroded. Early efforts at managing the forest were directed at controlling fires, stabilizing soils, thinning, and replanting trees. Many stands of Virginia and shortleaf pines have now reached old age and in normal forest succession would be replaced by hardwood stands. The southern pine beetle is hitting these stands hard. To counteract the beetle, the forest is replanting shortleaf pines.

OTHER HIKING OPTIONS

1. Short and Sweet. The round trip hike to Indian Fort Overlook is only 2.0 miles long.
2. Other fine overlooks at East Pinnacle (1.4 miles one-way), Eagle's Nest (1.6 miles one-way) and Buzzard's Roost (1.8 miles one-way) make fine day hikes.
3. Anglin Falls in the John B. Stephenson Memorial Forest State Nature Preserve is a 2.0-mile round-trip hike on well-maintained trail. The 75-foot-high falls fills the center of a spacious rockhouse at the head of a flower-filled hollow enclosed by sandstone cliffs laced with ornate patterns of iron concretions. The Forest is located off Anglin Fork Road near the old Disputanta Post Office.
4. The Berea College cross-country trails are located just south of the Boone Tavern on KY 595, at Brushy Fork Park.

24

Raven Run— Red Trail

TOTAL DISTANCE: A 4.8-mile loop on foot trail with several options for side trips

HIKING TIME: About 3 hours

DIFFICULTY: Easy

LOCATION: Raven Run Nature Sanctuary about 10 miles south of Lexington

MAPS: USGS Coletown and Raven Run Sanctuary

Raven Run Sanctuary hosts a gem of a trail system located just south of Lexington. These well-maintained trails explore historical sites, visit a scenic overlook above the Kentucky River, and offer one of springtime's most spectacular wildflower displays.

GETTING THERE

From Exit 97, off I-75 drive north on US 25 for 4.7 miles. Turn left onto KY 1975, which is Jacks Creek Road. At 8.5 miles, stay straight on KY 1976, where KY 1975 bears right. At 9.8 miles, turn left into Raven Run and reach the trailhead parking at 10.2 miles (37.88728N & 84.39733W).

THE TRAIL

Raven Run Sanctuary is packed with over 10 miles of hiking trails. The Red Trail, which circles the park, is the longest and most popular loop. The hike described here mostly follows the Red Trail, but it diverges off the Red Trail to visit the spectacular flower bowl and Mill Pond Dam.

From the northeast end of the trailhead, follow the paved path for 0.2 mile to reach the visitors center, (37.88857N & 84.3984W) where you can stop for trail information and then visit the displays inside. Continue past the visitors center on the bark chip Blue Trail to reach the trailhead for the Red Loop at 0.4 mile (37.89N & 84.39538W). Turn right to follow the loop counterclockwise and to encounter the various interpretive signs on the red loop in alphabetical order. The Red Loop is a wide dirt path that soon encounters a long section of distinctive stacked stone fencing, used by the early settlers to mark the edges of their fields.

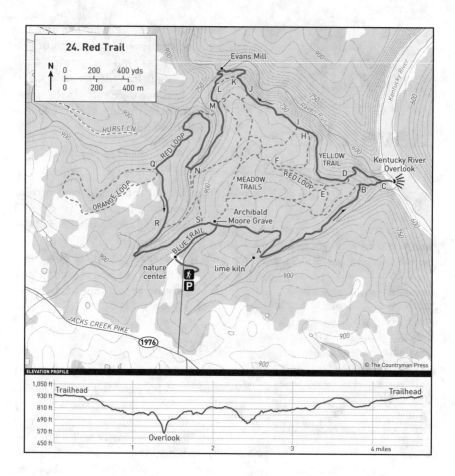

24. Red Trail

ELEVATION PROFILE

Spring flowers found here include phlox and larkspur. At 0.9 mile, a white-blazed trail leads right, to the site of an old lime kiln (37.88832N & 84.39243W). Be careful to avoid poison ivy if you decide to visit the kiln. Raven Run uses letters to mark the trail intersections on the Red Loop; the first of these, at the Lime Kiln, is designated "A."

Just beyond Junction B with a blue-blazed trail on the left, reach Junction C, which marks the side trail leading right to the Kentucky River Overlook at 1.5 miles (37.89243N & 84.38423W). The short path leads to a viewpoint above a graceful bend in the river.

Next, avoid an unofficial trail that leads right from a bench along the trail, and continue on the Red Loop to Junction D, with a yellow-blazed trail on the right at 1.7 miles (37.89258N & 84.38644W). This detour off the Red Loop visits the spectacular flower bowl, and it is a bit of a short cut as well. If you should happen to visit Raven Run at the right time in late April, you may be treated to perhaps the most impressive wildflower bloom in the region. The flower bowl hosts a diverse and prolific display of blooms, but most are overshadowed by the carpets of blue-eyed Mary, which cover the forest floor.

Rejoin the Red Loop at Junction H

THE FLOWER BOWL AT RAVEN RUN

at 2.0 miles (37.89508N & 84.38915W) as the trail passes along the rim of the gorge above Raven Run. Junction J marks a blue trail at the far end of a powerline crossing. At 2.4, miles reach Junction K, which marks a white-blazed side trail leading down to the site of Evans Mill (37.89808N & 84.39394W). Take this side trail down to a wooden platform above the mill site. Some flowers in this area may include Catesby's trillium, buttercup, and bishop's cap.

Rejoin the Red Loop again at Junction L at 2.7 miles (37.89763N & 84.39547W). Junction M next leads left to a blue-blazed trail just before a powerline crossing, and Junction N at 3.1 miles (37.89308N & 84.39711W) marks the end of another blue-blazed connector trail. Pass two more powerline crossings and Junction P before reaching Junction Q, which marks the start of the Orange Loop at 3.7 miles (37.89296N & 84.39969W).

From the Orange Loop, the trail descends to reach a small creek and Junction R (which marks another blue-blazed connector trail) at 3.9 miles (37.88975N & 84.39928W). The trail will cross the creek on a high wooden bridge. Before closing the loop at 4.4 miles, pass Junction S, the final junction, and pass the grave of Archibald Moore. From the end of the loop, retrace your inbound route back to the visitors center and the parking area at 4.8 miles.

Raven Run is a 734-acre nature sanctuary dedicated to preserving the natural beauty of the Kentucky River Palisades and early Kentucky history and is operated by Lexington Parks and Recreation. There is no fee to use the park, but hours vary seasonally, so be sure to call ahead. The park preserves a number of historical sites from the 1700s to the early 1900s and is home to over 300 species of wildflowers, 200 species of birds, and 40 species of trees. The Sanctuary was dedicated in 1977, and the current Nature Center was completed in 2010.

OTHER HIKING OPTIONS

1. Short and Sweet. The accessible Freedom Trails begins at the parking area.
2. Raven Run offers a complex of green-blazed Meadow Trails that are within the Red Loop.
3. The orange starts at Junction Q and is a 1.0-mile loop mowed into a grassy area on the west side of the park. The loop offers some good views, but should be avoided in tick season.
4. The white- and blue-blazed trails at Raven Run are generally very short connectors between the longer trails.

25

The Original Trail

TOTAL DISTANCE: This 3.3-mile loop hike includes a side trip to Lookout Point. The route uses the Original, Laurel Ridge, Rock Garden, and Battleship Rock hiking trails.

HIKING TIME: About 2.5 hours

DIFFICULTY: Easy/Moderate

LOCATION: Natural Bridge State Resort Park, about 3 miles east of Slade

MAPS: USGS Slade, Natural Bridge State Resort Park Trail Guide and Outragegis Mapping, Red River Gorge

Not surprisingly, the Original Trail was the first trail built at Natural Bridge State Park. And due at least in part to park signs calling it "the easiest trail to Natural Bridge," it is by far the park's most popular trail, and it may even be the most heavily-used trail in the state. The Original Trail deserves its fame. It is a historic, well-graded route to a spectacular arch and to a wonderful overlook.

GETTING THERE

From Exit 33 off the Mountain Parkway at Slade, drive south on KY 11 for 2.8 miles. Turn right into the main parking area for Natural Bridge State Park. The Original Trail starts at the far end of the parking area (37.77553N & 83.67813W) on a well-used walkway.

THE TRAIL

Since there are a number of routes leading to Natural Bridge from the same place, hikers should pay attention to the trails at the start. Almost every visitor first hikes up the Original Trail, but there are four other routes that can be used to return to the Lodge area. All are exciting and scenic, but the Rock Garden Trail is the longest, and least-used, so it may be the best match for the Original Trail.

The Original Trail begins at the far end of the parking area, by a large sign. Since the route is so heavily used, much of it is up stone steps, graveled, or fenced, to keep hikers on the route. Not far from the start, the trail splits, and a short cut to the Nature Center goes left. The Original Trail goes right and climbs to a paved walkway at 0.2 mile by some benches.

The walkway leads left to the Nature Center, where there are displays on the mammals of the Red River Gorge Area. To

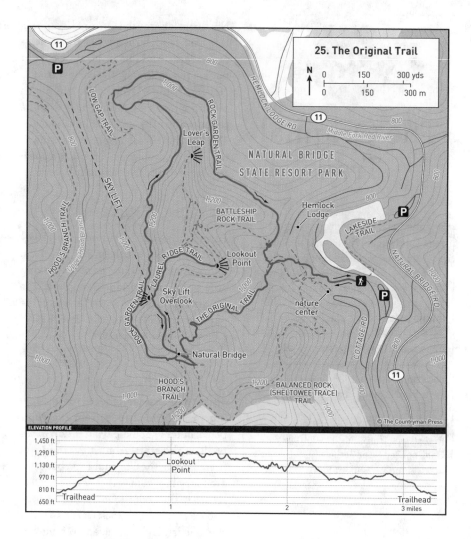

25. The Original Trail

N
0 150 300 yds
0 150 300 m

ELEVATION PROFILE

1,450 ft		
1,290 ft		
1,130 ft	Lookout	
970 ft	Point	
810 ft	Trailhead	Trailhead
650 ft		

1   2   3 miles

the right, the walkway leads to a parking area in back of Hemlock Lodge. Cross the walkway and go straight uphill to a junction with the Balanced Rock Trail (and Sheltowee Trace), which leads left. Go right and immediately come to another junction at 0.3 mile (37.77605N & 83.6817W), this time with the Battleship Rock Trail (your return route), which joins from the right, and the Balanced Rock Trail, which joins from the left. Stay straight, and continue to climb on the Original Trail.

The trail climbs past a trail shelter built in the 1930s by the Civilian Conservation Corps. Next is a small cave on the left side, which you can explore with the aid of a flashlight. Beyond this point, the trail continues a steady climb. The climb is not long enough, or steep enough, to trouble most experienced hikers, but it can seem far too long to those unused to walking on trails. Several other covered shelters make good resting points for the weary. Just before you reach the Natural Bridge, at 0.8 mile, there is a short cut to the right to the Battleship Rock Trail and Devil's Gulch (37.7738N & 83.68537W).

At 0.9 mile, the Original Trail reaches

NATURAL BRIDGE FROM LOOKOUT POINT

the base of Natural Bridge (37.773N & 83.68551W). On the opposite side of the front of the bridge is the upper end of the Battleship Rock Trail. On the back-side of the bridge are junctions with the Hood's Branch Trail on the left and the Rock Garden Trail on the right.

Your best close-up view of the bridge is from below. Here you can see the graceful curve of the top of the opening. To reach the flat top of the bridge, you must follow the trail up the thin crack on the far left side of the bridge. This long "squeeze" leads to some steps. To the right, at the top of the steps, is the upper end of the Balanced Rock Trail (which leads to the Sheltowee Trace Trail). Straight ahead is a large gazebo. To the left is the top of the bridge.

The top of Natural Bridge is not fenced, but it is wide enough to be safe for those who are paying attention to their surroundings. From the top of the bridge, you can see across the park, over the valley of Whittleton Branch to Red River Gorge. You will probably also see a prominent overlook to your left with many people on it. This is aptly named Lookout Point, a worthy destination for a large-scale view of Natural Bridge.

To reach Lookout Point, cross the arch and continue on the Laurel Ridge Trail to the top of the Sky Lift. The Sky Lift is a ski-type lift that climbs the back side of the park. Pass the Sky Lift and continue along the level trail until you reach the open views of Lookout Point at 1.3 miles (37.77598N & 83.68394W), which is the best vantage point for photos of Natural Bridge. From Lookout Point, return to the base of the Bridge to continue your loop on the Rock Garden Trail at 1.7 miles.

The Rock Garden Trail crosses under

THE SKY LIFT AT NATURAL BRIDGE

the Sky Lift and follows the base of the cliff band where Natural Bridge has formed. These cliffs offer one of the best displays of concretions visible to hikers in the park. The concretions form swirls or honeycomb patterns in the sandstone. They arise because the iron oxides that hold the individual sand grains of the rock together can be harder than the sand itself. As the sandstone is eroded, the concretions remain in relief as the sand is gradually worn away. These types of rocks also form rockhouses, the shallow overhangs that early peoples might have used as shelter. You'll see some rockhouses, too.

The trail next follows the ridgetop through an area of laurel and rhododendron, both plants that bloom wonderfully in summer. At 2.7 miles, reach a junction with the Low Gap Trail that leads left 0.5 mile down to the Sky Lift parking area (37.7811N & 83.68795W). The trail finally begins to descend down three narrow stairways carved into bare sandstone. Pass a house-sized boulder beside a wood bridge before coming to an area where there are views of Hemlock Lodge below.

As you leave Hemlock Lodge behind, the well-worn Battleship Rock Trail joins from the right at 3.4 miles. Just beyond, intersect the Original Trail, and turn

railroad, who built a campground, a picnic area, and the Original Trail. By 1926, the railroad had left the park business, and they donated Natural Bridge to the state to become one of the four original holdings in the Kentucky State Park system. The state built the original Hemlock Lodge in 1927, and by the late 1920's the park could be reached by a gravel road from Slade. The park built a new lodge in 1963. The original lodge burned in 1969.

Natural Bridge remains one of the state's most popular, and most beautiful, state parks. In addition to the park trails, Sky Lift, and Hemlock Lodge, the park contains two campgrounds at Middle Fork and Whittleton Branch (the site of the 1930s Civilian Conservation Corps Camp), cottages, and an immensely popular public swimming pool. There are also two snack bars, gift shops, and an activities center with nature displays. There is an active schedule of interpretative programs with several events per day offered in the summer. Red River Gorge is also one of the region's prime rock climbing areas. Though there is no rock climbing allowed on the state park lands, surrounding private and national forest lands in the Red River Gorge contain several exciting areas.

OTHER HIKING OPTIONS

1. Short and Sweet. Natural Bridge and Lookout Point can be reached from the Sky Lift in a one half-mile walk. However, the Sky Lift operates only seasonally.
2. The Lakeside Trail is a 0.6-mile round-trip hike along the lake that is also part of the Sheltowee Trace Trail.
3. The Battleship Rock and Balanced Rock Trails can be combined into a 2.0-mile loop that also leads to Natural Bridge.

left on it to return to the parking area (37.77605N & 83.6817W) at 3.8 miles.

Red River Gorge was still wild and unknown in the 1880s, when the Kentucky Union Lumber Company first built railroad tracks up the river. The forests were soon cut, and the logs hauled by oxen to the railroads, and brought to the huge mill at Clay City. The loggers came first for the prime hardwoods, mostly, white oak, chestnut, and yellow poplar. By the end of World War I, the logging boom was dead, the area almost completely cut over, and the rail lines and logging camps abandoned.

The park was established in 1895 by the

26

Hood's Branch and Sand Gap Trails

TOTAL DISTANCE: A 10.4-mile loop on foot trails which includes part of the Sheltowee Trace Trail and a visit to Natural Bridge.

HIKING TIME: About 5.5 hours

DIFFICULTY: Difficult

LOCATION: Natural Bridge State Resort Park, about three miles southeast of Slade

MAPS: USGS Slade, Natural Bridge State Resort Park Trail Guide and Outragegis Mapping, Red River Gorge

The hiking trails at Hood's Branch and Sand Gap form a backcountry loop on the back side of Natural Bridge State Park. The short trails on the Hemlock Lodge side of the park are heavily used and well worn, but few hikers explore the longer trails on the Sky Lift side of the park; a shame since these trails combine a backcountry sense of solitude with front country highlights.

GETTING THERE

From Exit 33 off the Mountain Parkway at Slade, drive 2.2 miles south on KY 11 to the entrance of Natural Bridge State Park. Cross the Middle Fork of the Red River and turn right. Drive 0.7 mile, past the Sky Lift, to a parking area by the snack bar and mini-golf area (37.78176N & 83.69076W).

THE TRAIL

The Hood's Branch and Sand Gap Trails form a 10.4-mile loop on the backside of Natural Bridge State Park, between the Sky Lift and Natural Bridge. This long walk is an all-day affair. Once hikers reach the Sand Gap Trail, there is no opportunity for an easy shortcut.

The Hood's Branch Trail starts behind the snack bar and mini-golf course just beyond the main parking area for the Sky Lift. Start the trail with a climb up some wood steps, then take a sharp left above the maintenance area where a path joins from the right. Hood's Branch begins as if the trail means to climb all 500 feet to Natural Bridge in one breathless gulp. But after the junction with the end of the Sand Gap Trail at 0.1 mile (37.78052N & 83.6907W), the grade eases.

Turn left to stay on the Hood's Branch Trail, which follows above the west bank

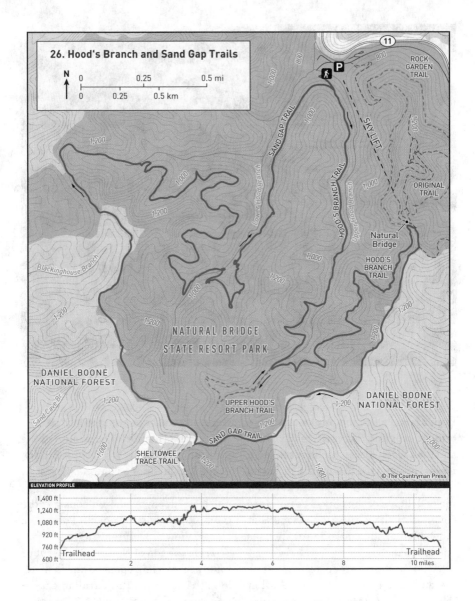

26. Hood's Branch and Sand Gap Trails

N

| 0 | 0.25 | 0.5 mi |

| 0 | 0.25 | 0.5 km |

ROCK GARDEN TRAIL

SKY LIFT

ORIGINAL TRAIL

Natural Bridge

HOOD'S BRANCH TRAIL

SAND GAP TRAIL

HOOD'S BRANCH TRAIL

Lower Hood Branch

Upper Hood Branch

NATURAL BRIDGE STATE RESORT PARK

Blackinghouse Branch

DANIEL BOONE NATIONAL FOREST

DANIEL BOONE NATIONAL FOREST

Sand Cave Br.

UPPER HOOD'S BRANCH TRAIL

SAND GAP TRAIL

SHELTOWEE TRACE TRAIL

© The Countryman Press

ELEVATION PROFILE

| 1,400 ft |
| 1,240 ft |
| 1,080 ft |
| 920 ft |
| 760 ft | Trailhead | | | | Trailhead |
| 600 ft | | 2 | 4 | 6 | 8 | 10 miles |

of Upper Hood's Branch through hardwood forest. At 0.6 mile there is a small wooden shelter to the right that was built in the 1930s by workers from the Civilian Conservation Corps and was restored in 1979. As you climb higher along the branch, the trail makes several crossings on wood bridges. The forest changes to a mix of boggy open areas and dark hemlock forests. Along some side branches

you'll find lush, bright green fern gardens. Even in midsummer you can spot flowers such as spiderwort in bloom.

At 1.6 miles, reach the junction with the upper loop of the Hood's Branch Trail (37.76491N & 83.69496W). This semi-loop trail adds an extra 0.7 mile to the hike, but it rewards the journey by visiting two deep rockhouses. Go left from the junction on a wood bridge over

LOOKOUT POINT FROM NATURAL BRIDGE

Upper Hood's Branch. Make one more bridged crossing of a very small stream and then reach a deep rockhouse. You'll now walk along the base of the cliff band that forms Natural Bridge, and the other rocky delights of the park. The cliffs are covered in thick rhododendrons that hide some of the trailside rockhouses and overhangs.

After a short, steep climb, reach the end of the Hood's Branch Trail at the base of Natural Bridge at 3.0 miles (37.773N & 83.68551W). In contrast with the solitude of Hood's Branch, the many front-side trails that converge here lead a horde of hikers to this scenic spot. But who could resist joining them, with a trip to the top of the Bridge so close? To reach the top of the arch, climb through the long, narrow crack at the base of the south side of the bridge and climb the stairs to the top.

Carefully walk out onto the bridge for a view of the Hemlock Lodge side of the park, and a look up Whittleton Branch in the Daniel Boone National Forest. If you haven't already walked the Original Trail hike, you should consider the 0.8-mile side trip to Lookout Point for a classic view of Natural Bridge.

From the top of Natural Bridge, your route passes a large gazebo and then follows the Balanced Rock Trail to a junction at 3.1 miles (37.77182N & 83.6845W). Here the Balanced Rock Trail (and the Sheltowee Trace to the north) goes left down to Hemlock Lodge, and the start of the Sand Gap Trail (and the Sheltowee Trace to the south) goes right. The next two miles are the easiest hiking on the loop. The trail follows a narrow ridge top along the south boundary of the park. In a short distance, the parkland also becomes part of the 994-acre Natural

Bridge State Nature Preserve, which was dedicated in 1981. The Preserve protects the habitat of the Small Yellow Lady's Slipper, a Kentucky endangered species, and the Virginia big-eared bat, a federally endangered species.

At 4.6 miles, just after entering the Daniel Boone National Forest, the Sheltowee Trace splits to the left, just short of a wooden gate (37.76103N & 83.70062W). Just beyond the gate, an old sign indicates the STT leads 7 miles south to Standing Rock and 16 miles south to the Kentucky River. From the gate, continue north along the ridgetop and cross back into the park at 5.4 miles. The forest here is typical of the dry ridgetop environment. Shortleaf pine, red maple, scarlet oak, and chestnut oak dominate the canopy, while sassafras is a common smaller tree. The trail veers off the left side of the ridge top to visit a small overlook with views through the forest at 5.8 miles. A few old mile mark-

VIEW FROM LOVERS LEAP IN NATURAL BRIDGE STATE PARK

ers can still been seen marking the way, a useful amenity for one of the longest stretches of trail in the state with no road or trail junctions.

After crossing to the right side of the ridge in a small saddle, reach a small pocket-cave above the left side of the trail that marks the start of a pretty bluff line segment. Begin the descent from the ridge at 6.3 miles. Turn sharply to the right after crossing a small stream on a wood bridge and begin a short steep climb. For the next few miles, the trail will climb in and out of the headwaters of Lower Hood Branch. Notice how the vegetation changes as the trail alternates between the wet valleys and dry ridgetops. At 8.7 miles, cross the headwaters of Lower Hood Branch on a wood bridge by a bench.

Make two more short climbs before reaching another, welcome bench at 9.3 miles. There's a high bridge on a side branch just before you regain sight of the main branch. After a double bridge, the trail begins to follow an old road. At 10.0 miles, leave the Nature Preserve, and at 10.3 miles, reach the intersection with the Hood's Branch Trail. Turn left onto the Hood's Branch Trail and reach the trailhead at 10.4 miles.

OTHER HIKING OPTIONS

1. Short and Sweet. Hikers can use the Sky Lift (for a fee) to ascend to Natural Bridge, and then they can enjoy a 3.0-mile downhill walk on the Hood's Branch Trail.
2. The new Low Gap Trail leaves from the north end of the Sky Lift parking area and leads 0.5 mile to the Rock Garden Trail and on to the Natural Bridge.
3. The Sheltowee Trace Trail leads 3.7 miles south from Natural Bridge to KY 1036. Much of the rest of the STT immediately south of the park is on roads or is open to ATVs.

Whittleton Arch

TOTAL DISTANCE: A 4.4-mile round trip on the Whittleton Arch (DBNF 217) and Whittleton Branch (DBNF 216) Trails which are for foot travel only.

HIKING TIME: About 2.5 hours

DIFFICULTY: Easy/Moderate

GENERAL LOCATION: Red River Gorge Geological Area, about 3 miles east of Slade

---

MAPS: USGS Slade, DBNF Red River Gorge Geological Area and Outragegis Mapping, Red River Gorge

---

Whittleton Arch is a good example of the high payoffs of hiking at Red River Gorge. Here is a scenic arch that is easy to reach from trailheads on both the Daniel Boone National Forest and Natural Bridge State Resort Park. In the early days of the timber boom at Red River Gorge, loggers built a branch of the logging railroad up the narrow valley of Whittleton Branch to extract the trees they'd harvested from the forests atop the gorge. Nowadays, all that remains from the railroad is a short section of corduroy along the trail, and a healthy stand of second growth forest. Don't merely consider the forest as background while you hike to the arch. Here is a chance to marvel at the power of nature to regenerate itself.

GETTING THERE

From the Slade Exit off the Mountain Parkway, drive 3.3 miles east on KY 15 to the junction with the DBNF Road 39, which is the Tunnel Ridge Road. On the right side of this junction is a small pullout, as well as signs for the Whittleton Branch and Sheltowee Trace Trails (37.79694N & 83.65428W). To reach the south trailhead at Whittleton Campground from the Slade Exit, drive 2.5 miles east on KY 11 to the campground entrance. You must park in the day use area, and not at site A37, where the trail begins.

THE TRAIL

Whittleton Arch can be reached from either a trailhead on KY 15, or from the Whittleton Campground on KY 11 in Natural Bridge State Resort Park. Though most hikers will return to the trailhead from the arch, the hike is short enough that many will want to hike the

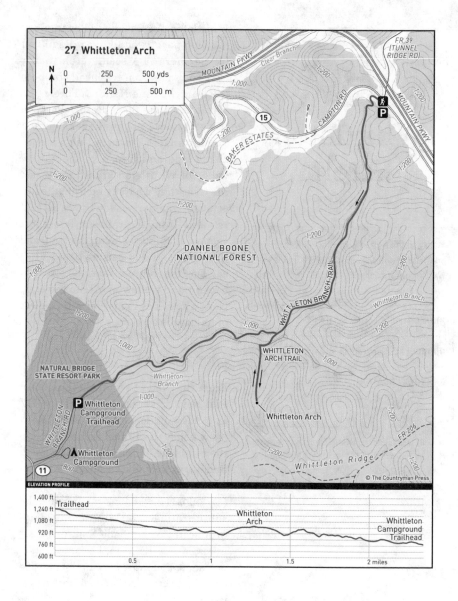

27. Whittleton Arch

N

| 0 | 250 | 500 yds |
| 0 | 250 | 500 m |

MOUNTAIN PKWY

Clear Branch

FR 39
(TUNNEL
RIDGE RD)

1,000

1,200

1,200

CAMPTON RD

MOUNTAIN PKWY

15

BAKER ESTATES

1,200

1,200

1,000

1,200

DANIEL BOONE
NATIONAL FOREST

1,200

1,200

1,000

WHITTLETON BRANCH TRAIL

Whittleton Branch

1,200

1,000

WHITTLETON
ARCH TRAIL

1,000

NATURAL BRIDGE
STATE RESORT PARK

Whittleton
Branch

1,000

WHITTLETON BRANCH RD

P Whittleton
Campground
Trailhead

Whittleton Arch

1,200

1,200

FR 206

1,200

Whittleton
Campground

11

800

1,200

Whittleton Ridge

© The Countryman Press

ELEVATION PROFILE

1,400 ft	Trailhead				
1,240 ft					
1,080 ft			Whittleton Arch		Whittleton Campground Trailhead
920 ft					
760 ft					
600 ft		0.5	1	1.5	2 miles

whole trail. The Whittleton Branch Trail is also part of the Sheltowee Trace Trail.

From the small parking area on KY 15, follow the foot trail south down steps that have been carved into the sandstone bedrock. The white diamond-shaped blazes lead down three switchbacks into the bottom of the narrow valley. This dark and damp area is dominated by hemlock, pitch pine, and rhododendron, with Christmas fern in the understory. The pines of Red River Gorge have not suffered from the southern pine beetle like their neighbors to the south, perhaps because colder winters have kept the beetles' population in check.

Once in the valley, you cross a small side branch. The next branch is unbridged, and it may flood the trail immediately after a hard rain. The val-

WHITTLETON BRANCH TRAILHEAD

ley is so narrow in places that the trail and stream must share the same route. In others, the trail is lined with moss and ground cedar, giving the trail the appearance of a narrow green tunnel.

At 0.5 mile, Whittleton Branch cuts through an especially thick and hard layer of sandstone. Rockhouses line both sides of the trail, and Whittleton Branch drops over a 6-foot cascade. Farther down the trail, the cliffs loom to nearly 60 feet high, and you can study the unusual concretions revealed in the deeply pockmarked sandstone.

Cross a wooden bridge by a leaning rock at 0.8 mile. Just beyond a split log bridge across a tributary on the right, reach the signed junction with the Whittleton Arch Trail (217) at 1.1 miles

(37.78598N & 83.66057W). Turn left onto Trail 217 and descend to Whittleton Branch before crossing on a sturdy wood bridge. Reach the arch at 1.4 miles (37.78266N & 83.66191W). Whittleton Arch appears to have formed from the collapse of the rear of a large rockhouse. There is a small wet-weather waterfall that pours over the right side of the opening of the arch. This impressive arch is about 55 feet long, 40 feet wide, and 30 feet high. The open and airy base of the arch is an ideal spot for a lunch break before starting your return hike back to the Whittleton Branch Trail at 1.7 miles.

To hike from the side trail junction to Whittleton Campground, continue south on the trail from the junction.

The trail drops from the side of the gorge down to Whittleton Branch, where traces of the old logging railroad grade are still visible. Here the trail makes many crossings of the stream on wood bridges, several of which were replaced in 2004. The bridges surely were a major challenge for both those who laid the first rail tracks through here and those now tasked with maintaining the hiking trail. Notice how the water in the stream disappears and reappears. The branch flows over limestone in the lower reaches, and its water comes and goes from underground passageways. At 2.5 miles, come to the Whittleton Campground Trailhead near site A37 (37.7827N & 83.67304W). To reach the parking area, you must walk through the campground to the day use parking area at the campground entrance station. If you have left your car at the upper trailhead, retrace your route back to end the hike at 4.4 miles.

The first rail line was pushed into Red River Gorge in the 1880s by the Kentucky Union Lumber Company. The track up Whittleton Branch was run by the Mountain Central Railway and operated until 1928, just two years after the establishment of Natural Bridge State Park.

The Red River Gorge Geological Area was designated in 1974 and protects 26,000 acres around the Red River. The Geological Area results from a bitter land-use battle fought over the gorge in the 1960s and 1970s. On one side was the Army Corps of Engineers, who proposed a $34 million dam that would flood 5,000 acres on the North Fork of the Red River for flood control. On the other side were conservationists and fiscal conservatives who felt that the dam would not be cost effective, would endanger or destroy critical habitats, and would benefit only a small number of downstream landowners. The dam project was killed in 1975 by a formal objection by Kentucky Governor Caroll.

Further protection of the area came in 1985 with the creation of the Clifty Wilderness, and in 1993 with the designation of the Red River as a National Wild and Scenic River. The river is home to sensitive fish species and twenty-three types of mussels. Along with the common white-tailed deer, bobcats, coyotes, and an occasional black bear have been spotted in the Area. The Geological Area contains over 100 arches. Of the approximately 5.5 million annual visitors to the DBNF, 500,000 per year visit the gorge.

OTHER HIKING OPTIONS

1. Short and Sweet. It is a slightly shorter trip to the arch by way of Whittleton Campground.

2. From Whittleton Campground, the 0.3-mile Henson Arch Trail leads to an unusual arch in the Natural Bridge State Resort Park. Instead of being formed from sandstone, Henson Arch is formed from limestone. It looks more like part of a collapsed cave than like an arch. Part of the roof remains over a cylinder-shaped hole. The smooth, fluted, and vertical walls remind one of the underground waterfall at Cascade Cave in Carter Caves State Park, or of a smaller version of Mammoth Dome in Mammoth Cave National Park. The arch is named for Clarence Henson, a former park superintendent.

3. From the trailhead on KY 15, the Sheltowee Trace Trail leads north about 0.7 mile to the Grays Arch Trailhead.

Courthouse Rock and Double Arch

TOTAL DISTANCE: An 6.4-mile loop hike on foot trails to Courthouse Rock, with an out-and-back leg to Double Arch. The hike uses the Auxier Ridge, Auxier Branch, and Double Arch Trails.

HIKING TIME: About 3.5 hours

DIFFICULTY: Moderate/Difficult

LOCATION: Red River Gorge Geological Area, Stanton Ranger District, about 8 miles north of Slade

MAPS: USGS Slade, DBNF Red River Gorge Geological Area and Outragegis Mapping, Red River Gorge

The trails on the west side of the Red River Gorge Geological Area pack the biggest punch of any of the trails in the area. Sure, they are packed with stone arches and rockhouses, but no other trails in the area, and perhaps in the state, can match the wide open views from Auxier Ridge. Here is a perfect escape from any claustrophobic feeling of being trapped in the woods.

GETTING THERE

From the Slade Exit off the Mountain Parkway, drive 3.3 miles east on KY 15 to Tunnel Ridge Road (DBNF Road 39). Turn left and drive 3.7 miles north to the end of the gravel road at the Auxier Ridge Trailhead (37.8202N & 83.68092W). Keep in mind that the Tunnel Ridge Road does not intersect KY 77. In fact, it crosses high above the Nada Tunnel and KY 77.

THE TRAIL

Since the publication of the first edition of this guide, the DBNF has completed an upgrade of the trails in this area. The section of Tunnel Ridge Road beyond the Auxier Ridge Trailhead was closed and is now part of the Double Arch Trail (201). The Auxier Ridge Trailhead was moved a bit to the east, and the first part of the Auxier Ridge Trail was relocated. These changes have made a loop hike possible that includes the Auxier Ridge and Double Arch Trails, and I've revised this hike to return via the Double Arch Trail rather than on the Courthouse Rock Trail.

From the parking area, walk north on the Auxier Ridge Trail (204) which is marked by the familiar white diamond-shaped blazes of the DBNF. The new section of trail starts on a narrow fin of rock,

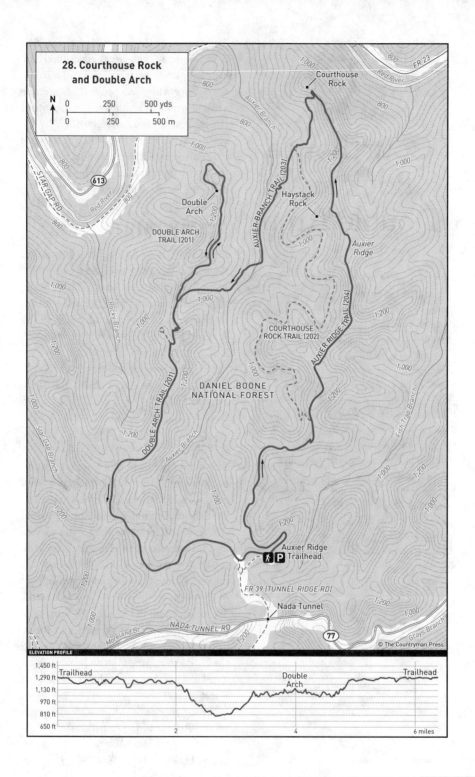

28. Courthouse Rock and Double Arch

N

| 0 | 250 | 500 yds |
| 0 | 250 | 500 m |

Courthouse Rock

Red River

FR 23

Auxier Branch

STAR GAP RD

613

Red River

Double Arch

Haystack Rock

DOUBLE ARCH TRAIL (201)

AUXIER BRANCH TRAIL (203)

Auxier Ridge

Rocky Branch

COURTHOUSE ROCK TRAIL (202)

AUXIER RIDGE TRAIL (204)

DANIEL BOONE NATIONAL FOREST

DOUBLE ARCH TRAIL (201)

Star Gap Branch

Auxier Branch

Fish Trap Branch

Auxier Ridge Trailhead

FR 39 (TUNNEL RIDGE RD)

Nada Tunnel

NADA TUNNEL RD

Moreland Br

77

Grays Branch

© The Countryman Press

ELEVATION PROFILE

1,450 ft		
1,290 ft	Trailhead	Trailhead
1,130 ft		
970 ft	Double Arch	
810 ft		
650 ft		
	2	4	6 miles

COURTHOUSE ROCK AWAITS AT THE END OF AUXIER RIDGE

and then it switchbacks sharply to the left to follow below a band of sandstone cliffs. In 0.4 mile, regain Auxier Ridge at a point where the old trail enters on the left. The trail leads north across the forested ridgetop to an intersection with the Courthouse Rock Trail (202) on the left at 0.9 mile (37.8266N & 83.67825W). The Courthouse Rock Trail leads 1.9 miles to the Auxier Branch Trail and provides an alternate return route for those who are just hiking to Courthouse Rock and back. Stay right and continue on the ridgetop on the Auxier Ridge Trail.

Approaching Courthouse Rock is a half-mile of unrestricted views from the narrow, cleared top of the ridge. You'll work your neck as much as your legs as you try to keep up with this "out west" scale scenery. But be sure to keep at least one eye on the path; there are no fences at these overlooks to protect the oblivious hiker. There are many dry campsites scattered along the ridgetop, but remember that Red River Gorge regulations prohibit camping within 300 feet of any roads or trails.

Courthouse Rock is one of those places you can spend all day exploring. Here long, narrow Auxier Ridge has been broken up into a series of high turrets and graceful towers nearly one hundred feet high. You'll need rock-climbing skills and equipment to climb to those points, but many great overlooks are easily accessible, and Courthouse Rock always appears enticingly ahead. To the west is the ridge containing Double Arch, which is occasionally visible; on the other side is the sheer dome of Raven Rock, capped with an unruly grove of trees, like a bad toupee. Two sets of wood-and-metal ladders mark the descent down to the saddle at the base of Courthouse Rock (37.84179N & 83.67784W) at 2.2 miles.

A number of unofficial "social trails" lead around the rock. These are safe to explore only for experienced hikers. Our route turns left off the ridge and begins a steady descent down the north end of the Courthouse Rock Trail (202). Look carefully here, and you can see Double Arch on the ridgeline to the west.

At 2.5 miles, reach the junction with the Auxier Branch Trail (203) (37.8392N & 83.67944W). Bearing left will take you more directly back to the trailhead on the Courthouse Rock Trail. To continue to Double Arch, bear right onto the Auxier Branch Trail. At the valley bottom, turn left and follow Auxier Branch upstream a short distance before crossing it near a spot others have used for a campsite. Climb gradually to the intersection with the Double Arch Trail (201) at 3.3 miles (37.83225N & 83.68613W) below a set of impressively high cliffs.

At this junction, the Double Arch Trail leads left 0.3 mile to the former trailhead on the now-closed portion of the Tunnel Ridge Road and is part of your return route. Go right and begin the side trip toward Double Arch. The trail stays nearly level as it traverses north along the base of a massive cliff band. You can see other arches in the making in the graceful, arched roofs of large rockhouses within the cliffs. If you keep a sharp eye out, and you're lucky, you'll spot Double Arch at the top of the cliff long before you reach it. The trail wraps around the nose of the ridge and traverses the west side for a short distance before reaching the arch at 4.0 miles (37.83753N & 83.68399W).

Double Arch is one of the most unusual arches in the Area. It is not uncommon for arches to occur side by side at Red River Gorge, but Double Arch is unique in that two arches are stacked on top of each other. The arches are similar in style to the "classics," like Natural Bridge or Grays Arch, that have formed by the erosion of thin ridges of highly resistant sandstone. The upper arch is a narrow slot, perhaps formed by the collapse of a single sandstone bed. The main lower arch is about 20 feet long, 15 feet wide, and 12 feet high. Framed perfectly in the opening of the arch is a view of Courthouse and Haystack Rocks on adjacent Auxier Ridge. Step carefully though as you enjoy the view. A fall from the arch over the cliffs below would certainly be fatal.

Once you've enjoyed all Double Arch has to offer, retrace your route back to the junction of the Auxier Branch and Double Arch Trails, just below the top of Auxier Ridge. At this point, you have walked 4.7 miles. Continue south on the Double Arch Trail. This section of trail is heavily used and uses switchbacks and wooden ladders up a steep fissure in the rocks to climb to the old trailhead site at 5.0 miles (37.83031N & 83.68677W). The rest of the hike uses the section of Double Arch Trail that was created from the closure of the old end of the Tunnel Ridge Road. The old road makes for fast, easy hiking and the number of side tails leading to dry campsites attest to its popularity with backpackers. At 6.2 miles, reach the former Auxier Ridge Trailhead near a gate. Here the trail turns sharply left to follow the new trail back to the current trailhead at 6.4 miles.

OTHER HIKING OPTIONS

1. Short and Sweet. The trip to Courthouse Rock and back from the Auxier Ridge Trailhead is 4.4 miles round trip. It is not necessary to hike the

entire distance to enjoy the fine overlooks from the ridgetop. A return trip via the Courthouse Rock Trail is 5.3 miles.

2. Koomer Ridge Campground on the east side of the Area has a similar system of short, high-impact trails. The Silvermine Arch Trail (DBNF 225) is a 1.3-mile trail to Silvermine Arch. In 2001, the trail was rebuilt around a set of collapsed stairs. The 1.2-mile Hidden Arch Trail (DBNF 208) can be combined with the Koomer Ridge Trail past this small arch. The Cliff Trail (DBNF 206) is a 0.5-mile connector along the bluff line between the campground and the Silvermine Arch Trail.

Grays Arch— Rough Trail Loop

TOTAL DISTANCE: This 9.1-mile loop on foot trails also includes the Buck Trail and parts of the Koomer Ridge and Pinch-Em-Tight Trails.

HIKING TIME: About 5 hours

DIFFICULTY: Difficult

LOCATION: Red River Gorge Geological Area, Stanton Ranger District about 4 miles northeast of Slade

MAPS: USGS Slade, DBNF Red River Gorge Geological Area and Outragegis Mapping, Red River Gorge

Of all the stonework on display at Red River Gorge, Grays Arch is perhaps the most impressive. This colossal arch has all the graceful curves and rugged beauty that hikers desire in a backcountry arch. The arch also anchors one end of the only hiking loop in the main gorge area long enough for overnight trips. The full loop is mostly of interest to backpackers. You don't need to take a long hike to see Grays Arch, but likely you'll be inspired to stay in the woods as long as you can. The loop has several stream crossings that could lead to wet feet for hikers in high water.

GETTING THERE

From Exit 33 from the Mountain Parkway at Slade, drive 3.3 miles east on KY 15 (37.79694N & 83.65428W). Turn left on the Tunnel Ridge Road (DBNF 39), and drive 0.9 mile to the Grays Arch Trailhead (37.80809N & 83.65758W). This trailhead may fill up on popular weekends, but there are other nearby parking areas along the Tunnel Ridge Road.

THE TRAIL

From the trailhead at Grays Arch, start north on the Grays Arch Trail (DBNF 205). At 0.3 mile, reach a junction with the Rough Trail (DBNF 221) (37.80914N & 83.66013W). The Rough Trail leads left 1.3 miles to KY 77, while our trail to the right continues to Grays Arch. This next section is part of both the Rough and Grays Arch Trails and is marked with white diamond-shaped blazes. Beyond the junction the trail is wide and sandy, a result of the heavy use this route receives. In about 0.5 mile, pass through a cleared area kept open for wildlife habitat.

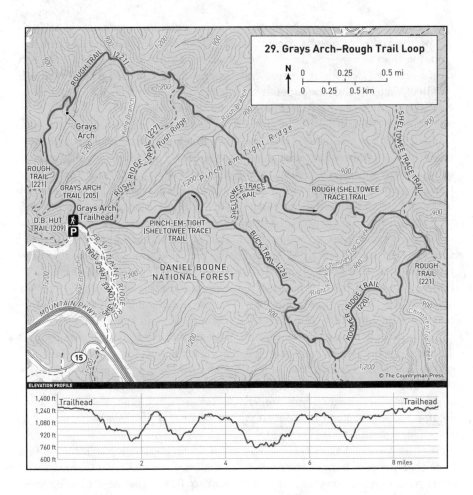

29. Grays Arch–Rough Trail Loop

ELEVATION PROFILE

Don't expect to see Grays Arch until the trail has dropped off the ridgetop. You'll descend past a shallow rockhouse and down several flights of wood stairs before reaching a trail junction at 1.1 miles (37.81762N & 83.65788W). This spot offers a great topside view of the Arch. The spur trail right leads about 500 feet to the base of Grays Arch. The arch sits at the narrow end of a long sandstone ridge. The rock is a massive bed of sandstone, dotted with pebbles of clean white quartz. Extending 80 feet long and 50 feet high, Grays is also one of the largest in the area and is a rare backcountry arch that approaches

the size of Natural Bridge in the state park or Natural Arch near the Big South Fork. Ruchhoft reports that Grays Arch was well known to loggers during that era, but the subsequent regrowth of the forest hid the arch until the 1930s, when it was relocated after a summer of searching.

Return to the main trail at 1.3 miles, and hike below the massive sandstone layer that forms the gorge rim. Many of the boulders along the trail are laced with unusual patterns of iron concretions in the sandstone. The concretions are harder than the surrounding sandstone; as the rock weathers, the concretions appear to resemble a bas-relief. Below the rim, evergreens are more common than above. You'll see abundant hemlock (look for the short flat needles), laurel, and rhododendron. Near the confluence with King Branch, you'll see many areas where others have camped. But remember, the Forest Service asks that campers stay at least 300 feet from any developed trail or road. Camping is prohibited within 100 feet of the cliff line or within rockshelters.

Turn up King Branch, and then turn up a side branch. After ascending two sets of wood stairs, reach the signed junction with the Rush Ridge Trail (DBNF 227) at 2.4 miles (37.81915N & 83.64628W). You can take a short cut here by following Rush Ridge to the right for 1.2 mile back to the trailhead. To complete the longer loop, stay left on the Rough Trail, which soon begins to earn its name. After a long, graceful rockhouse, reach a steep and eroded section leading to Rush Branch. Next there is a high rockhouse on the right, which fills the end of a box canyon. The trail goes directly down to the bottom of the box canyon where there are some blazes. Do not follow any of the false trails on the left side of the canyon wall. Though these look as well traveled as the main trail, they lead to precarious ledges.

The descent eases somewhat as the trail approaches Rush Branch. The overused campsites next to the creek should be avoided in favor of less visible and impacted sites. The climb out of Rush Branch is tough at the start, but it becomes easier close to the ridgetop. During the climb, you can see that there are two main rock layers that form rockhouses in the canyon. The most obvious layer is the one that forms both the rim of the gorge and Grays Arch. But there

is also a similar layer closer to the valley floor. True to form, on this climb you can see a small rockhouse in it. As you approach the rim, a short side trail will lead you right to a larger rockhouse in the upper layer.

At 3.6 miles, reach the junction with the Pinch-Em-Tight Trail (37.81068N & 83.63611W), which here is also part of the Sheltowee Trace Trail. This is your second chance for a shortcut. A right turn will lead you back to the parking area in 1.6 miles. This trail's unusual name comes from a gap to the north of the trail that was so narrow that anyone passing through was pinched. To continue on the longer loop, keep left on the combined Rough and Sheltowee Trace Trails and enjoy some level trail across the ridgetop. The ridgetop supports a pine-oak forest with some hemlock trees, common in many of the drier ridgetops in the Area. Many of these pines are white pine. They are easy to recognize, since the needles occur in clusters of five.

Part of the ridgetop was burned in a 1999 arson-caused fire. Pines are resistant to all but the most intense fires, so many of the older trees survived the burn. Most of the plants growing in the understory did not. The race to repopulate this habitat is fierce, and new growth in the burn looks much thicker than that under the undisturbed forest.

Beyond the burn, the Rough Trail soon begins the descent toward Chimney Top Creek. You'll rock hop the Right Fork, then the main fork, before reaching the split between the Sheltowee Trace and Rough Trails at 4.9 miles (37.80805N & 83.62138W). From the junction, the STT leads left along Chimney Top Creek 1.3 miles to KY 715 along the Red River. Your loop keeps right and crosses back to the right side of the

MORNING LIGHT FROM THE INSIDE OF GRAYS ARCH

creek, reaching a signed junction with the Koomer Ridge Trail (DBNF 220) at 5.1 miles (37.80543N & 83.61876W). From this point, the Rough Trail leads left 0.6 mile to Chimney Top Road and 2.4 miles to KY 715. Your route goes right to follow the Koomer Ridge Trail.

The area around Chimney Top Creek has what many campers look for in a backcountry site. Water is close by; there are many smooth, level areas; and the pine- and hemlock-shrouded slopes are as beautiful as one could want. However, some of these sites are badly worn, and the forest service asks that campers stay at least 300 feet from the trail.

The Koomer Ridge Trail leaves Chimney Top Creek on the right bank with a sharp switchback to the right. The climb toward the rim is steep at first, and then it moderates. Along the way, you pass a small rock tower that has a bowling ball–sized hole through its base. The trail climbs one more steep pitch before reaching the ridgetop at an area where some have made a dry camp. At 6.4 miles, reach the signed junction with the Buck Trail (DBNF 226) (37.79636N & 83.62907W). From here, the Koomer Ridge Trail goes left one mile to the Koomer Ridge Campground. Stay on the Buck Trail to continue on the loop.

The Buck Trail descends to make our second visit to the steep narrow valley of the Right Fork of Chimney Top Creek. Turn right and follow the right bank of the creek making three rock hops of the creek. There are several old campsites here. Exit the creek to the left, and begin a steady climb. Pass below a high, overhanging rock tower, beyond which the trail steepens.

At 7.9 miles, reach the ridgetop junction with the Pinch-Em-Tight and Sheltowee Trace Trails (37.8077N & 83.64007W). To the right is the end of our second shortcut, leading 0.4 mile back to the Rough Trail. Go left at the junction and enjoy ridgetop walking for the rest of the hike. Watch to the left of the trail for a potential campsite and a side trail to an overlook.

At 8.9 miles, reach the signed junction with the Rush Ridge Trail and the end of our first shortcut (37.80786N & 83.65317W). Keep left to reach the gravel Tunnel Ridge Road within sight of the trailhead. Then turn right to reach the Grays Arch Trailhead, reaching the end of the loop at 9.1 miles.

OTHER HIKING OPTIONS

1. Short and Sweet. A trip to Grays Arch and back is an easy 2.4-mile round trip.
2. The D. Boon Hut Trail (DBNF 209) is a 0.7-mile trail leading to a protected rockshelter containing a small hut, perhaps used by Daniel Boone.
3. The loop can be cut short by taking either the Rush Ridge Trail for a 3.7-mile loop, or the Pinch-Em-Tight Trail for a 5.3-mile loop.
4. The main loop can also be accessed from KY 77 by hiking 1.3 miles on the west end of the Rough Trail.

Swift Camp Creek— Wildcat Loop

TOTAL DISTANCE: The loop is 5.5 miles on the Swift Camp Creek (DBNF 219) and Wildcat (DBNF 228) Trails, and it includes a short return hike on KY 715. Clifty Wilderness trails are foot travel only.

HIKING TIME: About 3 hours

DIFFICULTY: Moderate

LOCATION: Clifty Wilderness Area, Stanton Ranger District, about 7 miles east of Slade

MAPS: USGS Pomeroyton, DBNF Red River Gorge Geological Area and Outragegis Mapping, Red River Gorge

While most of the hiking trails in the main area of Red River Gorge are ideal for day hiking, it's the longer trails of the adjacent Clifty Wilderness that are perfect for backpackers seeking longer escapes. Here hikers can flee the often-crowded trails in the main gorge to enjoy the solitude and peace found only far from the trailhead.

GETTING THERE

From Exit 40 from the Mountain Parkway, drive 1.3 miles west on KY 15 to the community of Pine Ridge. Turn right on KY 715 and drive north. In 3.0 miles, pass the Wildcat Trailhead, passing the Angel Windows Trailhead in another 1.1 miles. In another 0.3 mile, reach the gravel Swift Camp Creek Trailhead which also serves the Rough Trail. (37.80218N & 83.59101W).

THE TRAIL

Trails in the Clifty Wilderness occur both north and south of the Red River, with no current connection between the two. Swift Camp Creek-Wildcat is the only loop in the south half of the wilderness. It is suitable for day hiking, or for backpackers.

The Swift Camp Creek Trail starts across KY 715, at the south end of the trailhead parking area. Like all trails in the wilderness, it is marked with white diamond paint blazes. The trail parallels the road for a short distance, then it drops into the head of White Branch, where an unmarked side trail from the Angel Windows Parking area joins from the right at 0.3 mile (37.79831N & 83.59065W). Just beyond, the ground is covered with big leaf magnolia.

The trail continues along a wide ridge through a forest of pine, maple, beech,

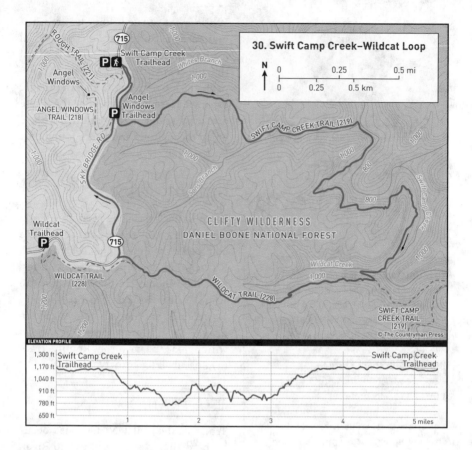

© The Countryman Press

and oak familiar to gorge hikers. When the trail turns right off the ridge to descend into the valley of Sons Branch, the forest changes quickly. Hemlock, laurel, and rhododendron are the most common trees where water is more abundant, and sunlight less so.

The trail crosses many side branches of Sons Branch in the upper reaches. As you descend further into the valley, the trail passes shallow rockhouses in the cliffs and overhanging boulders large enough to make their own "boulder houses." At 1.6 miles, the trail reaches Swift Camp Creek, on the north bank of Sons Branch (37.79857N & 83.57264W).

Many campers have used campsites located at the confluence, but these sites are now closed. The Forest Service now asks that campers stay 300 feet from any developed trail or road. Camping is not permitted within 100 feet of the of the base of cliff lines, or within rock shelters. There are other sites along Swift Camp Creek that are open to camping.

From the confluence, be sure to watch for white arrows to guide you down to the next section. Wriggle around two huge boulders in Sons Branch, then zigzag up and over a small bluff to end up beside Swift Camp Creek. The infrequently blazed trail along the creek will be tougher than trails you've experienced so far. Instead of winding along the narrow creek bottom, the trail stays along the midslope above the creek's west bank.

Still, there are cliff bands and small

IRON STAINS ON SANDSTONE ON THE SWIFT CAMP CREEK TRAIL

rockhouses, as well as glimpses of the creek, to entertain you. At 2.4 miles, there is a false trail on the right leading up to a rockhouse along a small branch. Swift Camp Creek Trail next takes a sharp turn to the left and switchbacks down to seasonal "Red Falls." At the falls, another small branch pours over the lip of a rusty iron-stained layer of sandstone.

You'll pass two more potential campsites between the trail and the creek before making an easy rock hop over Wildcat Creek at 3.1 miles. From the creek, climb to the signed junction with the Wildcat Trail at 3.2 miles (37.78933N & 83.57133W). The sign indicates that Rock Bridge Picnic Area is 4.5 miles ahead on the Swift Camp Creek Trail. Turn right here to follow the Wildcat Trail.

You've got a steady one half-mile climb ahead above Wildcat Creek

before the trail levels out along the ridgetop at a closed campsite. The rest of the trail will follow long abandoned dirt roads back to KY 715. There is an unmarked junction at 4.1 miles with an old road leading to the south. Its companion road to the north, just beyond, is hardly recognizable. Next, there is another road junction on the left, leading to a private cemetery that is not part of the Wilderness Area, but used by the Ashley and Baker families, at 4.4 miles (37.78997N & 83.58949W). The dirt road beyond this junction is in better shape. Stay on the road until it reaches KY 715 at 4.5 miles (37.79029N & 83.59094W). Don't make the left turn just before the road, which keeps hikers on the Wildcat Trail until it reaches the Wildcat Trailhead. You need only follow the Wildcat Trail to the end if you have left a car at the Wildcat Trailhead.

From KY 715, turn right on the paved

road and walk to the Angel Windows Trailhead at 5.2 miles. You can make the extra 0.6-mile round trip to the Windows, or you can continue straight on either KY 715 or Trail 219 to reach the Swift Camp Creek Trailhead at 5.5 miles.

The Clifty Wilderness was the second Wilderness Area to be designated in Kentucky. In 1985, the U.S. Congress protected almost all of the Red River Gorge east and north of KY 715 with this designation. At 12,646 acres, Clifty is almost three times as large as the state's other wilderness at Beaver Creek, in the Stearns Ranger District. Designation as wilderness protects the area against activities such as logging, mining, or road building. Motorized vehicles and mechanical vehicles, such as mountain bikes, are also prohibited. The goal of wilderness management is to minimize human impact on the land, and to allow the area to remain in a condition where people are only temporary visitors and leave no impact on the land. The DBNF manages these areas at a more primitive level, so that these trails tend to be a bit more rugged and challenging than other hiking areas in the forest.

OTHER HIKING OPTIONS

1. Short and Sweet. The Angel Windows Trail (DBNF 218) is a 0.6-mile out-and-back hike to the Windows, a pair of small arches at the end of a narrow ridge. This would be a great hike when blackberries are in bloom.

2. If you are able, leave a second vehicle at the Wildcat Trailhead, so you can combine the Swift Camp and full Wildcat Trails for a 5.0-mile one-way hike.

3. The Sky Bridge Trail (DBNF 214) and Whistling Arch Trail (DBNF 234) are 0.9-mile and 0.2-mile walks easily accessible from KY 715, just north of the Swift Camp Creek Trailhead. Long, delicate Sky Bridge is one of the signature features of the Red River Gorge. You shouldn't miss the arch, and the views from it. Whistling Arch is a comparatively smaller arch near the end of the thick sandstone layer that forms the cap of much of the gorge.

4. An alternate, and longer way, to approach the loop is from Rock Bridge Road and Picnic Area and the south end of the Swift Camp Creek Trail. From the picnic area, the Wildcat Trail is about a 4.5-mile walk.

5. The east end of the Rough Trail (DBNF 221) is also located at the Swift Camp Creek Trailhead. It is about 2.0 miles from the Trailhead to Chimney Top Road.

31

Gladie Creek Loop

TOTAL DISTANCE: A 9.2-mile loop on the Bison Way (DBNF 210), Sheltowee Trace (DBNF 100), Lost Branch (DBNF 239), and Osborne Bend (DBNF 240) Trails. Horses use part of the Lost Branch and Osborne Bend Trails. The loop includes a short walk on KY 715 between the two trailheads. It will be necessary to ford Gladie Creek if water is high.

HIKING TIME: About 5 hours

DIFFICULTY: Difficult

LOCATION: Clifty Wilderness, Stanton Ranger District, about 11 miles northeast of Slade

---

MAPS: USGS Pomeroyton, DBNF Red River Gorge Geological Area and Outragegis Mapping, Red River Gorge

---

The Clifty Wilderness north of the Red River now has its own excellent trail system. The Bison Way, Sheltowee Trace, Lost Branch, and Osborne Bend Trails can be accessed from trailheads near the DBNF Gladie Visitor Center; they offer the long loops through the wilderness that make backpacking so rewarding.

GETTING THERE

From Exit 40 off the Mountain Parkway, drive 1.3 miles west on KY 15 to the community of Pine Ridge. Turn right on KY 715 to the north. Drive 10.3 miles and park just beyond the bridge over Gladie Creek, at the signed trailhead (37.83682N & 83.60936W). If you have two cars, leave the other one 1.5 miles back on KY 715 at a small turnout at the mouth of Sal Branch, which is the west end of the Osborne Bend Trail.

THE TRAIL

Your loop starts outside of the Clifty Wilderness on the Bison Way Trail (DBNF 210), which connects the parking area near the Gladie Creek Bridge with the Sheltowee Trace Trail and is marked with white diamond-shaped blazes. The trail begins in a hardwood forest, interspersed with hemlock groves, typical of ridge areas in the Red River Gorge. The trail descends wood steps to make a bridged crossing of Sargent Branch just before intersecting the Sheltowee Trace Trail at 0.6 mile (37.84265N & 83.61135W).

Turn right on the wide Sheltowee Trace and enter a grove of hemlocks. Notice how little vegetation grows underneath these trees. Hemlock needles, and the needles of other conifers, are highly acidic, and so they change the chemistry of the soil when they decom-

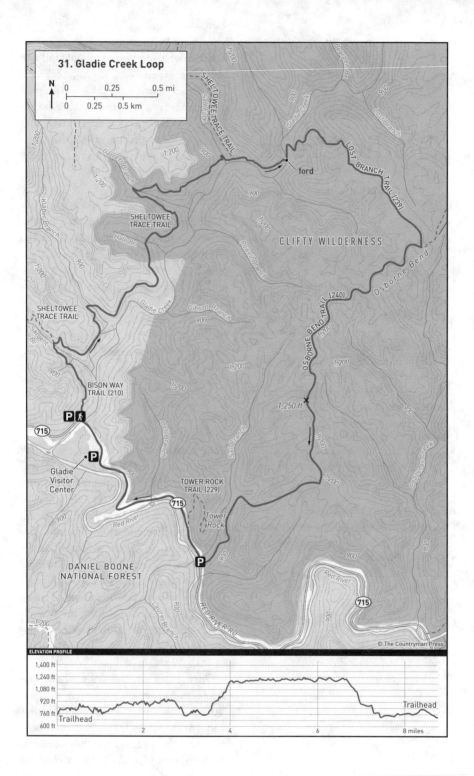

31. Gladie Creek Loop

N

| 0 | 0.25 | 0.5 mi |
| 0 | 0.25 | 0.5 km |

SHELTOWEE TRACE TRAIL

Sulphur

Garrett Branch

1,200

1,200

Halo Br.

SHELTOWEE TRACE TRAIL

900

Klaber Branch

1,200

900

Gladie Creek

SHELTOWEE TRACE TRAIL

Sargent Br.

900

BISON WAY TRAIL (210)

715

P

P

Gladie Visitor Center

900

Red River

900

Laurel Branch

DANIEL BOONE NATIONAL FOREST

1,200

Gladie Creek

Lost Branch

900

ford

LOST BRANCH TRAIL (239)

CLIFTY WILDERNESS

Powell Branch

Osborne Bend

OSBORNE BEND TRAIL (240)

1,200

1,200

1,200

Gibson Branch

900

1,200

Salt Branch

Bell Branch

1,200

1,250 ft.

1,200

1,200

TOWER ROCK TRAIL (229)

715

Tower Rock

P

RED RIVER RD

900

Red River

900

Copperas Creek

900

900

715

© The Countryman Press

ELEVATION PROFILE

1,400 ft						
1,240 ft						
1,080 ft						
920 ft					Trailhead	
760 ft	Trailhead					
600 ft		2	4	6	8 miles	

pose. Conifers and a few other plants, such as Christmas fern, can grow in the acidic soil, but many other plants cannot. The lack of underbrush allows the conifers and their allies to prosper; not coincidentally, the lack of underbrush also attracts campers who much prefer open conifer groves to the brushy campsites in hardwood areas.

The trail next makes an easy crossing of Klaber Branch on stepping-stones after a short, but steep, descent. The trail stays along the contour, too high above the creek for summer viewing. Look for the large leaves on the low shoots of big leaf magnolia. In summer, the light gray backs of these leaves provide the only break in the dense green carpet of the forest floor. You can tell big leaf magnolia from other similar magnolias by both the size of the leaf and by looking for a small notch in the base of the leaf where it connects to the stem. Big leaf and Fraser magnolias have this notch, while other magnolias do not.

After you cross into Clifty Wilderness, at 2.3 miles there is a side trail to the left up to a nice campsite on a small bench. Water is just beyond, at another small branch. Next, reach the huge

RESTORED CABIN NEAR THE GLADIE VISITORS CENTER

sandy expanse at the confluence of Salt Fork and Gladie Creek. Don't be fooled by the wide, deep pool in the creek below the campsite. In most places, the creek is not as wide and much shallower. Rock hop over Salt Fork and climb up the nose of a small ridge to the junction with the Lost Branch Trail (239) at 3.0 miles (37.8566N & 83.59377W). While the STT turns left and north at the junction, our route follows Lost Branch, which goes right. Follow the white-blazed trail down to Gladie Creek, where it intersects a well-used horse trail along the river at 3.3 miles.

Depending on conditions, the trail across the creek can be difficult to follow. Typically the water is less than knee-deep, but in high water it may not be possible to ford safely at this crossing. Ford the river to a point directly across from you, on the far bank. If all goes well, you'll find a few blazes and a small campsite in the small stream valley on the far side.

The trail exits the valley with a sharp right turn and begins a steep climb up a trail badly abused by horse traffic. The trail climbs up a steep, rock-strewn mud slope, pockmarked with hoof prints and sprinkled with horse droppings. Soon, the trail reaches the top of Osborne Bend Ridge and begins a level walk on another old road to a T-junction with the Osborne Bend Trail (DBNF 240) at 4.7 miles (37.84976N & 83.57541W).

The trail to the left turns east along Osborne Bend, luckily taking most of the horse traffic with it. Your route goes right and follows the Osborne Bend Trail toward Tower Rock. The trail generally stays along the crest of this narrow ridge, except when it makes a few slight detours.

At 6.7 miles, an abandoned trail splits to the left near the end of the ridge. Soon you begin a steep descent toward Sal Branch. At the end of the steep descent, turn left and travel above Sal Branch. The trail passes two old concrete block structures. The first is short and stubby with a heavy steel door that indicates it might have been used to store explosives, while the second is tall enough to walk into. Reach the signed end of the trail and KY 715 at 7.7 miles. If you were unable to leave a car here, you must walk 1.5 miles right on KY 715 to the Gladie Creek Parking Area to finish the hike at 9.2 miles.

OTHER HIKING OPTIONS

1. Short and Sweet. The Tower Rock Trail (DBNF 229) is one of the Red River Gorge's finest short walks. The 1.0-mile semi-loop climbs to the base of Tower Rock and then circles it. The entire loop offers views up the magnificent tower, which was the site of some of the gorge's earliest rock climbing activity. Even if there are no climbers, see if you can spot some of the routes they might use.

2. The Bison Way and Sheltowee Trace Trail to the south can also be combined into a 3.9-mile hike between trailheads that are 1.2 miles apart.

3. You can extend the hike by another mile by using the east leg of the Osborne Bend Trail, which reaches KY 715 at the concrete bridge over the Red River at the eastern edge of the wilderness. This is a great option for those with two cars, but otherwise it leaves a significant amount of road walking for those hiking back to the Gladie Creek Trailhead.

32

Cave Run Lake Loop

The hiking trails around Cave Run Lake are some of the best in the entire Daniel Boone National Forest. Here are trails both scenic enough for short journeys and long enough for overnight trips. This compact area has plenty of variety, and thanks to a new 2013 plan, there are trails for hikers, mountain bike riders, and horse riders. There are hikes along the lakeshore, trails hugging the ridgetops, tremendous vistas, and opportunities for solitude.

TOTAL DISTANCE: The 10.2-mile loop uses the Tater Knob, Buck Creek, Cross Over, Hog Pen, Buckskin, Connector, and Cave Run Trails which are shared with mountain bikes and horses, and a short section of the Zilpo Road.

HIKING TIME: This is a moderate overnight backpack or a 5.5-hour day hike on trails shared with mountain bikes.

DIFFICULTY: Difficult

LOCATION: Cumberland Ranger District, about 12 miles south of Salt Lick

MAPS: USGS Salt Lick and Daniel Boone National Forest Cave Run Lake

GETTING THERE

From the junction of US 60 and KY 211, drive 3.7 miles south on KY 211. Turn left on DBNF Road 129, which becomes the Zilpo National Forest Scenic Byway. Drive 3.9 miles and turn left onto DBNF 918, which is Zilpo Road. Continue for 4.7 miles to a pullout on the right side of the road with an interpretive sign for the Tater Knob Fire Tower (38.05592N & 83.54452W) just before the junction with DBNF 918B, which leads to the former parking area for Tater Knob. You can also access the loop at either intersection of the Crossover Trail (107) with the Zilpo Road.

THE TRAIL

The Cave Run Lake Loop explores the heart of the south side of the Cave Run Lake Trail system. This loop is not too long for most day hikers, but backpackers will enjoy the loop for its diversity, challenge, and scenery. From the trailhead, follow a gentle trail marked by white diamond-shaped blazes to the south. In 0.3 mile, intersect the former parking area for the Tater Knob Firetower (38.05361N & 83.5426W). This historic structure was burned in an arson fire on December 3, 2008,

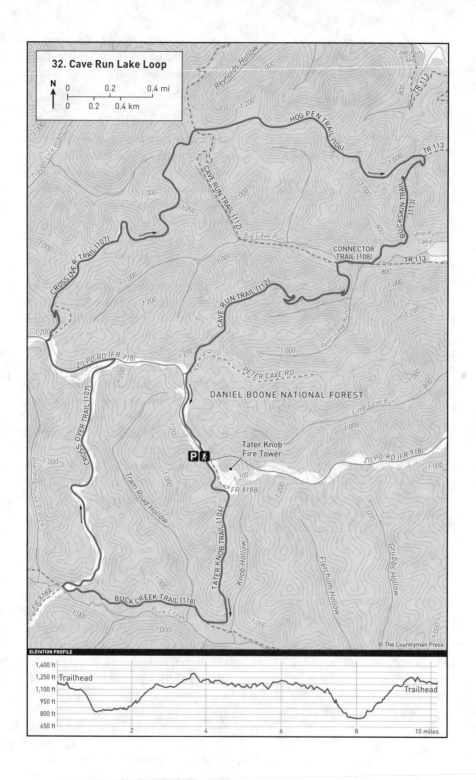

32. Cave Run Lake Loop

N

0   0.2   0.4 mi

0   0.2   0.4 km

Reynolds Hollow

Cave Run Lake

TR 113

HOG PEN TRAIL (106)

Trough Lick Branch

CAVE RUN TRAIL (112)

TR 113

BUCKSKIN TRAIL (113)

Cave Run Lake

CROSS OVER TRAIL (107)

Big Cave Run

CONNECTOR TRAIL (108)

TR 113

CAVE RUN TRAIL (112)

Peter Cave Run

ZILPO RD (FR 918)

PETER CAVE RD

DANIEL BOONE NATIONAL FOREST

Little Cave Run

CROSS OVER TRAIL (107)

Tater Knob Fire Tower

ZILPO RD (FR 918)

Boardinghouse Branch

Train Road Hollow

FR 918B

TATER KNOB TRAIL (104)

Knob Hollow

Fletchum Hollow

Grubbs Hollow

FR 918A

BUCK CREEK TRAIL (118)

Buck Creek

© The Countryman Press

ELEVATION PROFILE

1,400 ft
1,250 ft Trailhead
1,100 ft   Trailhead
950 ft
800 ft
650 ft

2   4   6   8   10 miles

and since then it has been closed by the Forest Service. Tater Knob was known until the 1930s for the small spring at the base of the Knob. Then in 1934, the Civilian Conservation Corps went to work. To ferry supplies to the tower site, nine men built a road (now the Tater Knob Connector Trail) from Buck Creek to the site in only six days. Think about that kind of productivity next time you're stuck in traffic because of one of those seemingly endless road construction projects. A new cab was added to the tower in 1959. The tower was manned to the mid-1970s, the last manned tower on the forest. Unfortunately, the 2008 fire completely destroyed the tower's cab. The stairs to the tower are still visible, and the interpretive signs for the tower and the spring used by the tower men are still in place.

From the tower, take the Tater Knob Trail (DBNF 104) south. The trail begins by following the ridge crest, but it soon drops off the left side to arrive at a junction with the Buck Creek Trail (DBNF 118) at 1.0 mile (38.04509N & 83.54437W). The orange-blazed Buck Creek Trail is an old road (formerly DBNF 1056) that is shared by hikers, mountain bikes, and horses in season. Turn right onto Buck Creek and enjoy some easy walking along the north side of the creek. You'll note that the Pioneer Weapons Wildlife Management Area supports a healthy wildlife population. Flocks of turkey as large as 12 birds have been spotted along the trail. The trail near the creek can be wet, and there is one small stream that must be rock hopped. Pass a large flat campsite to the left just before reaching a locked gate across the road at the crossing with DBNF Road 918A at 1.9 miles (38.04735N & 83.55674W). Here the Buck Creek Trail continues ahead and is open to horses. Our route now takes the Cross Over Trail (107) and turns right and follows the well-maintained roadway uphill toward the Zilpo Road. The Forest Service currently plans to build a new section of Trail 107 for hikers and mountain bikes that will bypass the upper portion of this road section.

At 3.4 miles (38.06232N & 83.55237W), reach the intersection with the Zilpo Road and turn left to walk the road shoulder. At 3.9 miles, turn right off the road (38.06353N & 83.55815W) at the start of road DBNF 1225. Trail 107 has been greatly altered by the new Forest Service plan for the Cave Run Area. The south half of Trail 107 formerly linked Buck Creek and the Zilpo Road with a foot trail up Boardinghouse Branch. That section was eliminated by moving Trail 107 onto Road 918 A. The north half of Trail 107 now consists of a short section of foot trail, and a longer section of Road 1225. Our route leaves the Zilpo Road to follow the foot trail section of Trail 107, which splits left from Road 1225 about 50 feet past the Zilpo intersection. This section may not be well maintained so be prepared for some blowdowns and brushy sections.

At 4.2 miles, turn left at an intersection onto DBNF Road 1225 (38.066N & 3.55763W). Much of the area around the road for the next mile was logged shortly before press time, and the slash piles and haul road associated with the cutting are still obvious. These areas are not pretty now, but the open forest and grassy meadows visible further along the trail from earlier cuts illustrate the power of the forest to regenerate. At 5.1 miles, a closed gate marks the end of the logging area.

At 5.7 miles (38.07737N & 83.54539W), our route crosses the Cave Run Trail

(DBNF 112). Go straight through the intersection and continue on what is now the Hog Pen Trail (DBNF 106). Shortly, you will see grass-covered Road 1225B on the left. The Hog Pen Trail is very nice ridgetop walking, with several open areas and occasional views through the trees of Cave Run Lake.

At 7.1 miles, reach a T-junction with the Buckskin Trail (DBNF 113) and

THE CROSSOVER TRAIL NORTH OF ZILPO ROAD

turn right (38.07578N & 83.52612W). To the left, a sign for the Buckskin Trail indicates that it is closed from December 1 through July 1 to protect a bald eagle nesting site. The Buckskin Trail

descends, steeply at first, down the right side of a narrow draw to the valley of Big Cave Run Branch. Once down in the draw, it turns right through the open woods, where potential campsites are plentiful. At 7.8 miles, turn right off of Buckskin onto the aptly named Connector Trail (DBNF 108) (38.06866N & 83.5307W). The Connector Trail leads a short distance along the valley floor to a junction, at 7.9 miles, with the Cave Run Trail (DBNF 112) (38.0688N & 83.53353W). Even if you're not staying overnight on the loop, this junction is a great spot to rest and have some lunch. An old weather-beaten forest service sign marks the junction. If you look closely, it appears that the "Daniel Boone" in the name of the forest is an inlay, indicating that the sign may originally date from before the 1960s, when the name of the National Forest was changed to "Daniel Boone National Forest" from "Cumberland National Forest."

Turn left onto the Cave Run Trail and begin a steady climb up to the Zilpo Road. Two pairs of switchbacks help to moderate the climb to the more gentle ridgecrest. At 9.7 miles, the trail intersects DBNF Road 1058, just short of the Zilpo Road (38.06156N & 83.54606W).

From the pullout at the end of gated DBNF Road 1058, look for the north end of the blue-blazed Cave Run Trail (DBNF 112) to the left, about 20 feet north of the paved Zilpo Scenic Byway. Despite the proximity to the road, both deer and wild turkey are easily seen on this trail. The trail stays within 100 feet of the north side of the Zilpo Road until closing the loop at 10.2 miles at the Tater Knob interpretive site.

In 1969, the US Army Corps of Engineers completed the Cave Run Dam on the Licking River. The Corps then transferred management of the area surrounding the 8,270-acre lake to the Daniel Boone National Forest. By the late 1970s, the forest began developing the area by replacing the former Cedar Cliffs Trail with the paved Zilpo Road. The trail system was expanded from 20 miles in the late 1970s to cover over 50 miles. There are now campgrounds at Zilpo, Clear Creek Lake, and Twin Knobs with around 400 campsites total, in addition to the horse camp at White Sulphur.

The Pioneer Weapons Wildlife Management Area (WMA) consists of 7,480 acres south of Cave Run Lake that are co-managed by the forest and Kentucky Department of Fish and Wildlife Resources. Hunting in the WMA is limited to longbow, crossbow, and muzzle-loading firearms only. For hunting information, contact the Kentucky Department of Fish and Wildlife Resources. Wild turkey and white-tailed deer are the primary game.

Recognizing that the Cave Run area was increasing in popularity and that a trail system designed in the 1960s and 70s was unable to handle the current recreation demands from hikers, bike riders, and horsemen, the Forest Service began a reevaluation of the Cave Run Trail System in 2009. In 2013, after years of work with various user groups, the final decision by the DBNF designated largely separate trail systems for horses and mountain bikes. The horse trails are located near horse camps on the south and west sides of the areas, while the bike trails are located for the best access to the existing campgrounds. Some new trails were opened and other existing trails were closed. In the first edition of this guide, I described a larger loop hike that extended west to include a segment of the Sheltowee Trace Trail. As part of the 2013 decision, part of the old loop along the shore of Cave Run Lake was removed from the trail system to isolate the horse trails from the mountain biking trails, causing a revision to the shorter loop described in this edition. Hiking and mountain biking are allowed year round on the Cave Run Trails. The horse trails are open from May 15 to December 15.

OTHER HIKING OPTIONS

1. Short and Sweet. The Clear Lake Trail (103) is an easy 1.0-mile trail around Clear Lake off of Forest Service Road 129.
2. Two modest variations on this loop are possible. Skipping the Hog Pen Trail and returning via the first intersection with the Cave Run Trail is 0.7 mile shorter for a 9.5-mile loop. Skipping the Hog Pen Trail and returning via the full length of the Buckskin Trail adds 2.6 miles for a 12.6-mile loop, and should only be walked outside of the December 1 through July 1 bald eagle nesting closure.
3. Much of the Sheltowee Trace Trail south of Forest Service Road 129 is designated foot travel only.

Carter Caves Cross Country Trail (4C'S)

TOTAL DISTANCE: A 8.3-mile loop hike that is also partly in the Tygarts State Forest. Some of the loop is shared with horses.

HIKING TIME: About 4.5 hours

DIFFICULTY: Moderate/Difficult

LOCATION: Carter Caves State Resort Park, about 7 miles northeast of Olive Hill

---

MAPS: USGS Wesleyville, Tygarts Valley, Grahn, and Olive Hill, and Carter Caves State Resort Park Hiking Map

---

Carter Caves is one of the state's oldest and most popular parks. Though the caves are the park's biggest draws, there are also exciting backcountry trails that visit stately arches and rockhouses reminiscent of Red River Gorge or the Big South Fork.

GETTING THERE

From Exit 161 off I-64, drive east 1.7 miles on US 60 to the intersection with KY 182. Turn north on KY 182 and drive 2.8 miles north to the park entrance. Turn left into the park and drive 1.0 mile to the Welcome Center (38.37732N & 83.12283W).

THE TRAIL

The 4C's Trail explores both the front country highlights and quiet backcountry of the 1,800-acre Carter Caves State Resort Park. If you add in the very short side trip to Raven Rock, you will pass three sandstone arches, in addition to crossing a state nature preserve and crossing the outlet of Smoky Valley Lake. This hike can be done as a long day hike or as an easy overnight hike by using the Johnson Homeplace Backcountry Campsite. Overnight campers will need to get a permit from the park's Welcome Center.

From the far end of the Welcome Center parking area, walk up the stone steps toward X-Cave. In 150 feet, bear right at the start of both the 4C's and the Horn Hollow Trails. The trails split in another 100 feet, at a point just above the cave where the 4C's goes left. Beyond, the 4C's the trail is marked with white and orange blazes and an occasional "4C's" diamond.

At 0.8 mile (38.38266N & 83.12727W), the trail intersects an old jeep road. To the left, the road leads 500 feet to the paved picnic shelter road. To the right,

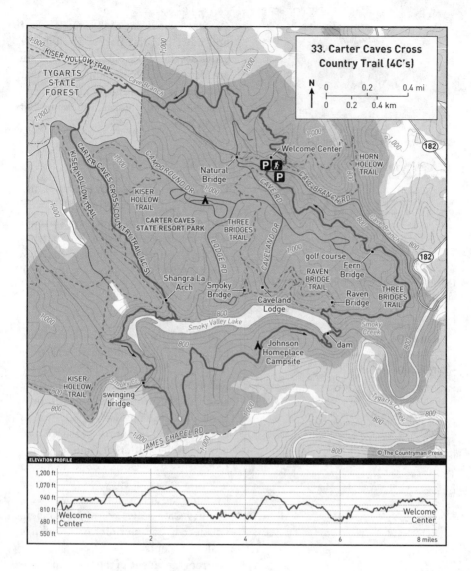

33. Carter Caves Cross Country Trail (4C's)

ELEVATION PROFILE

the trail enters the Carter Caves State Nature Preserve. Two small tracts, totaling 146 acres, within the park are managed as preserves to protect the federally endangered Indiana Bat and two plants rare in Kentucky, the mountain maple and the Canadian yew.

Reach a mowed area in a meadow at 1.3 miles (38.38135N & 83.13264W). To the left, the park maintenance area is only 500 feet away. To the right, the trail passes through a meadow blessed

with plentiful sunlight. Queen Anne's lace, butterfly milkweed, thistle, and black-eyed Susan are some of the summer flowers you may find here.

At 1.5 miles, leave the Nature Preserve in a stream bottom at an intersection where the Kiser Hollow Trail joins from the right (38.38288N & 83.13586W). The trail is now in Tygarts State Forest, and the next section of trail is shared by the 4C's and Kiser Hollow Trails. At 1.9 miles, cross the maintained

Cave Branch gravel road (38.37982N & 83.1404W). Here, an interpretive sign explains that many of the trees east of the road were harvested in the aftermath of a February 2003 ice storm. About 150 feet beyond the road is a former junction with the now abandoned Simon Kenton Trail that used to extend nine miles to the Jenny Wiley Trail. If you study the signs carefully, you can still see ghosts of the original lettering for the Simon Kenton Trail.

The 4C's Trail next turns right onto an old dirt road that it follows through a hardwood forest dominated by oak, maple, and beech trees. Soon a spur of

the Kiser Hollow Trail will branch left and lead toward the horse campground. This is a good spot to look for animals both fast and slow of foot. White-tailed deer and box turtles are both common. Soon, you should turn off the ridgetop and make another intersection with the yellow-blazed Kiser Tail at 2.5 miles (38.37345N & 83.13738W).

Arrive at Shangri La Arch at 3.0 miles. The arch seems more like a long natural tunnel. It is roughly 50 feet long, but it is only 6 feet high and 8 feet wide, and it was formed when its small stream eroded under a strong layer of rock. The top of the arch is formed from a thick

SHANGRI LA ARCH

layer of massive rock. You can see from the debris at the base of the arch that the layers below the arch were much thinner than the supporting span. Just below the arch, there is a small wet-weather waterfall. In 2015, a large slump at the far end of the arch shows that the formation of the arch is still active. Beyond the arch, turn left and sneak between the cliff and a huge boulder, then walk along the base of the cliffs.

At 3.1 miles, reach a signed trail junction with a 0.1-mile side trail to Smoky Lake Lane (38.36681N & 83.13151W) in a grove of pines. The 4C's Trail makes a sharp right at the junction and follows the lakeshore below an impressive set of cliff bands. Cross two small side streams before reaching a four-way intersection at Smoky Creek at 3.9 miles. This section marks the beginning of the 2001 reroute of the 4C's Trail that uses a new swinging bridge to make a dry crossing of the creek. The old trail route is now used by the unmapped but blazed horse trail which fords the creek.

Cross Smoky Creek on the swinging bridge at 4.1 miles, and start climbing out of the creek valley by some old roads. Part of the way up the hill, the blue-blazed horse route joins from the left, and it is now signed as the Collins Passage Trail. At 4.5 miles (38.35948N & 83.13167W), the Collins Passage turns right to reach the James Chapel Road, and the 4C's turns left, still following an old road. After some lovely flat walking, the 4C's leaves the road, turning to the right, and it eventually reaches the Johnson Homeplace Campsite at 5.5 miles (38.36491N & 83.12394W).

The campsite has a grassy, flat area for tents and a small rock shelter, but no water or latrine, perfect for a lunch stop. To stay at the campsite, it is necessary to get a permit from the park welcome center. From the campsite the 4C's Trail descends toward the outlet of Smoky Valley Lake. When you reach the cascades at the base of the spillway of the dam, make a sharp left, cross the creek, and climb toward the dam. If the trail is washed out, or if you get lost here, and you certainly won't be the first, simply climb to the embankment above, which is the Smoky Lake Dam. On the far side of the dam, reach a swinging bridge over the main spillway at 6.1 miles (38.36574N & 83.11724W).

Turn left after crossing the spillway, and begin a short but steep climb to the base of the bluff line. Pass beside another cliff band with an exceptional series of solution features, including two tiny arches, before climbing a flight of stairs that offers good views of Smoky Valley Lake. At 6.3 miles, reach a signed junction with the red-blazed Three Bridges Trail (38.36741N & 83.1186W). The Three Bridges loop is a popular trail that uses the same route as the 4C's from here to the Welcome Center, so expect plenty of company on the rest of the hike.

Go right at the Three Bridges junction, about one hundred yards, to reach a junction with the blue-blazed Raven Bridge Trail. Just 100 feet to the left, and barely out of sight up that trail, is Raven Bridge. This short side trail leads to a classic stone arch that formed in a narrow neck of a sandstone ridge. Notice on the view from the topside that one end of the arch looks as if it is perched precariously on a narrow fin of the underlying rock layer.

The 4C's Trail continues right from the junction with the Raven Bridge Trail. The trail follows just below the rim along the contour. Notice how many of the trees along the way have grown to have diameters of 3 feet or more. Some of these trees must be survivors of

NATURAL BRIDGE IN CARTER CAVES STATE RESORT PARK

early logging days. At 7.3 miles, reach the wood boardwalk under Fern Bridge (38.37171N & 83.11472W).

Fern Bridge is the largest of the bridges along the loop, stretching nearly 150 feet long and towering 84 feet high. The bridge formed from rock that has separated from the main cliff face, similar to Split Bow Arch in the Big South Fork. Someday this could be a double arch. There is another alcove behind the arch that may also separate from the main cliff band along a joint set, where you can see water slowly dripping.

Beyond the arch, climb up sets of both wood and stone steps to reach a junction with the side trail to the park cottages in 300 feet. Keep right at this junction, and walk along the rim while enjoying some more huge trees. At 7.7 miles, enter the designated rock-climbing and rappelling area and pass another spur trail leading left to the cabin area. Cross two wood bridges before descending to the park road at the entrance to Saltpeter Cave. At 8.3 miles, the Three Bridges Trail continues straight ahead while the 4C's descends to the Welcome Center parking area past Saltpeter Cave.

Carter Cave State Resort Park offers a full range of services. There is a lodge, a dining room, cottages, and a campground. You can also boat or fish, but not swim, on 45-acre Smoky Valley Lake. In addition to the guided cave tours, rangers also lead canoe trips on Tygarts Creek.

No one should visit this park without taking one of the cave tours. Tours of Cascade and X-Cave are offered year-round, and Saltpeter and Bat Caves seasonally. You must buy tickets for the tours beforehand at the Welcome Center. All tours are guided, charge a small fee, and take close to an hour. The happy coincidence of caves and arches in the area is in part the result of the stratigraphy of the geology here. The top rock layer is the Pennsylvanian Lee sandstone, the same rock type that forms the rock arches at the Big South Fork and Red River Gorge. Below the Lee formation are the Chester and St. Genevieve limestones, which are the hosts for the caves. The park contains at least six caves, plus some smaller ones surrounding Cascade Cave.

OTHER HIKING OPTIONS

1. Short and Sweet. The two largest arches in the park are not on the 4C's Loop. Natural Bridge is on a 0.5-mile semi-loop hike that also leaves from the Welcome Center and allows you to walk under, then across, the top span of this enormous arch. Smokey Bridge, with its 42-foot span and 50-foot height is on the Three Bridges Loop, or it can be accessed from the lodge on a short loop.

2. The Three Bridges Trail is a 3.3-mile loop that passes Fern, Raven, and Smoky Bridges. The last two miles of this loop follows the 4C's Trail.

3. The Raven Bridge Trail leads 0.7 mile to Raven Bridge from Caveland Lodge.

4. The Horn Hollow Trail is a 1.5-mile loop that starts from the park welcome center.

5. The Box Canyon Trail is a 0.8-mile semi-loop that starts near the entry to Cascade Cave. Though most folks use it to pass time while they wait for their cave tour, it is a worthy destination in its own right. The sheer walls and alcoves in the canyon are the highlights of the scenery.

6. The Kiser Hollow Multi-use Trail is a 8.6-mile loop through the park and Tygarts State Forest that begins at the Riding Stables. The trail was constructed in 2000, and it is administered by Carter Caves. The popularity of this loop has led to the development of the 2.5-mile Cave Branch Trail loop and the 3.6-mile Ridge Top Trail loop in Tygarts State Forest, as well as the 0.8-mile Collins Passage Trail.

34

Michael Tygart Loop Trail

TOTAL DISTANCE: A 10.1-mile semi-loop trail that uses short sections of a gravel road and a paved road. The trail is shared with mountain bikes and a short section with horses.

HIKING TIME: About 5.5 hours

DIFFICULTY: Difficult

LOCATION: Greenbo Lake State Resort Park, about 19 miles north of Grayson

MAPS: USGS Old Town and Argillite, and Greenbo Lake State Resort Park Trails Guide

Greenbo Lake State Resort Park is known primarily for the fishing and boating on 225-acre Greenbo Lake. But the park has a lot to offer hikers, including a rare long loop with backcountry camping options for overnight trips and two other long multi-use trails.

GETTING THERE

From Exit 172 off I-64 in Grayson, drive 15.1 miles north on KY 1 to KY 1711. Turn left onto KY 1711, and drive 2.7 miles to Buffalo Furnace Cemetery. Turn right at the cemetery, and drive 0.8 mile to Jesse Stuart Lodge. Park in the far end of the lodge parking area (38.48097N & 82.87225W).

THE TRAIL

The Michael Tygart Loop Trail is one of the rare Kentucky State Park hiking trails that is long enough for overnight trips. The loop is both diverse and scenic, visiting forests, creeks, and Greenbo Lake. Day hikers can shorten the loop to 7.5 miles by starting near Buffalo Furnace Cemetery.

Start the hike by the large signboard at the far end of the Jesse Stuart Lodge parking area. The trail begins as a wide gravel road, and you'll see both yellow blazes and interpretive markers for the Fern Valley Trail. This section of trail is closed to horses and mountain bikes. At 0.2 mile, the trails split (38.48354N & 82.8729W). The Fern Valley Trail loops right back to the lodge and the Michael Tygart Trail goes left in 0.5 mile.

From the split, the trail drops down to the lake side near some small buildings and then meanders along the shore. Here the forest is mostly hardwood; American beech, sugar maple, and oaks are the most common trees. At 1.3 miles, reach

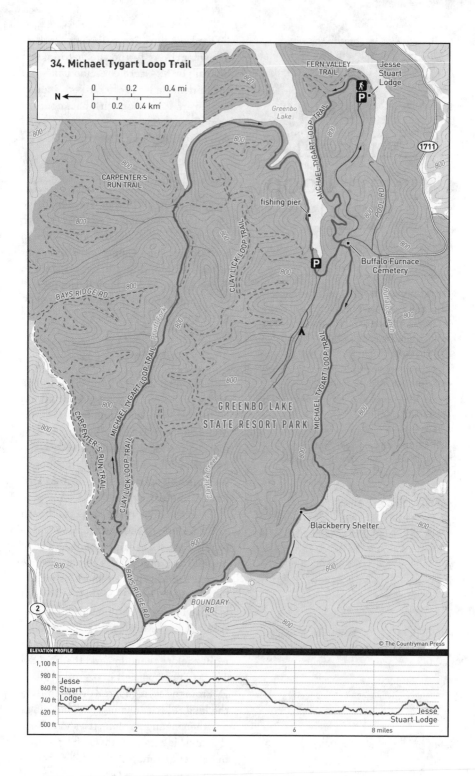

34. Michael Tygart Loop Trail

N ←
0   0.2   0.4 mi
0 0.2 0.4 km

FERN VALLEY TRAIL

Jesse Stuart Lodge

1711

Greenbo Lake

MICHAEL TYGART LOOP TRAIL

CARPENTER'S RUN TRAIL

POOL RD

fishing pier

CLAY LICK LOOP TRAIL

Buffalo Furnace Cemetery

Buffalo Branch

BAYS RIDGE RD

South Fork

MICHAEL TYGART LOOP TRAIL

MICHAEL TYGART LOOP TRAIL

CARPENTER'S RUN TRAIL

CLAY LICK LOOP TRAIL

GREENBO LAKE
STATE RESORT PARK

Clay Lick Creek

Blackberry Shelter

BAYS RIDGE RD

BOUNDARY RD

2

© The Countryman Press

ELEVATION PROFILE

1,100 ft
980 ft
860 ft   Jesse
740 ft   Stuart
620 ft   Lodge
500 ft

Jesse
Stuart Lodge

2   4   6   8 miles

a thick stand of pine trees and cross the paved road to the campground and boat dock near the split with the road to Jesse Stuart Lodge (38.48246N & 82.88653W).

Just beyond the road is the Buffalo Furnace Cemetery, which was established in 1851. Family names here include Kidd, Burton, and Kilburn, and there are graves as recent as 2014. Buffalo Furnace smelted iron from 1818 until 1856. The remains of the furnace are along the park entrance road beside Buffalo Branch. You may also spot deer who like to feed at the edge of the cemetery. From the cemetery, turn right and walk down the road 200 feet, then turn left onto an initially steep foot trail which climbs up the crest of a small ridge, then keep to the ridge crest under an open hardwood forest with scattered pines. At 2.0 miles, come to a faint side trail leading right to some small pits where iron ore was mined in the 1800s to feed Buffalo Furnace. These long, shallow pits look like short sections of long abandoned rail lines. The side trail will return to the main trail, so you don't have to retrace your steps if you visit the pits.

The trail remains on the ridgetop until it joins an old road in an area filled with blackberry and sumac. A slight detour to the right side of the ridge brings you to Blackberry Shelter, at 3.0 miles (38.4855N & 82.91162W). The Michael Tygart Trail was originally built as a side trail to the longer, now-abandoned Jenny Wiley Trail; the other shelter indicated on the trail signs here was part of the Jenny Wiley Trail system and has been abandoned. Blackberry is a three-sided Adirondack Shelter similar to those used along the famous Appalachian Trail. There is a picnic table, but no drinking water or latrine at the shelter. To use the shelter overnight, you must register at the front desk of Jesse Stuart Lodge.

Beyond the shelter, the Michael Tygart Trail, marked with yellow blazes, splits right from the dirt road (marked with blue blazes) and parallels it about 50 feet away. The trail will next leave the ridge crest to the right and pass a farm on the left, crossing a power line. At 3.7 miles, cross a gravel road that is gated on the left side and leads right down to the park camping areas, providing a useful connector trail for mountain bikers.

The trail then shadows the gravel boundary road and makes another power line crossing through thick pines before reaching the gravel Boundary Road at its intersection with the paved Bays Ridge Road at 4.2 miles (38.49722N & 82.92206W). Turn right onto the road and ignore the first side road leading right. Pass a large new trailhead for horses on the right side. At 4.7 miles turn right off the road at a trailhead for both the Carpenter Run and Michael Tygart Trails (82.92206N & 82.91608W). Red-blazed Carpenter Run is a ten-mile horse trail system on the north side of the park that will rejoin our loop near Greenbo Lake. The Michael Tygart Trail bears right along the ridgetop. At 4.9 miles, the seven-mile blue-blazed Clay Lick Loop splits off to the right (38.49938N & 82.9136W). Clay Lick is a favorite of local mountain bike riders as its ridgetop setting leads to a much drier and better-maintained trail. From this junction, the Michael Tygart Trail then turns left to descend steeply off the ridge crest to reach Pruitt Fork Creek and a junction with a connector to the Carpenter Run Trail at 5.0 miles (38.49957N & 82.91153W).

The dark, moist forest alongside Pruitt Fork Creek can produce prodigious numbers of mosquitoes, so it's a good idea to have some repellent, or

BUFFALO IRON FURNACE

you'll have to move fast in summer. Besides the pesky bugs, the creek supports prolific understory vegetation, including Christmas fern, ground cedar, poison ivy, sassafras, and tulip poplar. In pre-park times, several families lived along the creek; you may see relics of their homes, including the remains of a brick chimney and a two-story wood frame house and barn at 6.0 miles (38.49588N & 82.89541W). But the lush forest is rapidly reclaiming these signs of habitation. Occasionally, in summer, the dense bottom growth completely blocks views of the creek.

At 6.2 miles, reach an intersection with a connector trail for horses to the Clay Lick Loop on the right (38.49476N & 82.89083W). Next, make an easy crossing to the left bank of Pruitt Creek. You'll cross one side branch before returning to the right bank at 6.6 miles where another connector trail to the Clay Lick Loop also splits off to the right (38.49453N & 82.88555W). Just beyond is the grand entrance to the property of Boy Scout Troop 202, as well as the junction with the east end of the Carpenter Run Trail. Horses are not allowed further on the Michael Tygart Trail.

Just beyond this junction will be the first views of Greenbo Lake, along with a ring of benches in a cleared area. Lucky hikers can enjoy some bird watching and may even spot a great blue heron here. Beyond the benches, the Michael Tygart Trail follows the lakeshore closely, offering you nearly constant views and keeping you in touch with how the bass are biting. Watch the lakeshore trees carefully for signs of beaver.

At 8.2 miles, reach the accessible fishing pier located in another pine grove (38.48515N & 82.88418W). Continue to walk along the park road past the marina, and take the campground road back to the road junction near Buffalo Furnace Cemetery at 8.8 miles. At the junction, turn left onto the trail and retrace the first 1.3 miles of the hike back to the parking area.

In addition to the hiking trails and the lodge, Greenbo State Park offers camping and picnic areas, a dining room, tennis courts, and boat and canoe rentals. The Jesse Stuart Lodge is named for the famous Greenup County native and Kentucky Poet Laureate, who lived just north of the park. The lodge and restaurant were closed in October 2015 due to an electrical fire. Repairs are expected to be complete, and both lodge and restaurant reopened, by early 2017.

Michael Tygart was an eighteenth century explorer and scout who also appears in the novel *The Frontiersmen* by Allan W. Eckert. His namesake trail was originally constructed as a 24-mile-long connector from Greenbo to the Jenny Wiley Trail, which was completed in 1978. Much of the trail was lost when the state abandoned most of the Jenny Wiley Trail, which connected Jenny Wiley State Park to Portsmouth, KY.

OTHER HIKING OPTIONS

1. Short and Sweet. Greenbo is the rare state park with plenty of longer trails, but very few short ones. Your only choice for a short loop is the Fern Valley Trail, which is a 1.1-mile interpretive loop that also starts at the Jesse Stuart Lodge. You can check out the interpretive guide from the front desk of the lodge.

2. You can reduce the length of the trip to 7.5 miles by starting at the Buffalo Iron Furnace or the Greenbo Lake boat dock and just hike the loop section without the connecting trail to Jesse Stuart Lodge.

3. The Jesse Stuart State Nature Preserve is located just 6 miles north of the park, near Greenup on KY 1. The preserve contains about three miles of trails.

IV.

BLUEGRASS HEARTLAND

35

Main Trail

TOTAL DISTANCE: A 1.7-mile loop for hikers only

HIKING TIME: About 1 hour

DIFFICULTY: Easy

LOCATION: Boone County Cliffs State Nature Preserve, about 6 miles west of Burlington

MAPS: USGS Rising Sun and Boone County Cliffs State Nature Preserve brochure

This 74-acre pocket preserve is known for its prolific spring wildflower displays, festive fall foliage, and rocky cliffs formed from glacial conglomerates. But at any time of year, it is a pleasant walk and a welcome escape into serene woodlands. This small space packs a powerful biologic punch. Over 300 species of flowers, ferns, trees, and shrubs have been recorded in the preserve and over 90 species of birds have been sighted here.

GETTING THERE

From Exit 181 off I-75, take KY 18 for 10.7 miles west through Burlington. Turn left at a sign for Middle Creek Road. Drive for 1.7 miles east on this narrow, twisty paved road to the small trailhead on the north side of the road (38.9934N & 84.78449W).

THE TRAIL

The Main Trail begins at the west side of the parking area and follows a well-defined footpath. Be sure to observe the signs instructing you to stay on the trail to preserve fragile plant habitats. At 0.1 mile, there is a small signpost and then the trail climbs a set of wooden steps. At 0.2 mile, the trail reaches a hilltop with an outcrop of conglomerate where a short side trail leads left to a wooded overlook above the creek and hiking trail (38.99454N & 84.78315W). These outcrops are your best chance to observe the preserve's namesake cliffs.

A conglomerate is a type of rock composed of fragments of other rock that have been recemented together. Conglomerates can form by several processes; one common type is from the debris left behind by glaciers. The fragments in glacial conglomerates consist of pieces of any of the rock types that

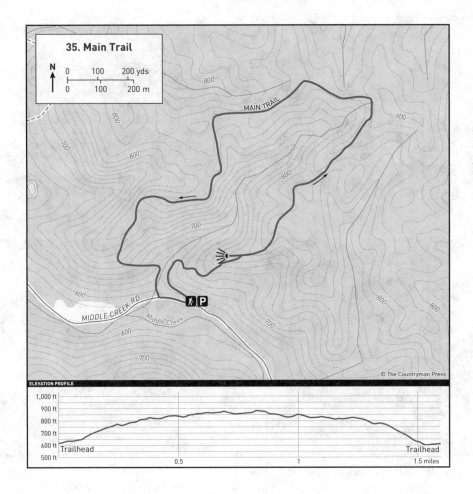

have been eroded from the previous path of the glacier. Some of the fragments in this conglomerate originated as far north as Canada. The matrix, or the material that holds the fragments together, is usually the very small remains of rocks that have been pulverized by the glacier. At the Boone County Cliffs, the conglomerate is composed of small fragments in a muddy brown matrix. The rock was deposited 700,000 years ago, during the last glacial period, very recently in geologic time.

Return to the junction to continue the loop, and in 0.4 mile, reach another signpost marking the north end of the now closed East Boundary Trail. The mature, open forest contains numerous sugar maple, beech, basswood, white oak, white ash, and slippery elm trees. The smooth gray bark of mature beech trees can be too much for vandals to resist. Carvings of names and initials left by thoughtless visitors mar one small ridgetop grove. Beechnuts are an important food source for bear, deer, squirrels, and wild turkeys and were an important food for some Native Americans. Beech leaves have large curved teeth and are deeply furrowed. Perhaps the best time to learn to recognize the leaves is in the winter. When most trees

A BOULDER OF GLACIAL CONGLOMERATE AT BOONE COUNTY CLIFFS

have dropped all their leaves, many young beeches keep their wrinkled brown ones.

At 0.8 mile, the trail crosses the head of the small creek, still following the ridge crest. Just beyond, you can see an old jeep road in the woods just outside the boundary of the preserve. Look for a worn path on the left at 1.3 miles that leads about 200 feet to another overlook above the creek. Leave the ridgetop at 1.5 miles and descend toward Middle Creek. The trail now ends on Middle Creek Road, on the west side of the creek, at 1.7 miles.

The Kentucky State Nature Pre- serves Commission was created in 1976 to help protect the state's natural heritage. The Commission seeks to find, acquire, and manage lands containing rare native species, rare natural communities, and special natural features. Through extensive survey work, the Commission has helped many landowners protect significant natural sites. The Commission manages 41 preserves, some in conjunction with either The Nature Conservancy or the Kentucky Department of Parks. While some preserves are too sensitive to be opened to the general public, others such as Boone County Cliffs and Bad Branch provide environmental education and recreation opportunities as well as established hiking trails.

In 1974, The Nature Conservancy purchased the first 46 acres of Boone County Cliffs when it became the Kentucky Chapter's first preserve. In 2010, ownership of the preserve was transferred from TNC to the Boone County Fiscal Court. Two important and sensitive species of salamanders live in the small creek on the property.

OTHER HIKING OPTIONS

1. Short and Sweet. A round trip hike to the conglomerate cliffs and overlook is only 0.5 mile. There are no other hiking trails at the preserve. The former East Boundary Trail is permanently closed.

2. The 107-acre Dinsmore Woods State Nature Preserve is located on KY 18 just west of the junction with Middle Creek Road. The preserve is open to day use only and has a 1.7-mile hiking trail. Hikers may park in the county park across the road from the preserve.

3. Big Bone Lick State Park, located off KY 338 west of Walton offers the 0.9-mile Big Bone Creek and Bison Trace Loop as well as the 2.0-mile Coralberry Trail. The park has several other trails, along with fossil exhibits.

36

Scott's Gap Loop Trail

TOTAL DISTANCE: A 3.5-mile loop on hiking trails

HIKING TIME: About 2 hours

DIFFICULTY: Moderate

LOCATION: Jefferson County Memorial Forest, south of Louisville, in Fairdale

MAPS: USGS Valley Station and Jefferson County Memorial Forest Scott's Gap Loop Trail Map

The Jefferson County Memorial Forest is a remarkable 5,400-acre area located just outside the I-265 beltway south of Louisville. The forest is dedicated to the area's war veterans, and it is used for a variety of public educational and recreation programs. There are trails in four sections of the forest, three of which are open to the general public. The Scott's Gap Loop is a special delight, because of its prolific spring and summer wildflower display, and for the historic Plymouth half buried along the route.

GETTING THERE

From Exit 3 on I-265 (the Gene Snyder Parkway), drive south 0.7 mile on Stonecrest Road to Blevins Gap Road. Stay right on Blevins Gap Road and drive 3.2 miles southwest to Scott's Gap Road. Turn left on Scotts Gap Road and drive 0.9 mile to the trailhead, which is located just beyond the western end of the Siltstone Trail. The small parking area is located on the west side of the road (38.05856N & 85.84222W).

THE TRAIL

From the far right end of the parking area, hike past a signboard on a single track trail and begin climbing Miller Hill. The loop is well marked with red paint blazes. Watch carefully to avoid the prolific poison ivy along the start of the trail. The three-leaved menace is in stiff competition here with the benign five-leaved Virginia creeper, which is also an important ground cover. At 0.1 mile, reach the intersection with the Siltstone Trail, which turns right to cross Scott's Gap Road on its 6.7-mile journey to the Tom Wallace Recreation Area in Jefferson Forest (38.05995N & 85.84205W). Next reach the start of the

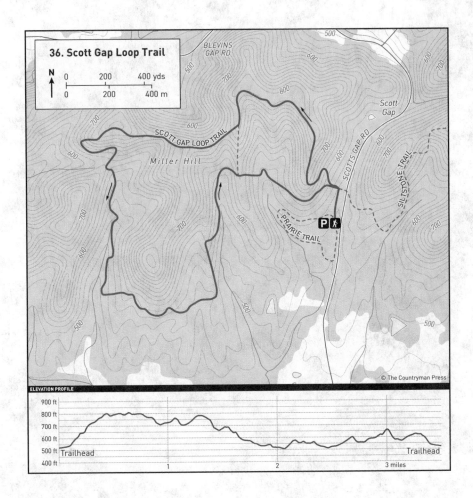

36. Scott Gap Loop Trail

N

| 0 | 200 | 400 yds |
| 0 | 200 | 400 m |

BLEVINS
GAP RD

SCOTT GAP LOOP TRAIL

Miller Hill

Scott
Gap

SCOTTS GAP RD

SILTSTONE TRAIL

PRAIRIE TRAIL

© The Countryman Press

ELEVATION PROFILE

900 ft
800 ft
700 ft
600 ft
500 ft Trailhead
400 ft

1   2   3 miles

Trailhead

loop and turn right to follow the loop counter clockwise.

Reaching the crest of the ridge earns the small reward of a tree-shrouded view. The ridgetop is covered in hardwood, including sugar maple and redbud. Purple redbud blossoms compete with the blossoms of dogwoods and some other domesticated trees to be the first sign of approaching spring. The buds appear well before the smooth, heart-shaped leaves. Later, the trees produce a long string bean–shaped fruit. Some of the common spring wildflowers that you might see along the trail include cut-leaved toothwort, May

apple, fire pink, wild geranium, chickweed, spring beauty, red trillium, bluets, rue anemone, hepatica, foamflower, and blue violet.

At 0.8-mile, reach a signed junction with the 0.2-mile short-cut tail leading left (38.0626N & 85.84744W). A left turn here will result in a 1.4-mile loop back to the Scott's Gap Trailhead. The main trail continues right along the crest of Miller Hill, but it does not appear too heavily used and it may be a bit brushy. Look for zigzag spiderwort and the light blue heads of common fleabane here. At 1.4 miles, drop off the right side of the ridge onto a drier slope covered in oak trees.

A RIDGELINE SECTION OF THE SCOTT'S GAP LOOP

Look here for the bright orange heads of butterfly milkweed. According to Seymour, the roots of this plant were used by Native Americans to treat respiratory diseases and the plant was also used to treat cuts, bruises, and sores.

The trail then begins to follow a tributary of Brier Creek. True to form, there are some briars and nettles mixed with Christmas fern, phlox, and May apple. This stretch is a favorite of box turtles, who favor the trail's easy terrain over other cross-country routes. After leaving this branch and swinging around the base of Miller Hill, you come to one of the trail's most amazing sights at 2.5 miles (38.05537N & 85.84945W). In a deep, but narrow draw, half-buried in decades of debris, is the body of an old Plymouth automobile. At one time, this small stream must have been accessible by car, and probably marked the edge of some farmer's field. Looking at the area now, it is just as easy to believe the car fell here from the sky.

After leaving the vehicle behind, climb up and over a small ridge, then follow up another small branch of Brier Creek. Cross two log bridges along trail in small draws that again have a few nettles. At 3.1 miles, reach the other end of the 0.2-mile connector trail at an unsigned junction (38.06043N & 85.84737W). Keep right to avoid repeating your loop. At 3.4 miles, reach the end of the loop, turn right, and descend to the trailhead at 3.5 miles.

The Jefferson County Memorial Forest is open for day use only. Mountain bikes are prohibited from all park trails. Pets must be kept on leashes at all times.

OTHER HIKING OPTIONS

1. Short and Sweet. Using the connector trail to short-circuit the main loop is a 1.4-mile trip.
2. The Prairie Trail leaves from the south end of the Scott's Gap Trailhead to traverse the perimeter of a mowed field in 0.5 mile. This is perfect habitat for deer and the ticks that feed off of them, so be sure to avoid this loop in summer.
3. The most popular hike in the forest is probably the 6.7-mile Siltstone Trail between Scott's Gap and the forest Welcome Center near Holsclaw Hill. The entire trail requires either a car shuttle or a 13.4-mile round-trip hike. There is an additional 4.1 miles of trail in the Tom Wallace Recreation Area within the Forest.
4. In addition to the Tom Wallace Area, two another recreation areas are open in the Forest. The Paul Yost Area has 6.4 miles of trails, and there are 10.4 miles at the Horine Reservation.

37

Tioga Falls National Recreation Trail

TOTAL DISTANCE: A 2.0-mile out-and-back hike on foot trail

HIKING TIME: About 1.5 hours

DIFFICULTY: Easy

LOCATION: US Army Armor Center and Fort Knox, about 6 miles north of Fort Knox

MAPS: USGS Fort Knox and Tioga Falls National Recreation Trail

The Fort Knox Military Reservation contains two National Recreation trails, possessing very different characters. The Tioga Falls Trail is a wooded foot trail leading to Tioga Falls. The Bridges to the Past Trail is an abandoned paved road which dead-ends at the boundary of the Military Reservation. Both are fairly heavily used, but they offer quick and convenient escapes into the woods. You should call ahead to the Fort Knox Hunt Control Office (502-624-7311/2712) to get the interpretive brochures, and to find out when the trails may be closed due to hunting season or military training.

GETTING THERE

From the junction of US 31W and KY 44 just south of Louisville, drive 3.8 miles south on US 31W. Make a left turn onto a narrow paved road on L&N Turnpike Road. Follow the road for 0.7 mile to the large parking area for Bridges to the Past and Tioga Falls (37.96878N & 85.96112W), in view of the first of two massive railroad trestles along the route. From the parking area, the left fork is the Bridges to the Past Trail and the right fork is Railroad Trestle Road. The Tioga Falls Trail begins in back of the large covered signboard at the end of the parking area, to the right of the railroad trestle.

THE TRAIL

Follow the foot trail for 0.1 mile, then cross a small stream on a footbridge. For its first half, the Tioga Falls Trail follows the route of the old Muldraugh Road through a thin strip between the railroad on the left and a paved road on the right. At 0.4 mile, carefully cross the rail line just short of a longer curving trestle before exiting into the woods on the left. Exercise caution around the

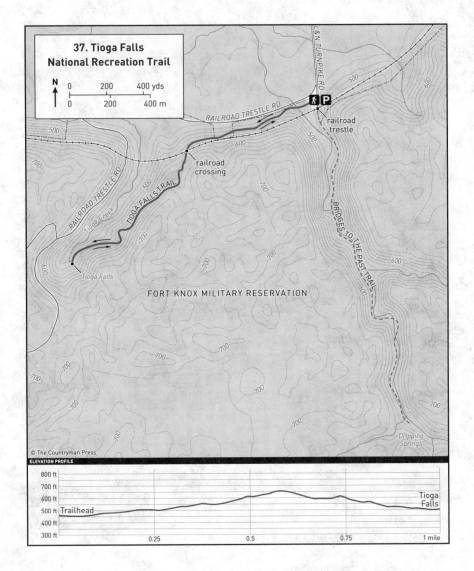

ELEVATION PROFILE

tracks, as the rail line is still active. The forest here is mostly hardwood with red maple, sugar maple, tulip poplar, beech, shagbark hickory, and sycamore. If you look closely, you can see where the forest has survived fires, tornados, and windstorms in recent years.

Beyond the tracks the trail is a little hillier, you'll climb over one small ridge that shows evidence of the intricate cribbing used by the original road builders before descending to Tioga Falls at 1.0

mile (37.96191N & 85.97479W). The Falls has two parts, an upper drop of 30 feet and a lower drop over a ledge of around ten feet. Both sets of falls are undercut, so you should avoid the temptation to climb to the top. Well above the Falls is the site of the 1800s–era Tioga Falls Hotel, a popular summer retreat for wealthy southerners. Unfortunately, nothing remains of this once-fine structure. Immediately downstream of the trail is another smaller series of

TIOGA FALLS

cascades. This small stream was once dammed to provide a swimming area for hotel guests.

Prior to the 2015 reopening of the trail after the reconstruction of the railroad trestles, Tioga Falls was a loop trail. However, since the completion of the trestle work the far side of the loop was not reopened, and you must trace your steps back to the parking area at 2.0 miles.

The trestle at the parking area was originally built in 1873, and it stands 85 feet high and 578 feet long. It has served a variety of railroads, and it is still used now by the Paducah and Louisville Railroad. The old L&N Turnpike under the trestle was a major transportation route between Louisville and Nashville from 1838 until the Old Dixie Highway was built to take travelers out of the range of the military exercises. The Old Dixie Highway, which includes the last half-mile of the Tioga Falls Trail, served until 1942, when US 31W was built.

After a closure of more than four years to replace the trestles along the Paducah and Louisville Railroad, the Fort Knox Garrison Commander reopened both the Tioga Falls and Bridges to the Past Trails on November 13, 2015.

Fort Knox is a 109,000-acre military base. It is perhaps best known as the home of the Gold Vault, where the US Government stores its supply of gold bullion (sorry, no free samples, or tours). But it is also the primary training site for the Army's Armored divisions and home to the 1st Armor Brigade and 16th Cavalry Regiment. 59,000 acres of the base are potentially open for recreation, including hunting, fishing, and hiking on the two trails described above. You can get access to these recreation areas through the Hunt Control Office, which you should contact before visiting. Birders should also enjoy this area. A 1998 survey identified 54 different species!

OTHER HIKING OPTIONS

1. Short and Sweet. The Bridges to the Past Trail along the historic L&N Turnpike is a 1.1-mile abandoned paved road that ends at the military reservation boundary near Siebolt Cave and Dripping Springs.

2. At Fort Duffield, near West Point, mountain bikers have constructed ten miles of single-track trails.

38

Otter Creek Trail

TOTAL DISTANCE: This 9.3-mile loop on trails shared with mountain bikes includes the side trip to Morgan's Cave and parts of the Valley Overlook Trail.

HIKING TIME: About 5 hours

DIFFICULTY: Moderate/Difficult

LOCATION: Otter Creek Park, about 15 miles south of Louisville

MAPS: USGS Rock Haven and Otter Creek Park Trail Map

Once a Louisville city park and now managed by the Kentucky Department of Forestry, Otter Creek is a wonderful resource for hikers, mountain bikers, and nature lovers from all over the state. The park contains around 15 miles of trails spread over 2,200 acres. Otter Creek is heavily used, but you may still have some of the park to yourself. The longest hike in the park follows the Otter Creek and Valley Overlook Trails in a 9.3-mile loop, which includes a side trip to Morgan's Cave, a visit to North Point Overlook, and a quiet stroll along Otter Creek. To avoid overlapping with trails used by horses, the east side of the loop described here follows the Valley Overlook Trail rather than the Otter Creek Trail. The many trail junctions in the park mean that you'll need to watch your map carefully.

The park is open Wednesday through Sunday, dawn to dusk. As of 2016, there is a $3 fee to hike, and a $7 high-impact fee applies to mountain bikers and horses.

GETTING THERE

From the junction of KY 44 and US 31W, south of Louisville, drive south on US 31W for 7.7 miles to the junction with KY 1638. Turn right on KY 1638 and drive 2.8 miles to the park entrance. Turn right again and drive past the former visitors center for 1.3 miles to reach trailhead parking (37.94029N & 86.04891W) at the site of the old park nature center.

THE TRAIL

From the trailhead, start north across the parking area on the Otter Creek Trail. You'll come to a junction in 0.1 mile where the Valley Overlook Trail branches to the right. The trails in

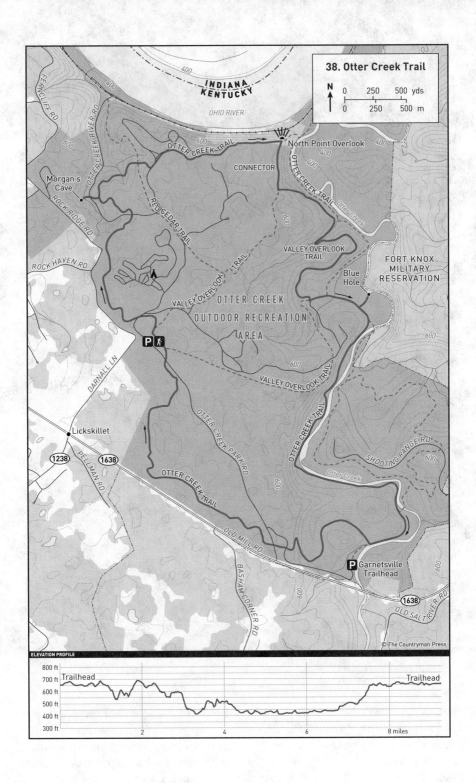

38. Otter Creek Trail

N · 0 · 250 · 500 yds
0 · 250 · 500 m

INDIANA
KENTUCKY

OHIO RIVER

FERNCLIFF RD

OTTER CREEK RIVER RD

OTTER CREEK TRAIL

CONNECTOR

North Point Overlook

OTTER CREEK TRAIL

Otter Creek

Morgan's Cave

ROCK RIDGE RD

RED CEDAR TRAIL

VALLEY OVERLOOK TRAIL

VALLEY OVERLOOK TRAIL

FORT KNOX MILITARY RESERVATION

ROCK HAVEN RD

Blue Hole

OTTER CREEK OUTDOOR RECREATION AREA

P

DARNALL LN

VALLEY OVERLOOK TRAIL

OTTER CREEK TRAIL

Lickskillet

1238 · 1638

PELLMAN RD

OTTER CREEK PARK RD

SHOOTING RANGE RD

Otter Creek

OTTER CREEK TRAIL

OLD MILL RD

BASHAM CORNER RD

P Garnetsville Trailhead

1638

OLD SALT RIVER RD

© The Countryman Press

ELEVATION PROFILE

800 ft Trailhead				Trailhead
700 ft				
600 ft				
500 ft				
400 ft				
300 ft	2	4	6	8 miles

FISHERMEN ALONG OTTER CREEK

Otter Creek are blazed with metal markers; the Otter Creek Trail (OCT), Valley Overlook Trail (VOT), and Red Cedar Horse Trail (RCT) are usually well marked. Next, cross the campground road and walk through shrubby hardwood and open pine forests. In the springtime, daffodils mark the location of old home sites. You'll cross a powerline, and a closed paved road near

stairs past an old roadside quarry. Turn right briefly on the park road, and then make another left turn to descend a set of log ladders. Cross an unnamed creek, and look for a path to the right of where a small tributary enters the creek. At 1.2 miles, reach the gated entrance to this small limestone cave. Morgan's Cave is formed in a rock called St. Louis Limestone, which formed during the Mississippian Period. Limestone of this age is common across the United States, but it is known by many other names, such as the Redwall in Grand Canyon National Park, the Paha Sapa in the Black Hills of the Dakotas, or the Madison of the Rocky Mountains in Montana.

Return to the junction of the side trail and Otter Creek Trail at 1.4 miles, and continue north around the loop. Many of the trees here are sugar maples. You can tell sugar maple from red maple by looking at the leaf in between the three major lobes. If the notch between the lobes is V-shaped, it is a red maple. If the notch is smooth and rounded like a "u," it is a sugar maple. To remind yourself, look for the "u" in "sugar" in between the lobes.

At 1.8 miles, come to an offset four-way junction with part of the Red Cedar Horse Trail (37.9529N & 86.05081W). The right branch is a 0.9-mile connector to the Valley Overlook Trail and the left branch leads to the Park Conference Center. Continue straight on the Otter Creek Trail to North Point Overlook.

Next, cross the park's cabin road and a powerline. The bedrock here is still limestone, and you can spot small sinkholes along the trail, evidence of the same type of karst activity that likely produced Morgan's Cave. The trail then begins to hug the line of bluffs high above the Ohio River, and it offers some nice views, particularly from Eagles

the campground, before reaching the side trail to Morgan's Cave at 1.0 mile (37.95063N & 86.0546W).

To visit Morgan's Cave, turn left at the junction and descend a set of log

Nest Overlook. Enjoy these views, since the North Point Overlook itself (37.95441N & 86.03742W, reached at 2.5 miles) is partly obscured by the rapidly growing forest. If you hear distant booms, and see no likely thunderclouds, you're probably hearing the troops at Fort Knox on maneuver or activity at the shooting range across Otter Creek from the park. Still, this is an ideal rest stop, with the best views along the loop.

From North Point leave the Otter Creek Trail on the connector trail that leaves to the right rather than continuing on the OCT. The descent to Otter Creek is very steep and difficult to maintain and once the trail reaches the creek, horses are allowed on the OCT to Blue Hole. To avoid these damaged sections of trail, use the connector and Valley Overlook Trail to reach Blue Hole. At 2.8 miles (37.95117N & 86.03781W) turn left onto the VOT and begin a gradual descent toward Otter Creek. At 3.1 miles (37.94959N & 86.03339W) cross the Red Cedar Trail in a utility cut, then pass a short spur down to the OCT on the left.

Enjoy some easy walking high above the creek before reaching the remains of a water filtration plant. At 4.2 miles the trail reaches a trailhead at the end of a gravel road (37.94335N & 86.0349W). Just beyond, the combined RCT and OCT trails enter from the left and will travel as one trail to Blue Hole. At 4.4 miles, a side trail leads 0.1 mile to Blue Hole, a lovely, wide stretch of the creek popular with fishermen. Return back to the start of the side trail at 4.6 miles, and continue south on the RCT and OTC. In about one hundred yards, the RCT will split left to cross the creek and join the Boone Hollow Horse Trails.

For the next few miles, the trail follows its namesake creek. This section offers prolific wild flowers in spring with sessile trillium, yellow violet, and wild geranium as some of the early bloomers. At the downstream end, Otter Creek looks sluggish, like a backwater of the Ohio River. As you progress upstream, the creek gains life, picking up current and rolling over small riffles. Occasionally the limestone along the trail will form small cliffs. The trail appears to be a favorite with both deer and mountain bikers. At 6.3 miles, reach another junction with part of the RCT leading left again to the Boone Hollow Horse Trails (37.92789N & 86.02633W).

At 6.6 miles, reach the junction with a spur trail leading left to the Garnetsville Trailhead and picnic area (37.92592N & 86.02951W). The OCT next loops around a small knob and uses one long switchback to reach a crossing with the Garnettsville access road at 7.4 miles (37.92559N & 86.03723W). Shortly you'll cross the main park road, within sight of both the entry station and KY 1638.

Beyond the park road crossing, the trees are mostly evergreens, such as pines and cedars. The cedars seem to grow best at the edge of the pine forest. These pines were planted in the early days of the park to reforest abandoned farmlands and stabilize soil. At 7.9 miles, you'll make the first of many crossings of the RCT as both trails reach the home stretch of their long loops back to the trailhead. You'll cross a small meadow before reaching the park road near the disk golf course. Close the loop at the trailhead at 9.3 miles.

The US Government originally purchased Otter Creek at the same time that it began acquiring lands for the Fort Knox Military Reservation. During the early 1930s this land was overused and eroded farmlands. Later, Civilian Conservation Corps Crews worked to convert the land into a park by building roads and structures. The US Government donated the park to the City of Louisville in 1947 in gratitude for the city's support of Fort Knox in World War II.

Few areas in this book have changed as much since the publication of the first edition as Otter Creek. In 2008, the City of Louisville announced that the park would be closed due to budget cuts. Fortunately for hikers and other lovers of the park, Governor Steve Beshear and Louisville Mayor Jerry Abramson announced that Otter Creek Park would be reopened in 2011 as an outdoors recreational area operated by the Kentucky Department of Fish and Wildlife Resources. By 2011, the park was reopened by Fish and Wildlife with some modifications to the trail system.

Mountain bikes are allowed on all park trails during dry weather. Bike traffic is normally not heavy and has not degraded the trails. Other facilities at Otter Creek include a campground, cabins, disc golf course, fishing, hunting, and an archery range.

OTHER HIKING OPTIONS

1. Short and Sweet. The hike from the former Conference Center Lodge Road to North Point and back is a 1.4-mile round trip.
2. You can combine the north legs of the Otter Creek and Valley Overlook Trails with the connector between them to make a 2.5-mile loop that also visits North Point.

39

Millennium Trail

TOTAL DISTANCE: A 13.7-mile loop on foot trails through beautiful forest

---

HIKING TIME: All day

DIFFICULTY: Difficult

LOCATION: Bernheim Arboretum and Research Forest, 6 miles south of Shepherdsville

---

MAPS: USGS Samuels and Shepherdsville, and Bernheim Trail System

---

Bernheim Arboretum and Research Forest has long been known to hikers for its beautiful, short interpretive trails. But forest hikers can now remember the celebration at the turn of the millennium in a big way, any time they set out on the Millennium Trail: a long excursion through parts of the Forest opened to the general public around the year 2000. Surprisingly, the new trail doesn't connect with any of the older foot trails so popular in the forest.

GETTING THERE

From Exit 112 on I-65, drive east 1.1 miles to the entrance to Bernheim Forest. If you are not an Arboretum member, and it is a weekend or holiday, you will need to pay an admission fee of $5 per vehicle. Drive 1.0 mile to the visitor center to register for the Millennium Trail and get a copy of the trail map. Then, take Guerilla Hollow Road to where it splits to make a loop in 0.9 mile, and go right. The start of the Millennium Trail is not signed, but is located where a cable gate blocks an old two-track road next to a prominent signboard (37.90987N & 85.66641W). You can park in a small area just ahead on the right side of the road.

THE TRAIL

The trail begins at a chain gate across an old road where you will immediately rock-hop across a small stream. In 250 feet, you'll see a grass-covered road enter from the left; this will be your return route. Follow the yellow trail markers into a small meadow at 0.3 mile, then cross the inlet to Lake Nevin on a wood bridge at 0.4 mile. Next, the trail joins paved Ten Toms Circle, a

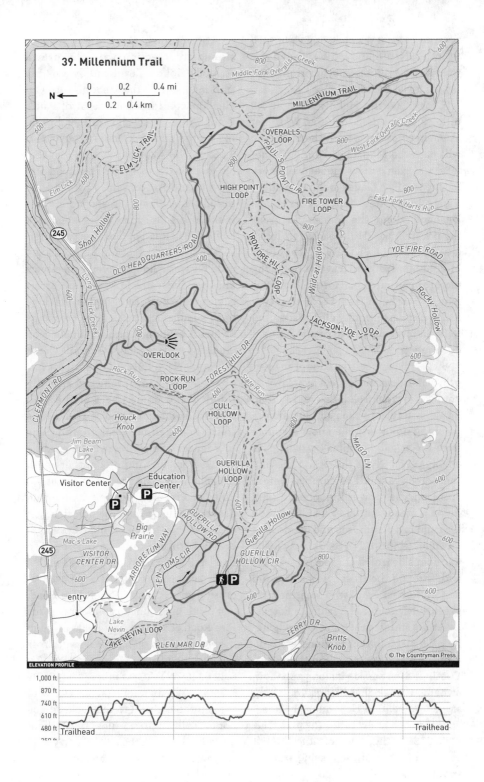

39. Millennium Trail

N ←

0   0.2   0.4 mi
0   0.2   0.4 km

MILLENNIUM TRAIL

Middle Fork Overalls Creek
West Fork Overalls Creek
East Fork Harts Run

OVERALLS LOOP

PAUL'S POINT CIR

HIGH POINT LOOP

FIRE TOWER LOOP

IRON ORE HILL LOOP

ELM LICK TRAIL

Elm Lick

245

Short Hollow

OLD HEADQUARTERS ROAD

Long Lick Creek

Wildcat Hollow

YOE FIRE ROAD

Rocky Hollow

JACKSON-YOE LOOP

OVERLOOK

Rock Run

ROCK RUN LOOP

FOREST HILL DR

Slate Run

CULL HOLLOW LOOP

CLERMONT RD

Houck Knob

Jim Beam Lake

GUERILLA HOLLOW LOOP

MAGO LN

Visitor Center

Education Center

P

P

Big Prairie

Mac's Lake

245

VISITOR CENTER DR

ARBORETUM WAY

GUERILLA HOLLOW RD

TEN TOMS CIR

Guerilla Hollow

GUERILLA HOLLOW CIR

entry

Lake Nevin

LAKE NEVIN LOOP

PLEN MAR DR

TERRY DR

Britts Knob

© The Countryman Press

ELEVATION PROFILE

1,000 ft
870 ft
740 ft
610 ft
480 ft
Trailhead   Trailhead

favorite of local walkers, at a right turn (37.91398N & 85.66746W). Leave the road at 0.7 mile on another right turn (37.91133N & 85.66348W).

Cross Guerilla Hollow Road at 0.8 mile (85.66348N & 85.66264W), just at the head of the loop in the road. You will pass the Magruder Family Cemetery, and then a more modest cemetery for the family's slaves, before reaching a gate in the deer fence at 1.1 miles. Descend along the fence and cross the paved Tower Hill Road at 1.7 miles (37.91436N & 85.65342W). Most of the Millennium Trail will travel through the mature open hardwood forest characteristic of Bernheim Forest. The trail typically wanders about, seldom seeming to be in any hurry to arrive at its next destination.

At 2.5 miles, reach the edge of an overgrown meadow and leave it by following an old two-track road. Leave this road on a sharp turn to the right just before reaching a powerline a short distance from KY 245 at 3.0 miles (37.92343N & 85.64958W). Cross the powerline and then cross a small streambed before crossing the powerline once again. Begin a steady climb to a side trail on the right to a picnic area and overlook at 4.0 miles (37.91519N & 85.64164W). The 400-foot side trail leads to a picnic table and, through the trees, views. The site honors Robert Paul, who was the first executive Director of Bernheim Forest.

At 4.9 miles, reach Jackson Cemetery. This small, fenced cemetery contains graves dating back to the 1800s. Continue a long descent along a shallow, unnamed creek that brings you along signed gravel Old Headquarters Road. Join the road at 6.2 miles (37.91143N & 85.62886W), then turn off it to the left at 6.4 miles, just after crossing another small creek.

At 7.1 miles, reach an important signed intersection with the gravel Ashlock Hollow Fire Road by a handy trail map sign at the junction with Old Headquarters Road just east of Paul's Point Circle Road and trailhead parking for the Elm Lick Trail (37.90702N & 85.62085W). West on Paul's Point Circle Road leads to Tower Hill Road and back to the Arboretum. East leads to the Elm Lick Trail, the second longest in the forest. Our route crosses Ashlock Hollow Fire Road and passes two intersections with the orange blazed 0.25 mile Overalls Loop. Beyond the Overalls Loop the trail follows a long, narrow ridge to the south. By 8.0 miles, the ridge has ended, and after several crossings of small branches and channels, you cross the middle fork of Overalls Creek (37.89325N & 85.6147W). In 2016 it was obvious that the stream had recently flooded and some parts of the trail had been washed out. The trail heads west, then it climbs over a small ridge to reenter the valley of the middle fork, before turning up another small branch. Leave the creek bottom at 9.0 miles and reach a monument honoring Steven Andrew Rone, which lies just below the top of the climb. At the next creek, turn left onto an old roadbed and then cross the creek in 50 feet.

At 9.6 miles (37.89997N & 85.62548W) cross gravel Wilson Creek Fire Road, just south of its junction with gravel Yoe Fire Road. The trail now leads through the woods south of Yoe Fire Road. Cross Yoe Fire Road at 10.2 miles (37.89818N & 85.63486W). At 10.7 miles (37.89636N & 85.6417W), an unofficial path leads to the right to connect to the Jackson-Yoe Loop Trail. At 10.9 miles, the Millennium Trail crosses the head of Log Cabin Hollow, then it climbs up and follows the crest of a ridge through some particu-

THE BERNHEIM MILLENNIUM TRAIL IS MARKED WITH YELLOW BLAZES

larly scenic woods with "winter" views to the north. Two false trails will lead off the main path, so be sure to keep watch for the yellow blazes.

At 12.4 miles, cross Guerilla Hollow. Cross through a gate in the deer fence at 13.4 miles (37.90802N & 85.67054W), then turn right to follow an old two-track road. Turn left away from the deer fence at 13.6 miles, before finally reaching the end of the loop at 13.7 miles.

Bernheim Arboretum and Research Forest has a long and distinguished history. This is one of the rare protected pieces of land in what is known as the Kentucky Knobs, the series of hills bordering the Bluegrass Region. Though the hills are not that high, a full day of climbing up and over them will tire out all but the fittest hikers.

Isaac W. Bernheim, a German immigrant who made his fortune distilling whiskey with the brand I.W. Harper, purchased the 14,000-acre site in 1929. Distilling is still important to the area: The modern Jim Beam Distillery is just west of the forest off KY 245. Bernheim was grateful for his success and bought the logged and farmed-out land for the people of Kentucky to make a park and arboretum.

Twelve thousand of the 14,378 acres of the property are used in the research forest. Current projects include studies of decline in frog and toad populations; the impact of non-native cowbirds on songbirds; and surveys of insects, snakes, and small mammals. Bernheim's forests are more diverse than they may appear to the casual hiker to be at first. Researchers have identified six distinct forest types on the property. Sycamore, sweet gum, and tulip poplar dominate the rich riparian areas along streams. On moist slopes where the bedrock is limestone, beech and sugar maple are the dominant trees, and wildflowers can be especially abundant. Three types of oak forests cover the remaining drier or steeper slopes or cover areas with more acid soils. Some ridgetops, where conditions are especially harsh, may be covered in Virginia pine.

Bernheim is open 7 a.m. to sunset daily except on Christmas and New Years Day. The visitor center is open 9 a.m. to 5 p.m. and the café is open 11 a.m. to 4 p.m. In winter, both close an hour earlier.

OTHER HIKING OPTIONS.

1. Short and Sweet. Most of the other trails at Bernheim are short loops that are ideal for nature study. The Forest has a total of 35 miles of trails. To exit the Millennium Loop where it crosses Guerilla Hollow Road and return to the parking area would be about a one-mile loop. The 1.2-mile Guerilla Hollow Loop Trail also starts on the loop road.

2. A number of short trails leave from the visitor center and Arboretum Way. Perhaps the most scenic of these is the 1.3-mile Lake Nevin Loop.

3. Some of the arboretum's favorite trails leave from trailheads along Forest Hill Drive, including Cull Hollow (1.5 miles), Jackson-Yoe (2.0 miles), and Rock Run (0.5 mile).

4. Farther to the east near Paul's Point Circle Road are several other trails, including the popular five-mile Elm Lick Trail and the 0.5-mile Fire Tower Loop.

5. The four-mile Bike Hike Trail is located off of Happy Hollow Road off KY 245.

V.
CAVE COUNTRY

40

Echo River Loop

TOTAL DISTANCE: This a 3.3-mile loop on hiking trails. You can shorten (or lengthen) the hike, depending on how many of the numerous side trails and overlooks you care to visit.

HIKING TIME: About 2 hours

DIFFICULTY: Easy/Moderate

LOCATION: Mammoth Cave National Park (hike starts at visitor center)

MAPS: USGS Mammoth Cave and National Geographic/Trails Illustrated Mammoth Cave National Park

---

The most popular surface trails at Mammoth Cave National Park are those that leave from the park visitor center. A number of scenic loops lead to Green River and back. By following the River Styx, Echo River Spring, and Mammoth Dome Trails, hikers can see the surface expression of many of the features they might later see close up inside the cave.

GETTING THERE

The loop starts at the park visitor center (37.18678N & 86.10122W). To reach the visitor center from I-65, take Exit 48 and follow the South Entrance Road for seven miles to the parking area.

THE TRAIL

Though the main trail corridor from the visitor center past the Historic Entrance of Mammoth Cave down to the Green River is heavily used, the rest of this loop is not. Many people walk part of the loop while waiting for cave tours to start, but the crowds really start to thin out once you're more than one half mile down the trail. But those that have the time to continue around the loop can learn first-hand about the relationship of the park's surface features to the remarkable cave that lies beneath the trails.

From the porch on the backside of the visitor center, descend the stairs and follow the paved route down to the Historic Entrance of Mammoth Cave in 0.2 mile (37.18722N & 86.10353W). Many of the park cave tours start with this walk, so the route can be crowded. The first thing you'll notice at the entrance is a rush of the 54 degree air that pours from the cave. In summer, the feeling is like standing in front of a huge, natural air conditioner. No one should visit this park without a tour of the cave. For the

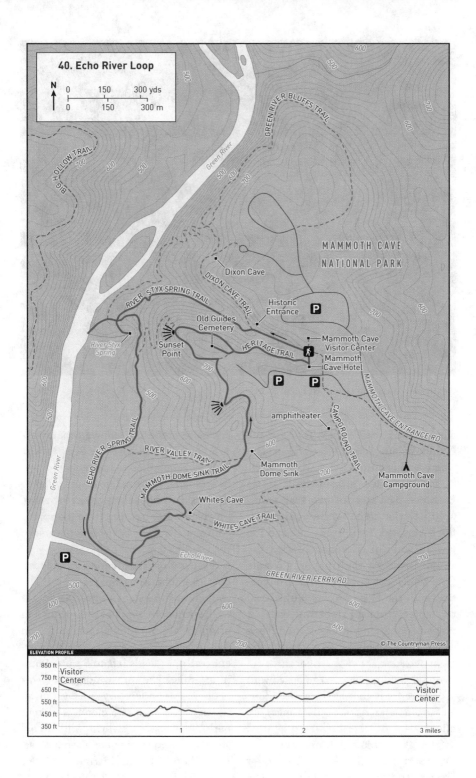

40. Echo River Loop

N

| 0 | 150 | 300 yds |
| 0 | 150 | 300 m |

GREEN RIVER BLUFFS TRAIL

MAMMOTH CAVE
NATIONAL PARK

BIG HOLLOW TRAIL

Green River

River Styx Spring

RIVER STYX SPRING TRAIL

DIXON CAVE TRAIL

Dixon Cave

Historic Entrance

Old Guides Cemetery

Sunset Point

HERITAGE TRAIL

Mammoth Cave Visitor Center

Mammoth Cave Hotel

MAMMOTH CAVE ENTRANCE RD

amphitheater

CAMPGROUND TRAIL

Mammoth Cave Campground

ECHO RIVER SPRING TRAIL

RIVER VALLEY TRAIL

MAMMOTH DOME SINK TRAIL

Mammoth Dome Sink

Whites Cave

WHITES CAVE TRAIL

Echo River

GREEN RIVER FERRY RD

© The Countryman Press

ELEVATION PROFILE

850 ft	Visitor Center				Visitor Center
750 ft					
650 ft					
550 ft					
450 ft					
350 ft		1		2	3 miles

JUNCTION OF THE ECHO RIVER AND RIVER STYX TRAILS

adventurous, the Historic Tour and the Grand Avenue Tour are described elsewhere in this guide.

Two trails leave from the Historic Entrance. The Dixon Cave Trail starts uphill to the right, while your route, the River Styx Trail, splits left and follows a wide gravel road toward the Green River. At the river in 0.6 mile (37.18754N & 86.10934W), reach a junction with the Green River Bluffs Trail that enters from the right and leads 1.4 miles to the picnic area by the visitor center. Straight ahead, a spur trail leads to an overlook above the river to an old riverboat-landing site next to beach with sycamore trees that have reached four feet in diameter. At rare quiet times, you might also see deer browsing nearby. To the left at this junction is the Echo River Springs Trail. Take the Echo River Springs Trail to an immediate fork. The right side of the fork follows a boardwalk to an overlook above River Styx Spring. This low-roofed cave and modest water flow look far too small to be an outlet to the world's longest known cave system. The blue water pouring from the spring contrasts with the pasty green water of the Green River.

Return from the boardwalk, and turn onto the Echo River Springs Trail. The trail climbs the slope above the boardwalk with more views of the spring and mingles among limestone bluffs on the hillside. At 1.1 miles, pass a shortcut trail that leads left to Sunset Point in 0.4 mile. The forest along the river is open, the understory grassy, giving the area the look of a clean, well-kept park. Next, reach a clearing with an old stone building where deer often browse. At the far end of the clearing, the River Valley Trail climbs left to the Mammoth

Dome Sink Trail at 1.3 miles (37.18334N & 86.10917W).

The Echo River Springs Trail exits straight across the clearing and follows the flat bottomland along the river. At the next junction at 1.7 miles (37.17951N & 86.10902W), Echo Spring is 0.1 mile to the right, and the trail ends in 0.4 mile at the Green River Ferry. Echo Spring is much different from the River Styx Spring and is worth the side trip. At Echo Spring, the water seems to boil straight from the ground, instead of pouring from the mouth of a cave.

Turn left at this junction, and take the Mammoth Dome Sink Trail. This well-maintained gravel path climbs steadily away from the river past low bluffs until it reaches a junction with the spur trail to the campground at 2.1 miles (37.18106N & 86.10667W), where the park service has installed a rest bench. Turn left at the junction, and soon come to the gated entry to Whites Cave nestled in the face of a shallow limestone bluff. The trail next loops around the nose of narrow ridge. Here are some unusual plants such as bedstraw and prickly pear cactus, which here is found far from its usual dry habitats.

At the next junction at 2.5 miles, the left fork is the top of the River Valley Trail leading up from the stone building. The right fork is a short spur that leads into Mammoth Dome Sink. The throat of the sink is choked with fallen timber, the floor covered with water-loving ferns. Sinks are the surface expressions of karst terrain, where the bedrock limestone has been leached away. This sink feeds magnificent Mammoth Dome, which is the final climatic climb of the Historic Cave Tour. Water entering the sink flows directly into the throat of the sinkhole and down into Mammoth Dome. Through time, this water wears away the rock through erosion and by dissolution, forming the tall, cylindrical dome.

Continue on the Mammoth Dome Sink Trail. Next, a side trail leads left to a bench beside an overlook that is being gradually reclaimed by the forest. To the right you'll pass some cabins and another pump house. The trail next passes the Sunset Terrace Rooms and intersects the handicapped accessible Heritage Trail at 2.8 miles (37.18631N & 86.10496W). To enjoy the view from Sunset Point, turn left and follow the loop. Beyond Sunset Point, take the wood boardwalk to the Old Guides Cemetery at the start of the Heritage Loop. The cemetery began as a resting place for slaves, and then it became used for guides, who were mostly African Americans in the early years. Many famous guides and cave explorers, including Stephen Bishop, who was born into slavery, are buried here. In some families, three generations rest in this spot.

To return to the visitor center from the cemetery, take the wood walkway past an overlook above the Historic Entrance, walk behind the Mammoth Cave Hotel, and then cross the concrete bridge to finish the loop in 3.3 miles.

White settlers probably rediscovered Mammoth Cave in the late 1700s. By the War of 1812, the cave was the site of an important saltpeter mining operation. Later, the cave was used and explored primarily for commercial tourism. By the early 1900s, public support for a National Park at Mammoth Cave was building. The US Congress authorized the park in 1926. In 1928, the Kentucky Legislature began efforts to purchase land. In 1941, Mammoth Cave National Park was formally dedicated.

In addition to protecting the cave, the park is an important home to many wild animals as well. 65 species of reptiles, including the northern copperhead and timber rattlesnake, have been found in the park. There are 43 mammal species here also. Besides the common possum, raccoon, squirrels, chipmunks, and white-tailed deer, you may also see signs of foxes, coyotes, or even bobcats. Over 200 species of birds have been sighted in the park. The list includes our national symbol, the bald eagle. The Green River supports an unusually diverse fish population. The park is also an important home to many species of freshwater mussels. Seven different mussels on the national endangered species list are found in the Green River.

OTHER HIKING OPTIONS

1. Short and Sweet. The Heritage Trail is a 0.6-mile handicapped accessible trail that leaves from the park visitor center.
2. From the visitor center, you can also make a loop with the Dixon Cave and Green River Bluffs Trails that is about 2.5 miles long. This loop also passes the Historic Entrance and emerges from the woods near the picnic area across the main parking area.

White Oak Trail

TOTAL DISTANCE: A 5.0-mile round trip hike on trail open to horses and mountain bikes

HIKING TIME: About 2.5 hours

DIFFICULTY: Easy/Moderate

LOCATION: Mammoth Cave National Park, about 14 miles northeast of the Mammoth Cave National Park Visitor Center

MAPS: USGS Mammoth Cave and National Geographic/Trails Illustrated Mammoth Cave National Park

The White Oak Trail follows the route of the long-abandoned Dennison Ferry Road. This trail is an easy backpacking trip or a moderate day hike. Because this is the only trail in the northeast part of the park, it is little used, especially by horses or mountain bikes. If you plan on camping in the park backcountry at the end of the trail, you must get a free permit at the park visitor center. The NPS limits backcountry sites to one party per night.

GETTING THERE

From the park visitor center, drive south to the Green River Ferry Road. Cross the river on the ferry, which operates from 6 a.m. to 9:55 p.m., and follow the North Entrance Road out of the park to KY 1827. Turn right on KY 1827, and drive 4.3 miles to signed Dennison Ferry Road. Turn right and follow the main road for 1.7 miles, until it turns to gravel beside a private house. Continue for another 0.3 mile to reach the signed trailhead at a gate across the trail (37.24373N & 86.06577W).

You can also reach the trailhead by driving 3.8 miles east on the gravel Little Jordan Road (also called the Ugly Creek Road) from the North Entrance Road. However, the Little Jordan Road is narrow, twisting, and slow.

THE TRAIL

Even in a backcountry as uncrowded as that of Mammoth Cave, it is nice to know of a few special trails that few others visit. The White Oak Trail is the only trail in the northeast corner of the park, and it sees very little use. As an added bonus, at the end of the trail is a backcountry campsite, one of only 12 in the entire park.

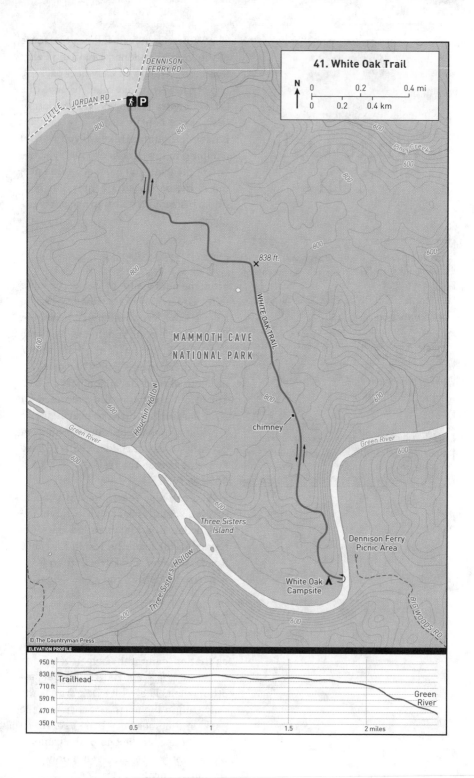

41. White Oak Trail

N

| 0 | 0.2 | 0.4 mi |
| 0 | 0.2 | 0.4 km |

DENNISON FERRY RD

LITTLE JORDAN RD

P

800

800

600

Piney Creek

600

838 ft.

WHITE OAK TRAIL

800

600

MAMMOTH CAVE

NATIONAL PARK

800

600

chimney

600

Houchin Hollow

Green River

Green River

600

Dennison Ferry
Picnic Area

600

Three Sisters
Island

600

White Oak
Campsite

BIG WOODS RD

Three Sisters Hollow

600

© The Countryman Press

ELEVATION PROFILE

950 ft				
830 ft	Trailhead			
710 ft				Green
590 ft				River
470 ft				
350 ft				
	0.5	1	1.5	2 miles

Cross the gate and begin hiking south on the old road. The trail has infrequent blue blazes, but there are no other roads or trails along the way that can be confused with the main trail. Most of the trail is in the hardwood forests typical of the ridgetops in the park, but in other areas where the forest is reclaiming old fields, cedars dominate the landscape. There is abundant poison ivy, particularly near the start, so make sure to watch your step if you venture off the trail.

At 1.0 mile, notice a faint old road leading to the left, where the trail makes a prominent right turn. If you look a few feet into the fork of the split, you can find a 1930s US Geological Survey benchmark, which gives your elevation at 838 feet.

At 1.7 miles, enter a grove of dense cedars and pass an old chimney to the right of the trail. At Mammoth Cave, cedars are the first trees to occupy abandoned farms or other clearings such as this old homestead. This old structure probably burned not long after it was abandoned. The chimney is a masterwork of elegant craftsmanship. Its profile, flared top, and huge lintel block are testaments to the care taken in its design and construction. Back in the days when the ferry attracted traffic, this was likely the site of a prominent home or inn.

At 2.0 miles, leave the flat, easy walking behind and begin a steady descent toward the Green River. Mountain bikers will find the descent a bit rough before reaching an overlook at the top of some bluffs above the river. From this vantage point, the color of the river looks little different from the bright green of the younger vegetation along it. Reach the White Oak Campsite, and the end of the trail at 2.5 miles. The campsite occupies a small bluff just above the river. You'll find the standard fire ring, hitching posts, and tent pad typical of Mammoth Cave backcountry campsites.

On the opposite bank is the Dennison Ferry Picnic Area and boat launch site. Occasionally the solitude of this campsite is broken by the clatter of boats being dragged down to the put in. One popular trip in the park during summer is the seven-mile paddle between Dennison Ferry and the Green River Ferry. Most paddlers use an outfitter for the shuttle to the launch from the Green River Ferry. Boats can be rented from outfitters also. Keep in mind that there is no longer a ferry at this site, and that there is no water or overnight camping allowed at the picnic area.

Mammoth Cave National Park receives over two million visitors per year. And though most are attracted to the park by the cave, only 500,000 of those choose to take a cave tour. A much smaller number will walk one of the front country trails near the visitor center. Only a tinier number still will visit the park backcountry. But at 53,000 acres, Mammoth Cave represents the only large block of protected land in the region. With much of the land undisturbed since the creation of the park in the 1920s, the successional forests are now maturing, and they harbor rich, diverse plant and animal life. Over 866 species of plants have been documented in the park, including 21 considered threatened, endangered, or of special concern by the Kentucky State Nature Preserves Commission. Seymour, with *Wildflowers of Mammoth Cave National Park*, has documented almost 200 species of flowering plants along the roads and trails. In addition, 65 species of trees, 30 species of shrubs, and five species of vines have been cataloged.

AN OLD HOMESITE ALONG THE WHITE OAK TRAIL

But not all the land in the backcountry of Mammoth Cave was cut for timber and planting. Just to the west of the White Oak Trail at Big Woods is one of the larger stands of old growth forest remaining in Kentucky.

OTHER HIKING OPTIONS

1. Short and Sweet. The park contains three other isolated trails, all on the south side of the Green River. The Turnhole Bend Nature Trail is a 0.5-mile loop off the West Entrance Road. The trail passes two huge sinkholes and an elevated platform with an overlook above the Green River at the Turnhole. The Youth Conservation Corps and park trail crews rehabilitated the trail in 2000.

2. The Cedar Sink Trail is a 1.9-mile round-trip hike into the depths of a sinkhole even larger than those at Turnhole Bend. There is a wood platform above the rim for those that may not want to climb down and out of the hole. This is also one of the better wildflower trails in the park front country. Look for false Solomon's seal, tall bellwort, bush clover, mistflower, ironweed, mountain mint, and black-eyed Susan among the summer flowers.

3. The Sand Cave Trail leads along a 0.2-mile boardwalk to the entrance to Sand Cave. In 1925, caver Floyd Collins was trapped by a rock fall in Sand Cave. The frantic, and ultimately unsuccessful, attempts to rescue him made national headlines at the time.

Mammoth Cave Railroad Hike and Bike Trail

TOTAL DISTANCE: The hike is an 8.2-mile out-and-back hike on trail shared with bicycles. If you can leave a vehicle at the trailhead for Sloan's Crossing Pond Walk (37.15119N & 86.09834W) the hike is only 4.5 miles.

HIKING TIME: About 4.5 hours

DIFFICULTY: Moderate

LOCATION: Mammoth Cave National Park, with hike starting at the visitor center

MAPS: USGS Mammoth Cave and National Geographic/Trails Illustrated Mammoth Cave National Park

The Mammoth Cave Railroad Hike and Bike Trail is one of the park's newest trails and offers a chance for hikers and bikers to explore the park's front country on a beautiful, well-maintained trail built between 2005 and 2007. The trail follows the route of the old Mammoth Cave Railroad from the gateway town of Park City north to the site of the modern park visitor center. The trail is wide with a crushed gravel surface that is perfect for enjoyable walking or riding. Though the trail follows the route of the old railroad line, the construction of the modern Mammoth Cave Parkway on top of some of the old railroad line means that the trail does not follow the rail bed exactly, and it will have a few turns and grades too sharp or steep for a train. This hike follows the trail from the north end at the visitor center south to Sloan Crossing Pond.

GETTING THERE

The hike starts at the park visitor center (37.18678N & 86.10122W). To reach the visitor center from I-65, take Exit 48 and follow the South Entrance Road for seven miles to the parking area. If you are able to leave a vehicle at Sloan's Crossing Pond (37.15119N & 86.09834W), this trailhead is located on the Parkway at the intersection with the Brownsville Road 3.5 miles south of the visitor center.

THE TRAIL

The hike begins at a relatively modest sign in front of the park visitor center. The start is paved and traces the edge of the main parking lot. After crossing the entrance to the Mammoth Cave Hotel, Railroad Engine #4 to the right of the trail stands as another reminder of the

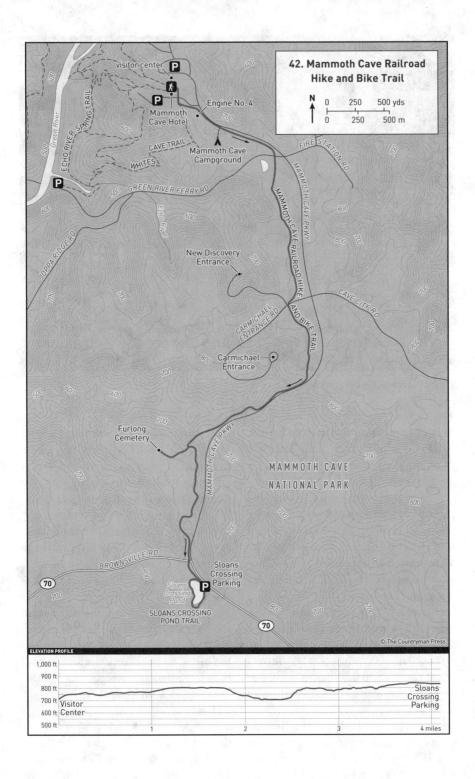

42. Mammoth Cave Railroad Hike and Bike Trail

N

| 0 | 250 | 500 yds |
| 0 | 250 | 500 m |

visitor center

Engine No. 4

Mammoth Cave Hotel

CAVE TRAIL

WHITES

Mammoth Cave Campground

ECHO RIVER SPRING TRAIL

Green River

GREEN RIVER FERRY RD

JOPPA RIDGE RD

Echo River

New Discovery Entrance

FIRE STATION RD

MAMMOTH CAVE PKWY

MAMMOTH CAVE RAILROAD HIKE AND BIKE TRAIL

CAVE CITY RD

CARMICHAEL ENTRANCE RD

Carmichael Entrance

Furlong Cemetery

MAMMOTH CAVE PKWY

MAMMOTH CAVE NATIONAL PARK

BROWNSVILLE RD

70

Sloans Crossing Pond

Sloans Crossing Parking

SLOANS CROSSING POND TRAIL

70

© The Countryman Press

ELEVATION PROFILE

1,000 ft				
900 ft				
800 ft				Sloans
700 ft	Visitor			Crossing
600 ft	Center			Parking
500 ft		1	2	3	4 miles

A GRAVE MARKER IN FURLONG CEMETERY

days when most visitors arrived here by rail. At 0.3 mile, Caver's Camp Store will be on the right, marking the end of the paved section of trail.

Cross the campground road and enter a narrow strip of woods between the campground and Parkway. Two spurs from the campground will join the main trail at interpretive signs. Once into the woods, the trail is marked by the same blue blazes used in the park backcountry. Though the trail is wide, most of it is well shaded and pleasant through the heat of the summer.

At 0.8 mile (37.18164N & 86.0918W) cross Ferry Road and begin a quieter section where the trail is well away from the Parkway. Cross a trio of boardwalks and look for the blooms of May apple here in late spring. At 1.6 miles, cross Carmichael Entrance Road (37.17132N & 86.09052W). As the trail approaches the Parkway, a long boardwalk spans a deep ravine on the right. The ravine is the edge of a sinkhole leading into Mammoth Cave and illustrates the difficulty of building the original 1886 railroad through the rugged karst terrain of the park. A trestle stood on this site until the construction of the parkway in 1961. Across the road from the boardwalk is the Doyel Valley Overlook.

As the trail again pulls away from the Parkway, it makes the only significant climb of this trip. At the top of the hill is an intersection with the spur trail to Furlong Cemetery at 2.8 miles (37.16105N & 86.09978W). Turn right on the spur to reach the cemetery at 3.0 miles (37.16084N & 86.10248W). Prior to the establishment of the park, the Doyel, Furlong, and Sloan families lived here. These families are remembered by the park and its visitors in the names they left on the park's geography.

Return to the main trail at 3.2 miles and turn right to continue hiking south towards Sloan's Pond Crossing. Emerge from the woods and cross the Brownsville Road at 3.9 miles. Just beyond, reach the paved trailhead for the Sloan's Pond Crossing Trail (86.10248N & 86.09834W) at 4.1 miles. This interpretive trail loop follows an accessible boardwalk completely around the lily pad–covered pond. The pond is an anomaly in karst terrain; typically water here finds easy access to the open cave spaces below the surface, so creeks and ponds are relatively rare. Close the loop at 4.5 miles.

To return to the trailhead by the visitor center, retrace your route back on the main trail. If you skip Sloan's Pond Crossing Trail and the spur to Furlong Cemetery, you will reach the trailhead in 3.7 miles, for a total hike of 8.2 miles.

Early travelers to Mammoth Cave had a much more daunting trip than we do today. Visitation to the cave was spurred by the construction of the L&N Railroad in 1859. After the Civil War, 40-50,000 visitors a year were taking the railroad to Park City and then stagecoaches to the cave. By 1886, the 9-mile railroad was in place, going to the cave, but it was only profitable for a few years, as automobile traffic gradually became more popular. By 1931, the railroad shut down and Engine #4 was placed on display at the end of the line.

OTHER HIKING OPTIONS

1. Short and Sweet. The most popular section of the trail is the 0.8 mile between the visitor center and the campground.
2. From Sloan's Pond Crossing Trail, the Mammoth Cave Railroad Hike and Bike Trail extends another 5.0 miles south to the park boundary at the town of Park City, where it connects to the Park City Bicycle and Walking Trail, which in turn ends at Bell's Tavern Historic Park.

Big Hollow Trail

TOTAL DISTANCE: Hiking both loops of the Big Hollow Trail covers 12.4 miles on trails shared with mountain bikes.
HIKING TIME: About 6.5 hours
DIFFICULTY: Moderate/Difficult
LOCATION: Mammoth Cave National Park, about 5 miles north of the park visitor center
MAPS: USGS Rhoda and Mammoth Cave and National Geographic/Trails Illustrated Mammoth Cave National Park

Big Hollow is the newest trail in Mammoth Cave National Park and the first to be built for mountain bike riders. The park has isolated this trail from those used by horses, and consequently this trail remains the gem of the Mammoth Cave backcountry. The trail's gentle grades and pleasant forests make it a favorite of hikers as well.

GETTING THERE

From the visitors center, drive south to the Green River Ferry Road. Cross the river on the ferry, which operates from 6 a.m. to 9:55 p.m., and follow the Green River Ferry Road north. Turn left onto the Maple Springs Road and proceed 0.8 mile to the large parking area and trailhead (37.20575N & 86.13857W).

THE TRAIL

The area around the Maple Springs Trailhead has changed as much as any place in the Mammoth Cave Backcountry. The Sal Hollow and Buffalo Creek Trails still leave to the southeast from here, but there is no longer a hiking trail out to Good Spring Church. The trailhead is much larger, and there are now picnic tables and bathroom facilities. Instead of being used primarily by hikers, the trailhead is now used primarily by horses and mountain bikers. Big Hollow Trail is barbell-shaped, with north and south loops separated by a mile-long connector trail, and the trail can only be accessed via the mile-long Maple Springs Trail.

The hike begins on the east side of the trailhead on the Maple Springs Trail, a wide gravel blue-blazed path shared with horses and mountain bikes. In 0.1 mile, a spur trail on the right leads to the Maple Springs Group Campground and

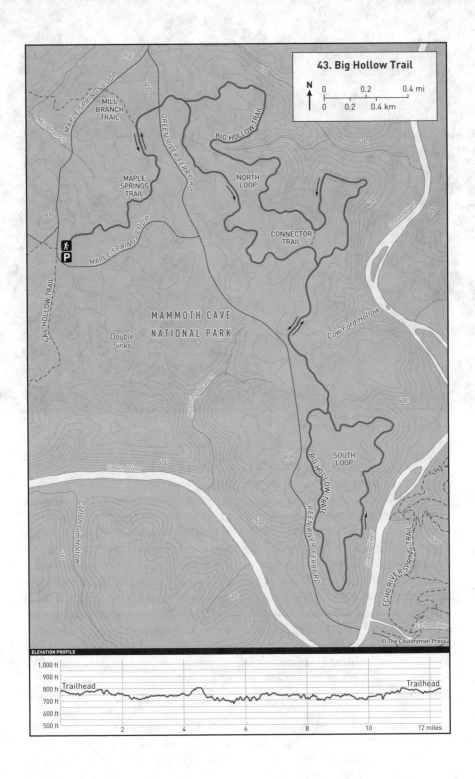

43. Big Hollow Trail

N

| 0 | | 0.2 | | 0.4 mi |
| 0 | 0.2 | | 0.4 km | |

MAPLE SPRINGS LOOP

Mill Branch

MILL
BRANCH
TRAIL

GREEN RIVER FERRY RD

BIG HOLLOW TRAIL

MAPLE
SPRINGS
TRAIL

NORTH
LOOP

MAPLE SPRINGS LOOP

CONNECTOR
TRAIL

Green River

SAL HOLLOW TRAIL

MAMMOTH CAVE
NATIONAL PARK

Double
Sinks

Cow Ford Hollow

Running Branch

Green River

SOUTH
LOOP

BIG HOLLOW TRAIL

GREEN RIVER FERRY RD

Cotton Gin Hollow

ECHO RIVER SPRING TRAIL

Green River

Echo River

© The Countryman Press

ELEVATION PROFILE

| 1,000 ft |
| 900 ft |
| 800 ft | Trailhead | Trailhead |
| 700 ft |
| 600 ft |
| 500 ft |

2   4   6   8   10   12 miles

THE NORTH LOOP OF THE BIG HOLLOW TRAIL

at 0.5 mile (37.20857N & 86.13238W), another spur leads right to the Maple Springs Research Center. As with many of the trails at Mammoth Cave this is prime habitat for poison ivy, so be careful to stay on the trail. At 1.0 mile, the Maple Springs Trail ends at a junction with the Mill Branch and Big Hollow Trails (37.21364N & 86.13237W).

At the one-mile junction, the horse traffic will exit left on Mill Branch Trail, while the hikers and bikers go right on Big Hollow Trail, which is now a smooth dirt surface. Big Hollow remains blue-blazed, and you may also see mileage markers along the way. At 1.2 miles, cross the Ferry Road, and at 1.3 miles (37.21532N & 86.12814W), reach the start of the north loop. Stay right to go counterclockwise around the loop.

Once on the loop, Big Hollow really begins to shine. The trail is well built for bikers and hikers; there is little climbing as it winds around contours on the edge of Big Hollow. Much of the forest is open and appears more mature than many of the stands in the backcountry west of the Ferry Road. Near the far end of the loop, you'll skirt a small creek that feeds a sinkhole before reaching the junction with a short-cut trail at 3.0 miles. Continue right to reach the north end of the connector trail at 3.1 miles (37.2042N & 86.11665W).

Turn right on the connector and continue south. The trail will approach close by the Ferry Road and then follow the remnant of a forest road. At 4.1 miles, reach the start of the South Loop (37.1944N & 86.11595W). Keep right again to follow this loop counterclockwise. The south loop caters in particular to mountain bikers. Occasional short splits in the trail allow bikers to ride more challenging features, while the main trail remains smooth and suitable for beginning riders. Near the south end of the loop, you may begin to hear noise from the ferry traffic before you turn east to ride a section high above the Green River. Beyond this turn, there are a few rocky sections along the trail.

At 6.9 miles, close the South Loop and hike north back on the connector to the south end of the North Loop at 7.9 miles. If you would like to save a mile of hiking, you can go left here for 0.1 mile and take a right turn on the shortcut trail for another 0.1 mile to shorten the hike. To keep on the main route, go right and continue counterclockwise on the North Loop.

At 9.0 miles (37.20677N & 86.11648W), reach the north end of the shortcut trail and continue to the right. The cedar and pine trees in this part of the forest often mark old homesites or fields. Pines and cedar are usually the first trees to appear in disturbed areas and will survive for a generation or so before they are overtaken by hardwoods. At 11.1 miles, reach the end of the north loop. Keep right here to reach the Maple Springs Trail, and then follow it back to the trailhead to end the hike at 12.4 miles.

The Mammoth Cave backcountry has changed considerably over the years. The trails north of the Green River were first opened in 1974 and quickly were expanded to a 50-mile system. The trails were mostly used by hikers, built and maintained at a level to support foot traffic. By the time of the first edition of this guide in 2001, the trails were in good condition, but horse groups were just starting to use the trails.

Mammoth Cave National Park then conducted a formal planning process for their roads and trails. For a few years, some of the backcountry trails, including Sal Hollow and Turnhole Bend, were opened on an experimental basis to mountain bikes, while the rest of the trails north of the river remained open to horses. Unfortunately, the formal process ultimately led to allowing horse use on all the existing backcountry trails and excluding mountain bikers from the trails that they had been maintaining. Local horse riders were vocal enough during the process to force the park to continue access for them on the First Creek Loop, even though the park's analysis recommended no horse use on that loop. Horse use has continued to increase in the park and as a result many of the existing backcountry trails have been essentially destroyed. Horses continue heavy use in wet weather and widen and extend muddy and boggy stretches of trail, and continue to ride in areas where they are not allowed. The establishment of commercial horse camps on the north boundary of the park suggests that these practices will continue.

Based on my last scouting trip to the park, I removed the two backcountry loops at First Creek and Raymer Hollow from this guide. Long stretches of the First Creek loop are now continuous mud holes in wet weather and, according to rangers, conditions are similar in much of the backcountry. The park continues to maintain and rebuild trail sections in the backcountry, but without some help from horse groups in improving their sustainability, these conditions are likely to persist. Spring and summer are likely the wettest seasons. Drier conditions in the fall and freezing weather in winter may make those seasons more appealing for backcountry visits.

Fortunately, the park has been proactive in providing trails for mountain bikers, opening the Big Hollow Loop in 2014. The trail was built to be sustainable and to protect park resources.

OTHER HIKING OPTIONS

1. Short and Sweet. The Maple Springs Trail is a 2-mile round-trip hike. Using the shortcut trail to walk just the North Loop is a 6.4-mile loop.
2. Due to other changes in the backcountry trail system, the First Creek-McCoy Hollow-Wet Prong loop described in the first edition of this guide is now a 16.4-mile loop. Heavy horse traffic leaving from horse camps near the First Creek and Lincoln Trailheads can make these hiking these trails tedious.
3. The Raymer Hollow-Mill Branch loop also formerly described in the first edition of this guide has also been relocated and can be accessed from the Maple Springs Trailhead for a 10.7-mile loop.
4. Also, from the Maple Springs Trailhead, a loop with the Sal Hollow and Buffalo Spring Creek Trails with the side trip to Turnhole Bend covers 7.9 miles.

44

Historic Cave Tour

TOTAL DISTANCE: This guided cave tour covers about two miles of the cave. You must pick up a tour ticket at the park visitor center. Contact the park for the current tour schedule and fee information.

HIKING TIME: This tour takes about 2 hours, and it can include up to 120 people.

DIFFICULTY: Easy

LOCATION: The tour starts at the Mammoth Cave National Park Visitor Center.

MAPS: The Mammoth Cave National Park Brochure Historic Cave Tour

No visitor to Mammoth Cave should leave before taking one of the park's many cave tours. Perhaps the most popular, and the most impactful, is the Historic Tour, parts of which have been a hit with visitors since the early 1800s. The Historic Tour enters the cave at the Historic Entrance and explores many of the huge open passages that made the cave famous in the days long before it was known to be the world's longest. The tour visits remains of a mining operation that took place during the War of 1812, and it finishes with a climatic climb up a steel tower in Mammoth Dome. These passages are generally large. However, for many, Fat Man's Misery and Tall Man's Misery are the most memorable parts of the trip.

You must purchase a ticket to go on any cave tour in the park. You can order tickets online at www.recreation.gov or by calling 877-444-6777. Same day or advance tickets can also be bought at the ticket counter at the visitor center. Cave tours often are sold out on weekends, or during the busy summer season, so it is best to make your reservations early.

GETTING THERE

To reach the visitor center from I-65, take Exit 48, and follow the South Entrance Road for seven miles to the parking area.

THE TRAIL

The Historic Cave Tour begins in the breezeway outside the main entrance to the visitor center. You should be ready at least five minutes before the scheduled starting time. Keep in mind that the only bathrooms along the route are at Great Relief Hall. Temperatures inside

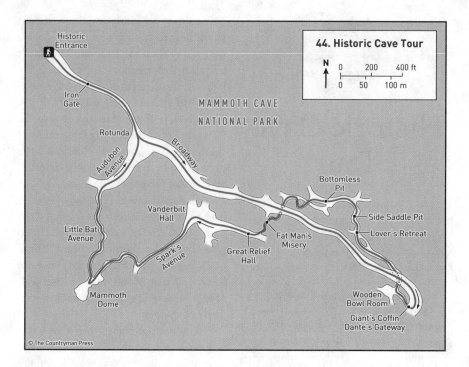

the cave average 54 degrees, which can feel uncomfortably cold for those used to summer heat. A jacket and long pants are usually enough to stay warm. It shouldn't be necessary to remind hikers to wear sensible shoes. Flash photography is not permitted on cave tours.

Your tour guide will lead the group down the paved walkway to the Historic Entrance. Your first stop will be a talk about safety, for both you and the cave. If your tour is full, you will need to stay near the front to hear what the guide says once you are in the cave. You will next enter the cave down a long set of stairs. The initial passages are very large, resembling slightly flattened tubes with a level floor. The first room you come to is called the Rotunda. Here are the remains of niter mines that operated during the War of 1812. Miners collected calcium nitrate from the cave, mixed it with water, pumped it out, and treated it to produce potassium nitrate. The nitrate was critical to the war effort, as it is one of the main ingredients in gunpowder. You can see much of the miners' equipment in a lower level of the room, and you will have already passed many of the hollow logs they built to bring water into the mine and pump the nitrate out.

From the Rotunda, the tour follows another large passage called Broadway. The gentle meanders of this wide passage seem very similar to the turns of a gentle river. The main passages in Mammoth Cave formed as surface water flowed into the cave system and was concentrated in underground rivers that cut their way downward until they reached the level of the Green River. The main passageways were once as much as 80 feet high, but they have been partially filled by breakdown from the cave roof and sediment from the underground rivers.

THE GREEN RIVER FROM THE OLD RIVERBOAT LANDING BELOW MAMMOTH CAVE

Well before the rediscovery of the cave in the late 1700s, Native Americans also used Mammoth Cave. From a period between 4,000 and 2,000 years ago, they explored as much as 12 miles of cave passages using only reed torches. They apparently removed gypsum and other salt crystals, for reasons not yet completely understood. Several bodies, including one left as the result of a rock fall from mining, have been found in the cave. Archaeologists have learned much about the diet of these early visitors from the feces they left behind.

The tour makes a right turn off Broadway at Giant's Coffin into the narrow passage called Dante's Gateway. It then descends through the middle level of 70-foot high Sidesaddle Pit, and then along a boardwalk at the edge of Bottomless Pit. Beyond the pits are the narrow, winding passages of Fat Man's Misery and the lower passages of Tall Man's Misery. These passages were enlarged by early cave operators, whose clients must have been shorter than modern visitors. Besides their smaller size, the meanders in these passages are more pronounced and closer spaced. The shape of these passages are similar to many of the slot canyons of the Colorado Plateau, in which the passages are carved by infrequent flooding rather than the gradual erosion of steady streams. If you look up in the passages, you can see that some of the walls are overhanging, and in other places, rocks have fallen from the roof or walls to become wedged in the narrow openings.

At the end of the "Misery," you will come to the welcome space of Great Relief Hall, where you are 310 feet below the surface. Just beyond this room, at River Hall, a passage leads down to the Echo River. The park service once led underground boat tours on the river, but this was found to disturb the endangered Mammoth Cave shrimp, so the tours were discontinued. The cave is home to 130 different animals, and several of these are endangered, including the cave shrimp and several species of bats.

The climax of the Historic Tour is the climb up the steel tower inside of Mammoth Dome. At the lower part of the Dome, you'll see the flowstone and stalactites that are the only cave formations on the tour route. The Dome is a complex arrangement of vertical shafts nearly 200 feet high, with smooth, fluted walls. A stairway spirals up the side, offering close-up views of the entire height. If you walked the Echo River hike, you would have seen the huge sinkhole that is the surface expression of Mammoth Dome.

The top of the Dome leads to a small, undistinguished passage that would give explorers approaching Mammoth Dome no indication that the wonders of the Dome might lie ahead. This passage leads into larger Audubon Avenue and then joins the inbound route at the Rotunda Room. Turn left at the Rotunda Room to exit the cave and return to the visitor center.

After the War of 1812, exploration of Mammoth Cave was rather haphazard until Franklin Gorin bought the cave in 1838. He turned guiding and exploration of the cave over to his slave Stephen Bishop. Bishop became the first and foremost of a long line of cave explorers. He was the first to push beyond the easy walking passages, the first to cross the feared bottomless pit (he used only a wooden ladder), and the discoverer of the Echo River. His explorations extended the length of the known cave from 4 to 27 miles.

In 1908 German Engineer Max Kemper teamed with Bishop's grandnephew Ed to produce the first high-quality map of the cave. Their map showed 35 miles of passages, and it is still a convenient guide for modern cavers. In the late 1910s and early 1920s, G. D. Morrison bought the southern end of Mammoth Cave and blasted the New and Frozen Niagara Entrances to the cave. Shortly afterward Mammoth Cave National Park was authorized and land acquisition began.

Meanwhile, serious exploration of a number of caves was also ongoing underneath Flint Ridge, just to the east of Mammoth Cave. Dedicated explorers were able to tie together the many originally separate caves into a network nearly as long as Mammoth itself. Through the 1960s and early 1970s explorers worked to find the connection between the Flint Ridge system and Mammoth Cave. In 1972, they were successful; the Mammoth Cave-Flint Ridge system was then the longest in the world, at 144 miles.

Through dedicated exploration and linkage with other caves, Mammoth is now the world's longest cave at 405 miles, with no signs of its exploration stopping soon. The world's second largest cave, Sistema Sac Acton in Mexico, has only 208 miles. Jewel Cave National Monument in South Dakota's Black Hills is our nation's second longest, with 181 miles of passages.

In 2016 the park renovated the Historic Tour route, which was originally constructed 75 years ago by the Civilian Conservation Corps.

OTHER CAVING OPTIONS

1. Short and Sweet. Please note that the cave tour schedule changes by season, and not all tours are offered year-round. If you have arrived without a reservation at a crowded time, you'll end up on the self-guided Mammoth Cave Discovery or Mammoth Passage tours which are offered as visitation warrants. Both include portions of the Historic Tour. The Mammoth Cave Discovery Tour is 30 minutes long and covers three quarters of a mile. The Mammoth Passage Tour lasts 75 minutes and also covers three quarters of a mile.

2. The Trog Tour treats children 8-12 to a 30- to 45-minute adventure including crawling through cave passages. Some special clothing is needed.

3. The Gothic Avenue Tour (2 hours, 1 mile) visits Gothic Avenue on a slightly shorter version of the Historic Tour.

4. The Violet City (3 hours, 3 miles) and Star Chamber (2.5 hours, 2 miles) explore Mammoth Cave by lantern.

45

Grand Avenue Tour

TOTAL DISTANCE: This guided cave tour covers about four miles of the cave. You must pick up a tour ticket at the park visitor center and reservations are recommended. Contact the park for the current tour schedule and fee information.

HIKING TIME: This tour takes about 4 hours and can include up to 120 people. The tour was formerly called the Half Day tour.

DIFFICULTY: Easy/Moderate

LOCATION: The tour meets at the Mammoth Cave National Park Visitor Center.

MAPS: The Mammoth Cave National Park Brochure Cave Tours

The Grand Avenue Tour explores Mammoth Cave between the Carmichael and Frozen Niagara Entrances. This long walk features a lunch stop at the underground Snowball Dining Room, the climb up Kentucky's version of Mount McKinley, and finishes with a visit to the fantastic formations at Frozen Niagara.

You must purchase a ticket to go on any cave tour in the park. You can order tickets online at www.recreation.gov or by calling 877-444-6777. Same-day or advance tickets can also be bought at the ticket counter at the visitor center. Cave tours often are sold out on weekends, or during the busy summer season, so it is best to make your reservations early.

GETTING THERE

The tour starts at the Mammoth Cave National Park Visitor Center. To reach the visitor center from I-65, take Exit 48, and follow the South Entrance Road for seven miles to the visitor center parking area.

THE TRAIL

The Grand Avenue Tour begins with a bus ride to the cave's Carmichael Entrance. You should be ready at least five minutes before the scheduled starting time. Keep in mind that there are only two brief restroom breaks. Temperatures inside the cave average 54 degrees, which can feel uncomfortably cold for those used to summer heat. A jacket and long pants are usually enough to stay warm. It shouldn't be necessary to remind hikers to wear sensible shoes. Flash photography is not permitted on cave tours. You can buy lunch along the route or bring it with you in a small pack.

After a brief safety talk at the Carmichael Entrance, you'll descend a narrow man-made passage down stairs to enter

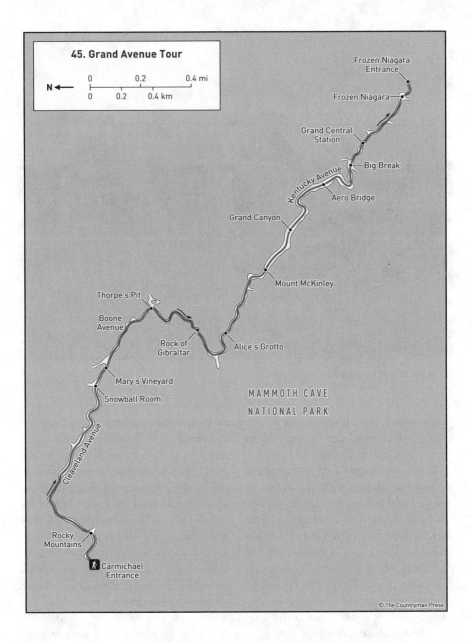

the cave at Sandstone Avenue. You soon turn into a larger passage called Cleaveland Avenue (named for a geologist, not the President). The roof of this passage is coated with crystals of gypsum, a soft, white mineral formed from calcium and sulfate. Native American explorers entered the cave 4,000 to 2,000 years ago to collect this and other minerals for reason still not yet fully understood.

You'll pass signs of previous explorers, who may not have been as sensitive to the ideals of cave preservation as modern visitors. Writing on the walls or leaving trash behind was acceptable in the early years, when the cave was pri-

THE MAMMOTH CAVE NATIONAL PARK VISITOR CENTER

vately owned. Now, however, the cave is fully protected and any damage to the cave is punishable by fines, or even jail.

The tour's longest stop is one mile in at the Snowball Dining Room. Here you can buy a boxed lunch, drinks, snacks, and soup if you need to warm up. There may be some bats in this room to entertain you. The room is named for the abundant white gypsum "snowballs" that coat the ceiling. The Snowball Room is also your last chance to use the bathroom. Be prepared to go the next three hours without facilities.

Beyond the Snowball Room, the huge passage of Cleaveland Avenue begins to change. You'll enter a more complicated multi-level passage called Boone Avenue, even though the famous Kentucky explorer never saw Mammoth Cave. Boone Avenue is a long, narrow slot, much like an underground version of the sandstone slot canyons of the Colorado Plateau. Past Boone Avenue is Kentucky Avenue, and then the climb up Mount McKinley. The climb is necessary because the formerly smooth and level floor (level for a cave, that is) has been buried here by piles of rock fallen from the roof. Here you can see that although the cave passages were originally carved by water, collapse of rock from the roof of the cave has played a major part in shaping the modern structure of Mammoth Cave.

Though the climb is a challenge for many cave visitors, it will not be a problem for trail-tested hikers. There are many switchbacks, and although the grade is steep and climbs 92 feet, there are no obstacles to climb over. But unfortunately, Mount McKinley is only the first of three climbs on the trip. The 87-foot climb up Heart Attack Hill on Aero Bridge follows in quick succession.

Your next stop will likely be at Grand Central Station. These next passages require some bending and stooping to pass through. Make the final ascent of the tour up Big Break. Once this climb is behind you, you may begin to see some cave crickets on the walls or ceiling. These unusual creatures use long feelers to move about the cave. They are very sensitive, so avoid touching them, or taking up-close flash photos.

Next, you begin to see some of the formations that have made this part of the cave so famous. You will descend to the bottom of the Drapery Room, the base of a large dome with walls covered in red travertine. There is some cave bacon here; the red-stripped form of flowstone must have been named by an awfully hungry explorer.

For protection, many of the formations are fenced off from the walkways. The climax of the tour is at Frozen Niagara, a 70-foot high flowstone formation that visitors climb past on a broad stairway. The tour leaves the cave by the Frozen Niagara Entrance, and returns to the visitor center by bus.

Mammoth Cave is developed in limestone of Mississippian age. Three different formations named the St. Louis, Ste. Genevieve, and Girkin host part of the cave. Overlying the limestone is the sandstone and conglomerate of the Pennsylvanian age Caseyville Formation. These rocks are very similar to those forming the ridge tops in the Big South Fork or Red River Gorge. No cave is formed in the overlying rocks.

The cave was formed as surface water began its long journey toward sea level. At Mammoth Cave, the quickest route to the sea is via the Green River. On the surface, water will first follow small streams, and then larger ones, until reaching the river. When streams flow over limestone,

small cracks and other points of weakness in the rock are eroded by stream action and slowly dissolved as water flows across the rock. Naturally occurring rainwater is slightly acidic, and can react and very slowly dissolve limestone. The surfaces between rock layers, called bedding planes, are one weak area that may initially divert water from a surface to a subsurface passage.

"Karst" is the term geologists use to describe limestone areas where water flow is underground. Sinkholes, which connect the surface to underground passageways, are the characteristic surface feature of karst landscapes. As you see at Mammoth Dome, a sinkhole can collect surface water and feed it directly into a cave system. Once underground, the water at Mammoth Cave tends to flow along a single rock layer. This results in the tubular shape of many of the passages. The floor of the cave is scoured and dissolved by flowing water, while the sides of the cave are opened by the same processes, but at a slower rate. The roof of the cave may be covered by water only during rare floods. The roof is expanded by breakdown of blocks onto the floor of the cave.

As the Green River has gradually cut its way down into the plateau around Mammoth Cave, the base level for water flow has also dropped. There are five different levels in the cave, each corresponding roughly to the outside factors that have controlled the rate of erosion of the Green River. The lowest level of Mammoth Cave now contains several major rivers that are still working to expand the cave.

Above the lowest levels, and on most of the tourist routes, Mammoth Cave is a dry cave. While this makes for comfortable cave tours, it does not make for spectacular cave formations. In areas where the cave is capped by sandstone, little groundwater leaks into the cave to form drapery and flowstone and other decorative features. These formations are formed from travertine, a mineral identical in composition, but different in structure, to calcite, the basic building block of limestone rocks. Travertine forms when the waters that have dissolved limestone are exposed to the atmosphere in a cave. When the water reaches the cave opening, some of the dissolved carbonate from the limestone is deposited on the cave walls as travertine. So, if there is little groundwater flow into a cave, there will be few travertine formations. The origin of other cave formations, such as gypsum and nitrate, is less understood.

OTHER CAVING OPTIONS

1. Short and Sweet. Visitors can see most of the cave formations along this route on either the Cleaveland Avenue (2 miles, 2.5 hours out and back to the Snowball Room), Frozen Niagara (1.25 hours, 1.25 mile), or Domes and Dripstones tours (2 hours, 0.75 mile).

2. If the Grand Avenue Tour was not enough adventure for you, try the Wild Cave Tour. This 6-hour, five-mile epic travels on some of the route used by Grand Avenue, but then ventures off the tourist routes to slither through tight and tiny passages that will test your fear of claustrophobia. This tour requires special gear, is offered only once a day, and is limited to 14 people, so make your reservations well in advance. The tour is limited to those 18 or over, or 16–18 year–olds accompanied by an adult. You must check in 30 minutes prior to the scheduled start of this tour.

3. The Introduction to Caving Tour (3.5 hours, 1 mile) is designed to teach responsible caving techniques to those over 10 years old. Those 10- to 15-years old must be accompanied by an adult. This tour requires special gear, is offered only once a day, and is limited to 20 people, so make your reservations well in advance.

VI.

LAKES AND RIVERS

46

Backcountry Loop

TOTAL DISTANCE: 4.2 miles of loops on hiking trails	
HIKING TIME: About 2.5 hours	
DIFFICULTY: Easy/Moderate	
LOCATION: John James Audubon State Park, near Henderson	
MAPS: USGS Evansville South, IND-KY: John James Audubon State Park Guide Map	

John James Audubon State Park honors the legacy of one of the country's most renowned early naturalists with a 692-acre park in Henderson, the artist's home from 1810-1819. Here Audubon did much of the work that led to his breakthrough publication, *Birds of America*, still regarded as one of the world's masterpieces of wildlife art. The park also contains a 325-acre State Nature Preserve centered on Wilderness Lake, which is laced by eight hiking trails that cover 5.7 miles. This hike picks the best of those trails and combines them into a series of loops.

GETTING THERE

From the north end of Pennyrile Parkway on the outskirts of Henderson, drive 1.5 miles north on US 41. Turn right onto the park entrance road, and park in front of the park office (37.88244N & 87.55705W).

THE TRAIL

Your first stop at the park should be a visit to the John James Audubon Museum and Nature Center. The museum contains some of the artist's original work, as well as a detailed series of displays about his life and his contributions to both the arts and conservation. The CCC-era museum and park office are two of the prettiest buildings in the Kentucky State Park system. The graceful turrets of the museum building are masterpieces of stonework.

The park trails begin in back of the Museum and Nature Center. Begin on the Museum Trail, an interpretive trail constructed as part of an Eagle Scout project. Signs along the trail identify white ash, black locust, and hackberry trees. At the first junction, the Museum

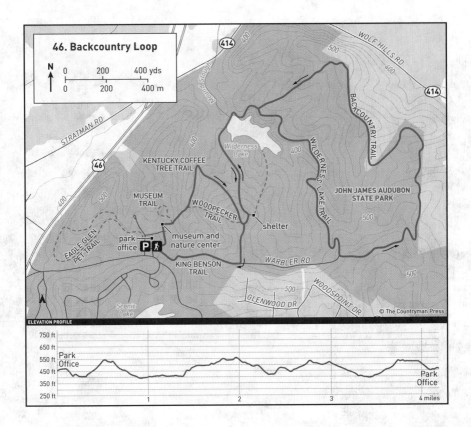

46. Backcountry Loop

N
0   200   400 yds
0   200   400 m

ELEVATION PROFILE

750 ft
650 ft
550 ft Park
450 ft Office
350 ft
250 ft
          1   2   3   4 miles
                                                Park
                                                Office

Trail splits left to make a short loop, while your main route goes right on the Kentucky Coffee Tree Trail (37.8831N & 87.55634W). The dense ground cover along this trail includes Virginia creeper, May apple, and a variety of ferns.

Arrive at a second signed junction at 0.2 mile where the Kentucky Coffee Tree Trail merges with the Woodpecker Trail, which enters from the right. Unless you want to get a taste of what stinging nettles feel like, avoid touching the plants around the sign. Go left at this junction, and cross a small wood bridge. Go left again when the trail splits. The Kentucky Coffee Tree Trail follows a tiny stream for a while before beginning the climb to a small ridge. On the ridgetop, the trail rejoins the Woodpecker Trail

and an old dirt road. Turn left onto the road, and reach a stone shelter at 0.8 mile (37.88359N & 87.55193W). The small shelter has benches and a fireplace. Look for wild ginger, May apple, and spiderwort here in springtime. Beyond the shelter, a side trail leads 0.2 mile down to the shore of Wilderness Lake. Our route will offer more open views of the lake than the side trail, which may be clogged with poison ivy and saw briers near the shore.

From the shelter, turn left onto the Wilderness Lake Trail, and descend gradually down flights of wood steps to the dam across Wilderness Lake. The lake's clear waters harbor a healthy population of very vocal frogs. The dam site and the trail along it are cleared by the park. At the second wood bridge over an

THE VISITOR CENTER AT JOHN JAMES AUDUBON STATE PARK

arm of the lake, reach the signed junction with the Backcountry Trail at 1.2 miles. The Backcountry Trail, combined with the remainder of the Wilderness Lake Trail, forms a 2.2-mile loop from this point. You should hike the Wilderness Lake leg first by turning right continuing to circle the lake.

Cross a few more wood bridges, where raccoons have left their mark, as you traverse the sunny north shore of the lake. At 1.6 miles, the trail joins paved Warbler Road, which is blocked to vehicle traffic at the park office. Pass one false trail leading left before turning left onto the Backcountry Trail at 1.8 miles

(37.88173N & 87.54739W). A carsonite post and shallow wood stairs mark the start of this trail.

The Backcountry Trail is marked by scattered red blazes, but it is easy to follow through the dense hardwood canopy of the Nature Preserve. Note how little sunlight makes it to the forest floor along much of the trail and, as a result, how sparse the undergrowth is here. Only on the tops of some of the ridges does the canopy thin, and understory plants, including poison ivy, flourish.

The Backcountry Trail returns to Wilderness Lake at 3.2 miles. Head back home across the dam and up to the stone shelter at 3.6 miles. From the shelter you can continue to retrace your route back, or follow the Woodpecker Trail to cover some new terrain on a shorter route. From the shelter, the Woodpecker Trail leads down a ridge crest through a dense growth of ferns. The largest trees here are American beeches, whose smooth bark has proved too great a temptation for vandals who have carved into the trees.

Pass two intersections with the Kentucky Coffee Tree Trail, each on either side of a short wood bridge, before reaching a T-junction with an old dirt road. This road is part of the King Benson Trail. Turn right on it, and climb to reach the Museum and Nature Center at 4.2 miles.

John James Audubon State Park is known as a sanctuary for the birds so beloved by Audubon. Over 200 species have been cataloged in the park. But the mature second growth forest has made it a sanctuary for hundreds of species of flowers, herbs, and shrubs as well. Some of the most striking spring blooms are bloodroot, Dutchman's breeches, bluebell, trout lily, trillium, blue-eyed Mary, and phlox.

John James Audubon moved to Henderson in 1810 from Louisville, where he had been operating a store with a partner. Their Louisville store was profitable enough for the two men to live on, but his partner felt that the growing city of Henderson offered more opportunity than they could find in an established town. Audubon had already begun sketching, painting, and studying birds while in Louisville, and he knew that Henderson was located along a major flyway beside the Ohio River. He realized that the new location would give him access to new and unusual birds, so he agreed to make the move.

During his time in Henderson, Audubon had already developed some of the traits that would later make him famous. He had begun banding birds to study their nesting habits. At this time, he also refined his unique style of painting by posing mounted specimens against their natural backgrounds and painting them life-sized. But the Henderson area was still too unsettled to support the partner's store. Audubon spent much of his time roaming the woods and sketching. He also built a small steam mill in Henderson, but that too was far ahead of his time. By 1819 bankruptcy had left Audubon with only the clothes on his back, his gun, and his original drawings. He then left Kentucky for a life of teaching, painting, and battles with the world of publishing.

His most famous work, *Birds of America*, took 14 years to complete. Each of the 435 engraved plates had to be hand-colored. The book was published in magnificent volumes, each 30" by 40", to accommodate the life-size portraits. Through his career, the artist described 23 species of birds previously unknown. He died in New York in 1851.

The remains of Audubon's mill burned in 1913, and with it the last traces of Audubon in Henderson almost disappeared. But local citizens began buying and donating land toward a park effort. By the 1930s, labor from the Civilian Conservation Corps and the Works Project Administration was available, and the park was developed. The museum and park offices were built, the trail system was constructed, and streams were dammed for fishing lakes.

The park also contains cottages, camping and picnic areas, a fishing lake, a golf course, and boat rentals. The Nature Center has a wildlife observation room, a hands-on discovery center, and rooms for instructional programs.

OTHER HIKING OPTIONS

1. Short and Sweet. The hike to Wilderness Lake and back can be done in two miles.

2. The King Benson Trail is a 0.3-mile loop that starts at the far end of the office parking area at the gate across Warbler Road.

3. The 0.9-mile Eagle Glen Pet Trail leaves from the back end of the parking area for the Museum and Nature Center.

Macedonia Trails

TOTAL DISTANCE: A 3.6-mile loop on hiking trails
HIKING TIME: About 2 hours
DIFFICULTY: Easy
LOCATION: About nine miles south of Dawson Springs in Pennyrile State Forest
MAPS: USGS Dawson Springs SW and Pennyrile State Resort Park Visitor's Guide

The Pennyrile State Forest and Pennyrile Forest State Resort Park hide one of the state's most underappreciated outdoor recreation areas. Here lies a wealth of trails for hikers and mountain bikers, just waiting to be discovered. The Macedonia Trails are three loops designed to let hikers pick the length of trail that best suits their time and ability. These trails are now shared with mountain bikes and connect to other mountain bike trails south of the loops.

GETTING THERE

From the junction of KY 62 and KY 109 in Dawson Springs, drive 6.8 miles south on KY 109 to a junction with KY 398. Drive 1.1 mile to the trailhead, which is located by Macedonia Cemetery.

THE TRAIL

The Macedonia Trail consists of three loops, each of which makes for a slightly longer hike. All three loops begin at the signed trailhead on the west side of KY 398, across from Macedonia Cemetery. Your route will extend through all three loops, but it is easy to make a shorter hike. In the thick pines just beyond the trailhead the trail immediately leads to Loop 1, which is blue-blazed. Turn right here to follow the loops counterclockwise. Look for young sassafras, Virginia creeper, Christmas fern, and poison ivy growing below the pines.

Keep your tree book handy here, you'll see Virginia, loblolly, shortleaf, and pitch pines at various points along the route. The pines are mostly nonnative trees. These fast growers were planted in the 1940s, shortly after the state acquired the land. This well-worn parcel of land was in danger of severe erosion. The pines stabilized the soil

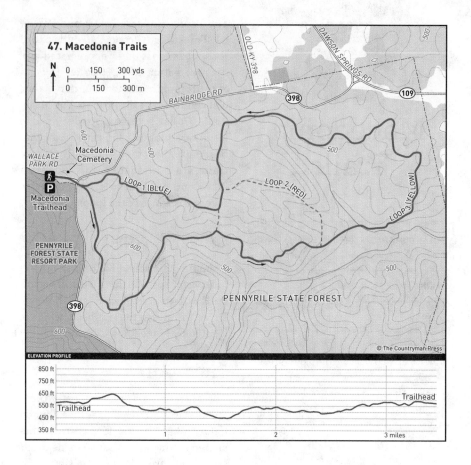

until the native oak-hickory forest could be reestablished. Now the pines are being decimated by the southern pine beetle, which has invaded most of the stands. The Pennyrile State Forest may be forced to thin some of these stands to reduce fire hazard. The demise of the mature pines will also let much more sunlight through the tree canopy and will make for shrubbier trails.

You'll soon leave the pines for a more typical young hardwood forest that provides food and shelter enough for a small deer herd. Loop 1 circles the headwaters of a small stream, which may be reduced to a series of shallow pools by early summer. Along the stream bottom, at 0.8 mile, reach a connector trail that turns right to join a white-blazed mountain bike trail. These mountain bike trails consist of an upper 1.7-mile loop and a lower 1.6-mile loop, which are also both accessed off a trailhead on KY 398. The Macedonia Loop is also now open to mountain bikes, but very few bikers, or hikers for that matter, are found.

At 0.9 mile, reach a signed junction with red-blazed Loop 2 and turn right. Soon, a collapsed chimney formed of blocks of native sandstone will mark the site of an old home site. The encroaching forest now means that deer, rather than people, make their homes here. The trail follows the course of a small stream with a set of sandstone ledges looming above it. You'll next turn from the

MACEDONIA TRAIL IN PENNYRILE FOREST STATE RESORT PARK

stream and reach the junction with the yellow-blazed Loop 3 at 1.4 miles. While the first two loops are well used and well marked, Loop 3 is now little used and may be overgrown in summer, a time when potential encounters with hungry ticks may make a shorter, two-loop hike the wisest choice. Loop 3 enters another grove of pines before descending into a dry branch. You'll briefly join a very old road, and then branch left from it before approaching the forest boundary, where you can spot cleared fields through the trees. When the trail joins another old road, be ready to make a left turn off it before crossing a dry creek. Many of the pines in this area have died, creating holes in the forest canopy that allow a variety of undergrowth to flourish and to obscure the trail.

At 3.0 miles, reach the signed junction with the far end of Loop 2, indicating that you should keep right. The far end of Loop 1 comes in at 3.1 miles. Keep right here also, and in a few hundred yards, reach a very faint side trail leading left to the heavily overgrown Collins Cemetery. Dr. Morgan Collins and E. B. Owen are buried here, along with at least six others. Finally, the trail reaches the pine grove near the trailhead and closes the loop at 3.6 miles.

The connector between Loops 1 and 2 is only 0.1 mile, making Loop 1 only 1.5 miles around. The connector between Loop 2 and 3 is 0.5 mile, making Loop 3 only 2.6 miles around. This connector is less used than the other trails, and hikers should be prepared for poison ivy.

The name Pennyrile comes from the small pennyroyal plant, a member of the mint family. The name, in its various spellings, has spread from the plant to encompass the entire region of low-rolling hills in south central Kentucky.

Pennyrile State Forest consists of 15,331 wooded acres acquired by the US Government during the Depression. During the 1930s, the Works Progress Administration built the cabins, lodge, and other buildings that are now part of the state park. The Commonwealth of Kentucky acquired the land in 1954. Nearby Pennyrile State Resort Park also contains a network of hiking trails. The park also has a 68-site campground, a lodge, restaurant, cottages, and a lake for swimming, fishing, and boating.

OTHER HIKING OPTIONS

1. Short and Sweet. Loop 1 is only 1.5 miles around.
2. There are seven short hiking trails in Pennyrile State Park. The main route is the 2.4-mile loop around Pennyrile Lake on the Lake Trail. Hikers could extend this loop, or they could make shorter loops by using the Pennyroyal or Cane Creek Trails that connect to the Lake Trail. The Indian Bluff, Clifty Creek, Camper's Trace, and Thompson Hollow Trails are all about one quarter mile long.
3. Pennyrile State Resort Park is also the southern end of the 13.5-mile Pennyrile Nature Trail, which connects the park to Dawson Springs.
4. Pennyrile State Forest also contains two new mountain bike loops, with a total of 3.3 miles, located just south of the Macedonia loops.
5. Pennyrile State Forest also contains 23 miles of horse trails in three main loops located south of the state park.

Canal Loop B

TOTAL DISTANCE: A 3.0-mile loop via connector B on trails shared with mountain bikes

HIKING TIME: About 1.5 hours

DIFFICULTY: Easy

LOCATION: Land Between the Lakes National Recreation Area, 2 miles north of the North Welcome Station

MAPS: USGS Birmingham Point and Land Between the Lakes National Recreation Area Canal Loop Trail

The Canal Loop Trails are some of the most convenient and most popular trails at the Land Between the Lakes, probably because it is so easy for hikers to find a loop exactly the length they want. Not only can you easily find a quiet walk nestled in deep forest, but the location close by Kentucky Lake, Lake Barkley, and the canal that joins them guarantees some lake views. It's also a safe bet that you'll be walking through woods thick with deer.

GETTING THERE

From the Trace just south of the canal between Lakes Kentucky and Barkley, turn west on one-way Kentucky Lake Drive and drive 0.4 mile to a signed parking area in a grassy field on your left. The Canal Trail begins at the far end of the field by a signboard (36.9865N & 88.22224W). Turn left at the sign to hike clockwise around the loop.

THE TRAIL

There are enough hiking options at the Canal Loops that a brief orientation is in order. The main loop here is a north-south oval split down the middle by the Trace (Road 100), which is the main north-south road through LBL. The north end of the loop is where the Trace Bridge crosses the canal between the lakes, and the south end of the loop is at the North Welcome Station. The loop connects to the very north end of the North/South Trail at the North Welcome Station. Then there are four connector trails (labeled A, B, C, and D from north to south) that let you short-circuit the loop. We'll skip Connector A on this loop and use Connector B. Connector C is parallel to the south end of Kentucky Lake Drive, and Connector D also begins at the North Welcome Station. Mountain bikers

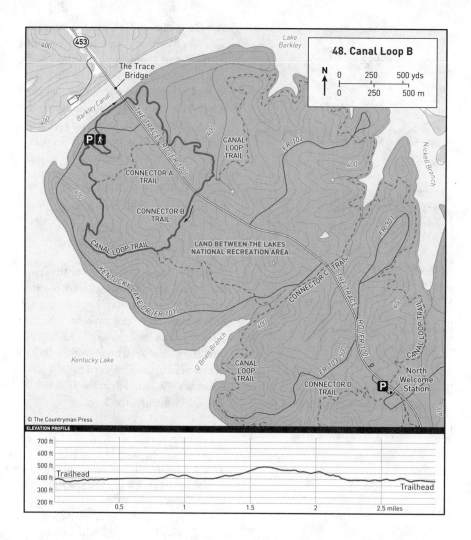

48. Canal Loop B

N
0   250   500 yds
0   250   500 m

ELEVATION PROFILE

700 ft
600 ft
500 ft
400 ft   Trailhead
300 ft
200 ft
         0.5   1   1.5   2   2.5 miles
                                              Trailhead

have been allowed on these trails since 1997, but the trails are in better shape than many hiking trails in other areas.

For a short hike that packs in a maximum of lake views, try starting from the north end of the trails and making a loop via Connector B. From the trailhead, turn left and walk north to a crossing of Kentucky Lake Drive. Many unofficial side trails lead down to the lake on this next stretch. Make sure you're careful to avoid poison ivy, should you explore any of them. At 0.4 mile comes the end of a pre-canal road. Cross underneath the highway bridge. The trail is marked by white diamond-shaped blazes.

At 0.8 mile, reach the signed east end of Connector A (36.98715N & 88.21687W). If you want to cut the loop short, the yellow-blazed Connector A is 0.5 mile, and you will return to the trailhead in 0.8 mile. You will also notice that some of the older signs on the loop indicate that the North/South Trail once continued all the way along the west side of the Canal Loop to our trailhead, and that the east side of the loop was once called the Barkley Trail.

While this was once true, the North/South Trail now officially ends at the North Welcome Station. To continue on the loop, keep left at this junction. The trail climbs very gradually through a thick hardwood forest to the signed junction with Connector B at 1.3 miles (36.98437N & 88.21304W).

Now, turn right on the yellow-blazed B connector trail. You'll next cross the Trace at the end of an abandoned asphalt road (be careful of fast-moving traffic here), then pass underneath a large line bringing power from the TVA dams. On the hilltop that marks the divide between Kentucky Lake and Lake Barkley, turn left onto a gravel road and follow it for 200 feet before turning right back into the woods. The gravel road is used to service a nearby microwave tower. The fenced off tower can be seen from the main loop, just south of the end of the B connector.

At 1.8 miles (36.97955N & 88.21754W), turn right onto the main loop at the west end of Connector B. You'll enjoy some views of Kentucky Lake to your left through the trees. The trail here is old enough that some less-used areas have thick coatings of moss that would not have been able to grow on newer trails, or on heavily traveled footpaths. At 2.6 miles, reach the west end of Connector A (36.98381N & 88.22247W). Connector A appears to be the least-used part of the Canal Loop, so expect that the trail may look a bit overgrown. Keep left at this junction, and at 3.0 miles finish the loop at the parking area.

The Land Between the Lakes is unique among America's National Recreation Areas. LBL occupies a wedge of land once known as "Between the Rivers" to the people who lived where the Tennessee and Cumberland rivers raced side by side to join the mighty Ohio.

Early white settlers were dependent on logging, farming, and the iron industry. However, the Great Depression of the 1930s hit the area hard, and many families were forced to try and sell their land. A New Deal program called the Resettlement Administration acquired the lands of the Hillman Land Company in 1936. In 1938, a 65,000-acre wildlife refuge was created from the Resettlement Administration lands along with TVA and US Army Corps of Engineers property.

The Tennessee Valley Authority recognized the hydroelectric potential of the rivers. In 1937, plans for the construction of the Kentucky Dam on the Tennessee River caused the removal of 3,500 families. This massive project allowed TVA to control flooding downstream, but it also resulted in the loss of farms along the fertile river bottoms to make way for the 134,000-acre lake. In 1966, the Barkley Dam across the Cumberland River and the canal joining the two lakes were competed. This dam displaced another 2,300 families.

By the 1960s, it was clear that any boom times from logging or iron smelting were long gone, and with the fertile bottom lands now underwater, farming, too, would never be the same. The Wildlife Refuge lands were transferred to TVA in 1964. The plan to convert the Land Between the Lakes into a recreation area required the removal of the remaining 2,300 people by the TVA, and the purchase of over 96,000 acres from private holdings. TVA was left with 170,000 acres for LBL stretching across Kentucky and Tennessee, and over 300 miles of shoreline to devote to outdoor recreation and environmental education.

LBL now contains over 500 miles of trails, including 260 miles of hiking

MICROWAVE TOWER NEAR CONNECTOR TRAIL B

trails and 70 miles of mountain biking trails. It receives 1.4 million visitors every year. There are 15 camping areas with over 1,400 sites as well as five different environmental education centers. There are hundreds of miles of old roads to explore on mountain bikes. Some of the other attractions in the Kentucky portion of LBL include the 700-acre Elk and Bison Prairie, which is a fee area.

In 2001, 25 elk from LBL were transferred to the Great Smoky Mountains National Park as part of a three-year experimental reintroduction of elk into that park. The Golden Pond Visitor Center, located at the junction of the Trace and US 68/KY 80, includes displays, a gift shop, and a planetarium. Hunting for white-tailed deer, wild turkey, and small game is popular in the Recreation Area, as is fishing for crappie, bass, sauger, catfish, and bluegill.

In October 1999, the management of LBL was transferred to the United States Forest Service. The Forest Service is committed to maintaining current services and facilities until a new Land and Resource Management Plan is developed.

OTHER HIKING OPTIONS

1. Short and Sweet. Using Connector A, you can walk a 1.5-mile loop.
2. Starting from the North Welcome Station and making a loop via Connector D is a 1.9-mile walk.
3. There are a total of 14 miles of trail in the Canal Loop system.

North/South Trail—North Welcome Station to Gray Cemetery

TOTAL DISTANCE: 11.1 miles one way on trail shared with mountain bikes. One-way hikers must leave a car for their return trip on Road 130.

HIKING TIME: About 6 hours

DIFFICULTY: Difficult

LOCATION: Land Between the Lakes National Recreation Area at the North Welcome Center

MAPS: USGS Mont and Birmingham Point and Land Between the Lakes National Recreation Area North End of the North/ South Trail

The North/South Trail is the premier hiking trail at Land Between the Lakes and the only long distance hiking trail in western Kentucky. The trail extends 58 miles from the North Welcome Station in Kentucky to the South Welcome Station in Tennessee. It connects to LBL's second and third largest trail networks at the Canal Loop and Fort Henry in Tennessee. Since the North/South Trail and the Trace, the main road through LBL, both run down the middle of the area, it is relatively easy to make a shuttle hike and avoid retracing your route if you cannot go all the way.

For the second edition of this guide I've changed the sections of the trail to showcase. Instead of the section of trail between Hillman Ferry Campground and Hatchery Hollow, I've moved the north starting point to take advantage of the parking, information, and bathroom services available at the North Welcome Station; I've also moved the south end to Road 130 near Gray Cemetery to keep the section distance about the same and use the better road access than is available at Hatchery Hollow. This also allows hikers to make a loop with the northern end of the route by following the paved hike/bike trail north from Road 110 back to the North Welcome Station.

Hikers share the entire North/South trail north of the Golden Pond Welcome Center with mountain bikers, but as with the Canal Loop Trail, conflicts are few and the trails remain in great shape. Overnight hikers must buy a permit at one of the welcome stations.

GETTING THERE

The route begins at the North Welcome Station, which is six miles south of I-24

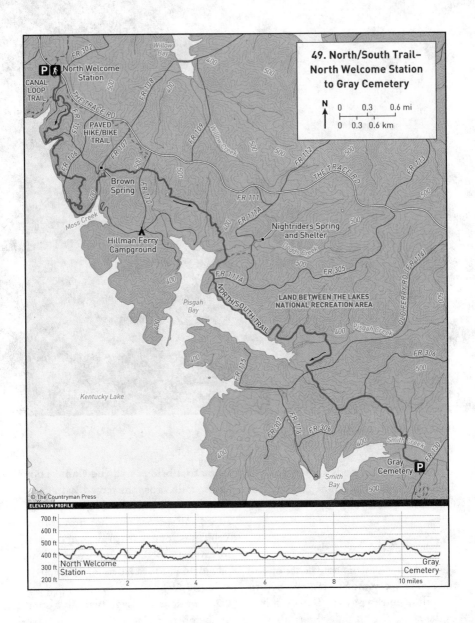

49. North/South Trail–
North Welcome Station
to Gray Cemetery

N

| 0 | 0.3 | 0.6 mi |
| 0 | 0.3 | 0.6 km |

ELEVATION PROFILE

via KY 53 and the Trace (LBL Road 100) (36.97082N & 88.19882W). Unfortunately, the trails that begin here are not well marked. The North/South Trail begins by following the paved hike/bike trail south of the Station along the west side of the Trace. Don't be misled by the Canal Loop which intersects the parking

area from the east, or the Canal D Connector which exits the parking area on the west side.

To leave a car at the south end of this trip, leave the Trace west on Road 130. Keep left at the junction with Road 309. At 2.0 miles, just before crossing the North/South Trail, turn right onto

AN INVITING BEACH ALONG PISGAH BAY

a gravel road that leads shortly to Gray Cemetery and an informal parking area (36.9102N & 88.12741W).

THE TRAIL

The tail starts at the southeast end of the North Welcome Station and begins by following the paved hike/bike trail to the south. In 0.1 mile the trails split (36.96982N & 88.19733W), with the North/South Trail bearing to the right. The North/South Trail is a well-defined footpath, often smooth enough for easy mountain biking, that is marked with older white metal rectangular and newer white diamond-shaped blazes. At 0.3 mile (36.96693N & 88.19866W), stay left at another split where the right fork leads to a bridge and the Canal Loop. At 0.4 mile, cross the paved Twin Lakes Road, where a gravel road also splits off. At 0.7 mile, cross another gravel road. You'll pass one more gravel access road for Kentucky Lake before reaching paved Road 106 at 2.0 miles (36.95463N & 88.1964W).

From Road 106, you'll climb a small hill before descending to a shoreline picnic area at 2.9 miles with a nice gravel beach and tremendous views of Kentucky Lake. Much of this north end of the North/South is a twisty, turny meander through the woods on trail that seems to be in no hurry to get anywhere fast. For day hikers, the lake views and scenic forest are enough, but long-distance hikers should pack their patience. At 3.7 miles, reach the junction with a yellow-blazed side trail leading east to Brown Spring (36.95453N & 88.18927W). While once this spring might have had appeal as a water source, it's likely most hikers will find treating lake water to be more appealing.

At 4.3 miles, cross paved Road 110 (36.95554N & 88.181W), which leads right to Hillman Ferry Campground and left to the Trace. If you would like to make a loop back to the North Welcome Station, turn left here and walk a few hundred feet up the road to the unsigned paved hike/bike trail. On the hike/bike trail it is 1.5 miles back to the North Welcome Station, giving you a 5.9-mile loop. The area around the campground is prime deer habitat, so keep an eye out for those not-so-elusive white tails. The trail follows the edge of a wide powerline cut where deer love to graze. Edges of forests and openings provide them with large quantities of the browse they love.

At 5.9 miles, come to the junction with the side trail leading east 0.6 mile to Nightrider Spring and backcountry campsite (36.9424N & 88.16495W). If you'd like to visit this unusual spot, follow the side trail and make a left onto a gravel road for 100 yards before turning back into the woods. The campsite looks like a half-buried quonset hut, but is a dry and comfortable place to spend the night.

From the Nightrider junction, continue south to reach gravel Road 111 near modern Lee Cemetery at 6.2 miles (36.9424N & 88.16495W). There is also access to Kentucky Lake here, and primitive camping is allowed at the Pisgah Point Backcountry Area. The trail beyond this point is one of the highlights of the trip. For much of the way, you'll walk along the shore of Pisgah Bay, past enticing campsites while enjoying constantly changing views of the bay. After crossing two small bridges and one huge new one, the trail crosses the marshy inlet of the bay and then joins a gravel farm road. The North/South Trail leaves the gravel road in a cluster of pine and cedar trees, but it stays parallel to it until crossing paved Old Ferry Road 114 at 8.8 miles (36.92481N & 88.149W).

To the east on Road 114, the Trace is 2.4 miles. Ferry Landing is 1.0 mile west. From this intersection, the trail makes a gradual climb to a hilltop, where it turns left onto dirt Road 306 at 9.4 miles (36.91893N & 88.14316W), which may be too rough for most auto traffic. From this hillside, the forest is interspersed with cultivated fields. Deer can often be found feeding nearby. Turn right off the road at a post and return to the woods. You'll turn right onto another farm road that has a huge new bridge at the end and climb a short, but steep hill.

The trail next turns left onto a gravel road with Isaac Gray Cemetery on the right. The cemetery holds the remains of two generations of Isaac Grays, and other graves as recent as 1998. Beyond the cemetery, reach a T-junction with gravel Road 130 where this hike ends (36.90806N & 88.12756W) at 11.1 miles. There is no parking at the crossing, but there are ample spaces near the Gray Cemetery.

Mountain bikes are allowed on the North/South Trail anywhere north of the Golden Pond Trailhead. Horses are allowed on the North/South Trail only from the junction with the side trail to the Colson Hollow Overlook Picnic Area south to the crossing of the Trace between the Cedar Pond Picnic Area and Road 201.

Although LBL has the finest trail systems in the area, it is also known throughout the region for something a little less appealing: its thriving tick population. LBL hosts Lone Star and American Dog ticks, though you'll most likely not want to try and tell them apart. Both mature ticks and larvae (seed ticks) can leave numerous itchy painful bites and in some cases can spread disease. LBL mows and sprays developed areas in summer, but the backcountry areas are too large to be controlled. Your best strategy for avoiding ticks is to use insect repellent and tuck in both long sleeves and long pants. Remove any ticks as soon as you find them. Ticks concentrate in grassy areas, especially those at the edges of openings and forests, where deer and their normal prey are common.

OTHER HIKING OPTIONS

1. Short and Sweet. The Hillman Heritage Trail, which leaves from near Hillman Ferry Campground, contains about 5.1 miles of trails. A hike from the trailhead near the campground entrance station to the overlook is 2.4 miles round trip.
2. Other major trail networks in the Kentucky portion of LBL include 4.8 miles at the Energy Lake Campground.

Honker Lake Trail

50

TOTAL DISTANCE: A 4.6-mile loop on foot trails

HIKING TIME: About 2.5 hours

DIFFICULTY: Easy/Moderate

LOCATION: Land Between the Lakes National Recreation Area, about 12 miles northeast of the Golden Pond Visitor Center

MAPS: USGS Mont and Land Between The Lakes National Recreation Area Nature Station Hiking Trails

The Woodlands Nature Station is the Land Between The Lakes' environmental education center. Two small lakes nearby are perfect for canoeing or wildlife watching. The Woodlands Nature Station is also the trailhead for five diverse hiking trails, including the Honker Lake Trail, which circles Honker Lake.

GETTING THERE

Nine miles south of the North Welcome Station at the junction of the Trace (the main north-south road through LBL) and Silver Trail Road (Road 133), drive 3.2 miles east on Silver Trail Road to the Woodlands Nature Station Parking Area (36.90177N & 88.03656W). The Nature Station is open from 9:00 a.m. to 5:00 p.m., and the gate locks at 5 p.m., so it may be wiser to park by the Center Furnace Trail, or near the picnic pavilion. If you plan to visit the Woodlands Nature Station, remember that it is a fee area.

THE TRAIL

From the north end of the parking area in front of the Nature Station, the Honker Lake Trail and the Woodland Walk both start with a descent of wooden steps past a gazebo and then a right turn into the woods. At 0.2 mile, reach a junction by an ironwood tree where the Woodland Walk turns to the right to make a 0.9-mile loop that also returns to the Nature Station Parking Area (36.90344N & 88.03571W). The Honker Lake Trail crosses a gravel road and then follows a mowed strip through fields, then up a hill where small pits were once dug to prospect for iron. Once past the Woodland Walk junction, the Honker Lake Trail is marked by white diamond-shaped blazes.

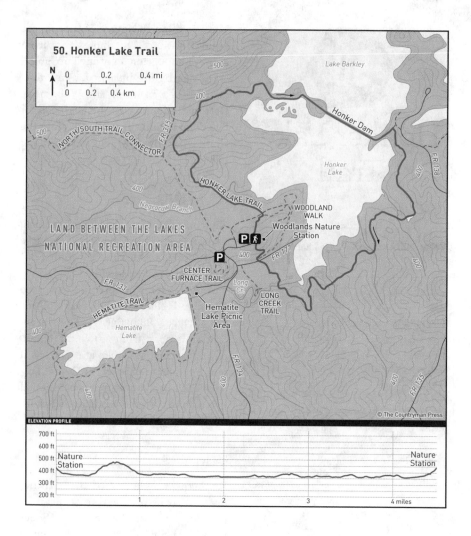

50. Honker Lake Trail

N

| 0 | 0.2 | 0.4 mi |
| 0 | 0.2 | 0.4 km |

Lake Barkley

NORTH/SOUTH TRAIL CONNECTOR

FR 315

Honker Dam

FR 138

HONKER LAKE TRAIL

Honker Lake

Negrorow Branch

LAND BETWEEN THE LAKES
NATIONAL RECREATION AREA

WOODLAND WALK

Woodlands Nature Station

FR 177

CENTER FURNACE TRAIL

Long Cr.

LONG CREEK TRAIL

FR 133

HEMATITE TRAIL

Hematite Lake Picnic Area

Hematite Lake

FR 134

FR 135

© The Countryman Press

ELEVATION PROFILE

| 700 ft |
| 600 ft |
| 500 ft | Nature Station | Nature Station |
| 400 ft |
| 300 ft |
| 200 ft |

1 2 3 4 miles

Your route is in a forest where sweet gum trees are especially common. Sweet gum is easily recognized by the five long points on its leaves and its small spiny fruits that some call "porcupine eggs." Sap from the tree can be made into chewing gum, but the tree is most valuable to furniture makers, who prize its hard wood.

Soon the trail will cross a small creek and begin a gradual ascent of a small ridge. Just beyond the crest of the hill, watch to your left for a small pit where iron ore was mined. A boulder of ore beside the trail is stained red, yellow, and brown by the various oxides of iron that comprise the raw ore. At LBL, raw ore like this was heated to extremely high temperature in ovens stoked with coal, then combined with small amounts of limestone, to separate the pure iron from the other elements in the ore. If you'd like to see where the ore was converted to metal, you can hike the short Center Furnace Trail, which also begins near the Woodlands Nature

Station. Iron smelting was the region's most important industry from the 1820s until the Civil War. After the war, steel production replaced traditional iron production, and there were few trees left in the region to make charcoal from. However, some small furnaces struggled on until 1912, when the iron industry disappeared from the region.

When the trail appears to split, keep right and head downhill. You'll then cross a small bridge and a power line right-of-way before joining a two-track dirt road within sight of Honker Lake at 1.6 miles (36.91284N & 88.03581W). The lake was named for the nasal call of the Canada Goose. The 190-acre lake was built in 1966 to provide a nesting area for migrating geese. Here, you are close to Goose Island, where the recreation area has constructed a special nesting area for these big birds.

On the other side of a small grove of pines, cross a small concrete dam. The pines were probably planted in the late 1930s both to prevent erosion and to provide shelter for wildlife at a time when the land had been overused. Next reach Honker Dam. With Honker Lake on your right, and Lake Barkley on your left, the views from the dam can't be beat. This perfectly flat walk is not quite as easy as you might expect. The dam is obviously a popular stop for wildlife, and you'll need to watch your step to avoid what they've left behind.

On the far side of the dam at 2.3 miles (36.90885N & 88.02547W), turn left onto gravel Road 138 for 500 feet. Look for a sign indicating a right turn onto a wide foot trail back into the woods. This side of the loop has a few handy mile markers to help you track your progress. Two old roadways will branch left from the trail; ignore both of these and keep to the right. The trail next crosses a power line opening at 3.2 miles (36.90322N & 88.02541W), where white-tailed deer often browse. Several types of trees are labeled here. Watch for a black cherry tree that has reached almost 1 foot in diameter. Seldom will you see one this large.

The trail crosses a shallow slough on a wooden bridge, then crossing another on a much larger, newer composite bridge at 3.7 miles (36.89846N & 88.02954W). After another composite bridge, reach gravel Road 177 near a parking area at 4.4 miles (36.90012N & 88.03621W). The far end of the Woodland Walk intersects our loop here. From the road, the Honker Lake Trail climbs the hillside past a small quarry to reach the southeast end of the parking area for the Woodlands Nature Station at 4.6 miles.

The Woodlands Nature Station includes the indoor Learning Center with displays about the plants and animals that live in LBL. The Backyard area contains animals that cannot be returned to their natural habitat and so must remain in captivity. Birds in the Backyard area include red-tailed hawks, bald eagles, wild turkeys, and several species of owls. There are also bobcats, coyotes, white-tailed deer, fallow deer, and red wolves. Fallow deer are a Eurasian species that thrives in captivity, and so they have been transplanted across the globe. The Hillman Land Company brought them to the area in 1918. Fallow deer are smaller than white tails, with spots and black tails. When excited, fallow deer run with a bouncy pogo-stick gait much like our western mule deer. Wild fallow deer can sometimes be seen near the Woodlands Nature Station.

A NEW COMPOSITE BRIDGE ON THE HONKER LAKE TRAIL

The Woodlands Nature Station is also the site of part of the captive breeding program for the endangered red wolf. This close cousin of the timber wolf and coyote once roamed much of the southeast, but it nearly became extinct because of loss of habitat and hunting. A small population was isolated and bred in captivity until the population was large enough to reintroduce back into the wild. A stable population of red wolves has now been established at Alligator National Wildlife Refuge in North Carolina on the Atlantic Coast. The Woodlands Nature Center is a fee area and is generally open 10 a.m. to 5 p.m. in season. It is closed from December through February.

OTHER HIKING OPTIONS

1. Short and Sweet. The Center Furnace Trail is a 0.3-mile interpretive loop that highlights the history of iron mining and processing in the Land Between The Lakes.

2. The Long Creek Trail is a 0.2-mile paved handicap accessible trail. The trail winds along Long Creek and is a good spot for watching wildlife or enjoying spring wildflowers.

3. Two other loop trails leave from the

Woodland Nature Station. Hematite Lake Trail is a 2.2-mile loop featuring observation decks for wildlife watching and a photography blind. The Woodland Walk is a 0.9-mile loop that starts and finishes with the Honker Lake Trail and leads to the boat dock on Honker Lake.

4. The Nature Station Connector leads 4.8 miles to the North/South Trail. A side trail to Token Trail Spring is located about halfway along this trail.

The Sheltowee Trace National Recreation Trail

The 280-mile-long Sheltowee Trace Trail stretches from Pickett State Park in Tennessee to the very northern tip of the Daniel Boone National Forest. On its journey across the state, it visits many of the premier hiking areas in the Kentucky Appalachians, such as the Big South Fork National River and Recreation Area, Daniel Boone National Forest, Cumberland Falls State Resort Park, Laurel River Lake, Natural Bridge State Resort Park, Red River Gorge Geological Area, Clifty Wilderness, and Cave Run Lake. There are other long distance trails in the region, but none are as long, as diverse, or as well suited to hikers.

The trail is named for Daniel Boone, who was given the name Sheltowee (Big Turtle) during his time with the Shawnee Indians. The route, which explores so much of the wild land remaining in Kentucky, is a fitting tribute to the state's most famous explorer. The trail is marked with a wide variety of turtle-shaped blazes in addition to white diamonds used by the DBNF.

Despite the unparalleled opportunity for long distance hiking that the Sheltowee Trace provides, until recently only a modest number of hikers attempted to walk the entire trail, and instead, the trail served as a main trunk line, linking together trail networks. But the Sheltowee has undergone a renaissance in recent years. Led by the Sheltowee Trace Association (STA), the trail is much better known through the hiking community, primarily through their Hiker Challenge, which promotes hiking on the entire length of the Sheltowee Trace. The STA has also signed an agreement with the Daniel Boone National Forest to contribute to the maintenance of the trail.

In the Big South Fork, the Sheltowee Trace has also changed as well. Working with trail advocates, park administrators have designated much of the John Muir Trail in Tennessee as part of the Sheltowee. While the 280-mile main line of the Sheltowee continues south from the state line to reach Pickett State Park, the trail now splits at the junction with the Rock Creek Loop just south of the state line. The new section of the STT now follows the John Muir Trail south and east to the junction with the Station Camp Creek Trail. From here the STT detours west then south to reach the Bandy Creek Area of the BSFNRRA. Bandy Creek is home to the park's main visitor center and largest campground. From Bandy Creek the STT travels east to Grand Gap, where it joins the John Muir Trail, which it follows to reach the end of both trails at Burnt Mill Bridge over the Clear Fork at the south end of the park. This version of the STT is listed at a healthy 319 miles.

But the Sheltowee Trace is not open to hikers alone. Much of the trail is open to mountain bikes and horses. Some sections are open to off-road vehicles, and a few sections follow maintained roads. If you look at a detailed map of the Daniel Boone National Forest, you'll see that the forest service actually owns little land in the middle third of the forest. For the trail to be continuous, many parts of it were routed onto active or abandoned old roads, so that the trail could cross areas where there is no public land. These sections mean that parts of the trail will be of less interest to hikers, except for those few that seek to walk the entire trail.

Management of the Sheltowee Trace is shared by the three forest districts that the trail passes through (the Stearns, London, and Cumberland), the three state parks (Pickett, Cumberland Falls, and Natural Bridge) and the Big South Fork NRRA. These agencies control which trail sections are open to mountain bikes, horses, or motorized vehicles. In practice, closures for vehicles or horses are not always clear, and may not be marked on the ground.

At least four ATV routes designated by the forest service use part of the STT. Just north of the Rockcastle Narrows hike, the Big Dog ATV route uses 2.7 miles of the STT between two intersections with DBNF Road 457. Near KY 80, the Pine Creek OHV Route uses 2.9 miles of trail between DBNF 747 and KY 1956. The 9 miles south of the Turkeyfoot Campground is the Turkeyfoot OHV Route. The 9.5 miles north of S-Tree Campground is the S-Tree OHV Route. These last two areas sometimes receive heavy ATV use.

The forest service issues a recreation guide for the trail, which is helpful for a large-scale view of the trail. The best sources of detailed information are the individual recreation guides for trails issued by the forest and the excellent maps produced by the folks at Outragegis.com. In the table that follows, I have summarized the recreation guide information into a mileage table for the Sheltowee Trace. The table should help section hikers on the STT plan their trips and should be equally useful to any potential through hikers. I used data from Dreaver et al. for the trail from Pickett to Cumberland Falls, since my measurements agreed well with theirs. Otherwise, I used mileages from the district recreation guides, unless I happened to wheel or drive a section myself. These data show the length of the main trail is 280 miles, though this overall length varies from year to year as various changes and relocations are implemented. One such example is the recent reroute near Bark Camp Creek. I've also tried to identify the trail sections that follow maintained roads.

SHELTOWEE TRACE NATIONAL RECREATION TRAIL MILEAGE TABLE

From	To	Section	Total	Roads	Manager
TN 154	Double Falls Tr.	4.2	4.2		Pickett SP
Double Falls Tr.	Rock Cr. Tr.	0.8	5.0		BSF
Rock Cr. Tr.	John Muir Tr.	0.8	5.8		BSF
John Muir Tr.	Access Divide Road	3.6	9.4		BSF
Access Divide Road	TN line/Parker Mtn Tr.	0.5	9.9		BSF
TN line/Parker Mtn Tr.	Great Meadows CG	3.1	13.0		BSF
Great Meadows CG	Gobblers Arch Trail	1.9	14.9		Stearns RD
Gobblers Arch Trail	Mark Branch Trail	0.7	15.6		Stearns RD
Mark Branch Trail	Peters Mountain Trailhead	1.6	17.2		Stearns RD
Peters Mountain Trailhead	Laurel Ridge Trail	1.6	18.8	Gravel Road	Stearns RD
Laurel Ridge Trail	Off Laurel Ridge Road	4.1	22.9	Gravel Road	Stearns RD
Off Laurel Ridge Road	Leave DBNF 6308	3.0	25.9		Stearns RD
Leave DBNF 6308	Devils Creek Road	2.8	28.7		Stearns RD
Devils Creek Road	Kroger Arch Tr.	0.8	29.5		Stearns RD
Kroger Arch Tr.	Kentucky Tr.	1.9	31.4		Stearns RD
Kentucky Tr.	KY92/Yamacraw Bridge	1.6	33.0		Stearns RD
KY92/Yamacraw Bridge	Lick Cr. Tr.	1.4	34.4		Stearns RD
Lick Cr. Tr.	Negro Creek Tr.	1.5	35.9		Stearns RD
Negro Creek Tr.	Alum Ford	3.3	39.2		Stearns RD
Alum Ford	Yahoo Falls Tr.M	1.8	41.0		Stearns RD
Yahoo Falls Tr.M	Big Creek	2.7	43.7		Stearns RD
Big Creek	US 27	3.2	46.9	Part Road	Stearns RD
US 27	US 27 TH	1.1	48.0	Part Road	Stearns RD
US 27 TH	E JCT TR 624	4.7	52.7		Stearns RD
E JCT TR 624	KY 700	4.2	56.9		Stearns RD
KY 700	Join KY 700	1.4	58.3		Stearns RD
Join KY 700	Thunderstruck Road	2.3	60.6	KY 700	Stearns RD
Thunderstruck Road	McKee Bend	1.1	61.7		Stearns RD
McKee Bend	Blue Bend Trail	2.5	64.2		Stearns RD
Blue Bend Trail	KY 90	2.2	66.4		Cumberland Falls SP

From	To	Section	Total	Roads	Manager
KY 90	Gift Shop	0.2	66.6	KY 90	Cumberland Falls SP
Gift Shop	Dog Slaughter Falls Tr.	2.9	69.5		London RD
Dog Slaughter Falls Tr.	Star Creek Shelter	2.2	71.7		London RD
Star Creek Shelter	Bark Camp Creek	2.8	74.5		London RD
Bark Camp Creek	KY 1277	4.0	78.5		London RD
KY 1277	Mouth of Laurel Boat Ramp	0.4	74.9		London RD
Mouth of Laurel Boat Ramp	Laurel Dam-S	2.4	80.9		London RD
Laurel Dam-S	Laurel Dam -N	0.5	81.4		London RD
Laurel Dam -N	Holly Bay Campground	4.2	85.6		London RD
Holly Bay Campground	KY 192	4.3	89.9		London RD
KY 192	Trail 401-South	2.7	92.6		London RD
Trail 401-South	Trail 401-North	1.1	93.7		London RD
Trail 401-North	DBNF Road 119	1.1	94.8		London RD
DBNF Road 119	DBNF Road 457-South	1.3	96.1	Part Road	London RD
DBNF Road 457-South	DBNF Road 457-North	2.7	98.8		London RD
DBNF Road 457-North	Sinking Creek	4.1	102.9	Part Road	London RD
Sinking Creek	DBNF Road 747-N	1.6	104.5	Part Road	London RD
DBNF Road 747-N	KY 80	2.9	107.4	Part Road	London RD
KY 80	DBNF Road 1956	0.3	107.7		London RD
DBNF Road 1956	Hawk Creek	1.7	109.4		London RD
Hawk Creek	DBNF Road 4095	1.5	110.9		London RD
DBNF Road 4095	I-75	3.5	114.4	Road	London RD
I-75	DBNF Road 760-S	1.4	115.8	Road	London RD
DBNF Road 760-S	DBNFRoad 736	3.2	119.0	Road	London RD
DBNFRoad 736	DBNF Road 760-N	3.0	122.0	Road	London RD
DBNF Road 760-N	Leave DBNF Road 4078	0.7	122.7	Road	London RD
Leave DBNF Road 4078	KY 490	2.8	125.5		London RD
KY 490	Rockcastle River	1.5	127.0	Road	London RD
Rockcastle River	On Road 489	3.3	130.3	Road	London RD
On Road 489	Off Road 489	0.8	131.1	Road	London RD

From	To	Section	Total	Roads	Manager
Off Road 489	Horse Lick Creek	1.3	132.4	Road	London RD
Horse Lick Creek	Wolf Pen Branch	3.6	136.0	Road	London RD
Wolf Pen Branch	DBNF @S-Tree CG	4.5	140.5	Road	London RD
DBNF @S-Tree CG	DBNF Road 43	2.0	142.5		London RD
DBNF Road 43	Leave DBNF Road 20	2.0	144.5		London RD
Leave DBNF Road 20	DBNF Road 3062	2.2	146.7		London RD
DBNF Road 3062	Leave DBNF Road 3062	1.0	147.7		London RD
Leave DBNF Road 3062	US 421	2.3	150.0		London RD
US 421	Road 443	1.3	151.3	Road	London RD
Road 443	KY 89	4.7	156.0		London RD
KY 89	DBNF Road 376	0.6	156.6		London RD
DBNF Road 376	Turkeyfoot CG	3.7	160.3		London RD
Turkeyfoot CG	War Fork	2.2	162.5		London RD
War Fork	KY 1209	7.2	169.7		London RD
KY 1209	Hale Ridge Road	0.5	170.2	Road	London RD
Hale Ridge Road	DBNF Road 3047	1.6	171.8		London RD
DBNF Road 3047	Copperas Branch	2.6	174.4	Part Road	London RD
Copperas Branch	Sturgeon Creek	0.3	174.7		London RD
Sturgeon Creek	Crestmont-Todds Road	2.6	177.3	Road	London RD
Crestmont-Todds Road	KY 399	2.7	180.0	Road	London RD
KY 399	Kentucky River	1.1	181.1	Road	London RD
Kentucky River	KY 52	3.6	184.7	Part Road	Cumberland RD
KY 52	KY1036	6.4	191.1	Road	Cumberland RD
KY1036	Sand Gap Trail	3.7	194.8		Cumberland RD
Sand Gap Trail	Balanced Rock Trail	1.5	196.3		Natural Bridge SP
Balanced Rock Trail	Lakeshore Trail	0.8	197.1		Natural Bridge SP
Lakeshore Trail	Whittleton Branch Campground	0.5	197.6		Natural Bridge SP
Whittleton Branch Campground	KY15	2.3	199.9		Cumberland RD
KY15	Gray's Arch TH	0.9	200.8		Cumberland RD
Gray's Arch TH	Jct Tr. 227	0.2	201.0		Cumberland RD
Jct Tr. 227	Jct Tr. 226	1.4	202.4		Cumberland RD

From	To	Section	Total	Roads	Manager
Jct Tr. 226	Join Tr. 221	0.4	202.8		Cumberland RD
Join Tr. 221	Leave Tr 221	1.3	204.1		Cumberland RD
Leave Tr 221	KY 715	1.3	205.4		Cumberland RD
KY 715	Trail 210	3.5	208.9		Cumberland RD
Trail 210	Trail 239	2.5	211.4		Cumberland RD
Trail 239	Corner Ridge TH	2.0	213.4		Cumberland RD
Corner Ridge TH	KY 77	1.0	214.4	Road	Cumberland RD
KY 77	US 460	2.8	217.2	Road	Cumberland RD
US 460	KY1274	5.4	222.6	Road	Cumberland RD
KY1274	Clear Lake TH	9.2	231.8		Cumberland RD
Clear Lake TH	White Sulphur Horse Trail	1.5	233.3		Cumberland RD
White Sulphur Horse Trail	Trail 113	2.9	236.2		Cumberland RD
Trail 113	White Sulphur Horse Trail	0.5	236.7		Cumberland RD
White Sulphur Horse Trail	Caney Loop Trail #226-W	1.5	238.2		Cumberland RD
Caney Loop Trail #226-W	Caney Loop Trail #226-E	2.5	240.7		Cumberland RD
Caney Loop Trail #226-E	KY 801	0.5	241.2		Cumberland RD
KY 801	Big Limestone Trail	3.8	245.0		Cumberland RD
Big Limestone Trail	US 60	1.7	246.7		Cumberland RD
US 60	KY 32	6.8	253.5	Road	Cumberland RD
KY 32	Martin Branch Trail	5.9	259.4	Part Road	Cumberland RD
Martin Branch Trail	KY 799	6.1	265.5	Road	Cumberland RD
KY 799	Holly Fork Road #779	2.2	267.7		Cumberland RD
Holly Fork Road #779	Dry Branch Road	2.3	270.0		Cumberland RD
Dry Branch Road	N TH on KY 177	9.9	279.9		Cumberland RD

Contact Information

US Government Agencies

Abraham Lincoln Birthplace National
    Historical Park
2995 Lincoln Farm Road
Hodgenville, KY 42748
270-358-3137
www.nps.gov/abli

Big South Fork National River and
    Recreation Area
4564 Leatherwood Ford Road
Oneida, TN 37841
423-569-9778
www.nps.gov/biso

Cumberland Gap National Historical Park
91 Bartlett Park Road
Middlesboro, KY 40965
606-248-2817
www.nps.gov/cuga

Land Between The Lakes National
    Recreation Area
238 Visitor Center Drive
Golden Pond, KY 42211
800-525-7077
www.landbetweenthelakes.us

Mammoth Cave National Park
P.O. Box 7
Mammoth Cave, KY 42259-0007
270-758-2180
www.nps.gov/maca

Reelfoot National Wildlife Refuge
4343 Highway 157
Union City, TN 38261
731-538-2481
www.fws.gov/reelfoot

Daniel Boone National Forest
1700 Bypass Road
Winchester, KY 40391
859-745-3100
www.fs.usda.gov/dbnf/

Cumberland Ranger District
KY 801 South
Morehead, KY 40351
606-784-6428

London Ranger District
761 S. Laurel Road
London, KY 40744
606-864-4163

Stearns Ranger District
3320 US 27 North
Whitley City, KY 42653
606-376-5323

Redbird Ranger District
91 Peabody Road
Big Creek, KY 40914
606-598-2192

Kentucky State Agencies

Kentucky Department of Parks
Capital Plaza Tower 10th floor, 500
    Mero Street
Frankfort, KY 40601
502-564-2172
parks.ky.gov

Big Bone Lick State Historic Site
3380 Beaver Road
Union, KY 41091
859-384-3522

parks.ky.gov/parks/historicsites
/big-bone-lick/

Breaks Interstate Park
627 Commission Circle
Breaks, VA, 24067
276-865-4413
parks.ky.gov/parks/recreationparks
/breaks-interstate/

Carter Caves State Resort Park
344 Caveland Drive
Olive Hill, KY 41164
606-286-4411
parks.ky.gov/parks/resortparks
/carter-caves/

Cumberland Falls State Resort Park
7351 Highway 90
Corbin, KY 40701
606-528-4121
parks.ky.gov/parks/resortparks
/cumberland-falls/

Dale Hollow Lake State Resort Park
5970 State Park Road
Burkesville, KY 42717
270-433-7431
parks.ky.gov/parks/resortparks
/dale-hollow/

Dawkins Line Rail Trail
Hwy 825
Swamp Branch, KY 41240
502-564-8110
parks.ky.gov/parks/recreationparks
/dawkins-line/

Green River Lake State Park
179 Park Office Road
Campbellsville, KY 42718
270-465-8255
parks.ky.gov/parks/recreationparks
/green-river/

Greenbo Lake State Resort Park
965 Lodge Rd.
Greenup, KY 41144
606-473-7324
parks.ky.gov/parks/resortparks
/greenbo-lake/

Jenny Wiley State Resort Park
75 Theatre Court
Prestonburg, KY 41653
606-8869-1790
parks.ky.gov/parks/resortparks
/jenny-wiley/

John James Audubon State Park
3100 US Hwy 41 North
Henderson, KY 42410
270-826-2247
parks.ky.gov/parks/recreationparks
/john-james/

Kingdom Come State Park
502 Park Rd.
Cumberland, KY 40823
606-589-2479
parks.ky.gov/parks/recreationparks
/kingdom-come/

Lake Barkley State Resort Park
3500 State Park Rd.
Cadiz, KY 42211
270-924-1131
parks.ky.gov/parks/resortparks
/lake-barkley/

Levi Jackson Wilderness Road State
Park
998 Levi Jackson Mill Road
London, KY 40744
606- 330-2130
parks.ky.gov/parks/recreationparks
/levi-jackson/

Natural Bridge State Resort Park
2135 Natural Bridge Road
Slade, KY 40376

606-663-2214
parks.ky.gov/parks/resortparks
/natural-bridge/

Pennyrile Forest State Resort Park
20781 Pennyrile Lodge Road
Dawson Springs, KY 42408
270-797-3421
parks.ky.gov/parks/resortparks
/pennyrile-forest/

Pine Mountain State Resort Park
1050 State Park Road
Pineville, KY 40977
606-337-3066
parks.ky.gov/parks/resortparks
/pine-mountain/

Pine Mountain State Scenic Trail
606-589-2479
parks.ky.gov/parks/recreationparks
/pine-mountain-trail

Kentucky State Nature Preserves
    Commission
801 Teton Trail
Frankfort, KY 40601
502-573-2886
naturepreserves.ky.gov

Kentucky Department of Fish and
    Wildlife Resources
1 Sportsman's Lane
Frankfort, KY 40601
800-858-1549
www.kdfwr.state.ky.us
fw.ky.gov

Kentucky Department of Fish and
    Wildlife Resources
Hunt Control Office
Wilson Road, BLDG 9297
Fort Knox, KY 40121
502-624-2712
www.knox.army.mil/fw

Kentucky Division of Forestry
627 Comanche Trail
Frankfort, KY 40601
502-564-4496
forestry.ky.gov/Pages/default.aspx

Otter Creek Outdoor Recreation
    Area
850 Otter Creek Park Road
Brandenburg, KY 40108
502-942-9171
fw.ky.gov/Pages/Otter-Creek-Outdoor
    -Recreation-Area.aspx

Other Organizations

Berea College
Forestry Department
Berea, KY 40404
859-985-3587
www.berea.edu/forestry/

Bernheim Arboretum and Research
    Forest
PO Box 130
Clermont, KY 40110
502-955-8512
bernheim.org/

Blanton Forest
Kentucky Natural Lands Trust
877-367-5658
knlt.org/blanton/

Jefferson County Memorial Forest
11311 Mitchell Hill Road
Fairdale, KY 40118
502-368-5404
louisvilleky.gov/government/jefferson
    -memorial-forest

The Nature Conservancy, Kentucky
    Chapter
114 Woodland Avenue

Lexington, KY 40502
859-259-9655
www.nature.org/ourinitiatives
/regions/northamerica
/unitedstates/kentucky/

Pine Mountain Trail Conference
www.pinemountaintrail.com

Raven Run Nature Sanctuary
3885 Raven Run Way
Lexington, KY 40515
859-272-6105
www.lexingtonky.gov/raven-run
-nature-sanctuary

Robinson Forest
Department of Forestry, University of
Kentucky
711 Clemons Fork Road
Clayhole, KY 41317
606-666-5034
www2.ca.uky.edu/forestry/robfor.php

Sheltowee Trace Association
STA Livingston Visitor and Training
Center
P.O. Box 360
Livingston, Ky. 40445
606-386-3636
www.sheltoweetrace.org

References

Cumberland Gap National Historical Park, General Management Plan/ Environmental Impact Statement, 2010.

DeLorme, *Kentucky Atlas and Gazetteer*, 2010.

Dreaver, B. G, H. R. Duncan, and J. A. Smith. *Hiking the Big South Fork*. Knoxville, TN: The University of Tennessee Press, 2005.

Kremer, Deborah Kohl. *Explorer's Guide Kentucky*. New York: The Countryman Press, 2013.

Lander, Arthur B. *A Guide to the Backpacking and Day-hiking Trails of Kentucky*. Birmingham, AL: Menasha Ridge Press, 1979.

Manning, Russ. *The Historic Cumberland Plateau: An Explorer's Guide*. Knoxville, TN: The University of Tennessee Press, 1999.

McConnell, Jeannie. *The History of Cumberland Falls*. Kentucky: Kentucky State Parks, 1982.

McDade, Arthur. *The Natural Arches of the Big South Fork: A Guide to Selected Landforms*. Knoxville, TN: The University of Tennessee Press, 2000.

National Geographic/Trails Illustrated. Big South Fork National River and Recreation Area Map # 241. 2013.

National Geographic/Trails Illustrated. Mammoth Cave National Park Map # 234. 2015.

Outragegis Mapping. Cumberland Gap National Historical Park. www.outragegis.com, undated.

Outragegis Mapping. Red River Gorge. www.outragegis.com, undated.

Pine Mountain Trail Conference. Pine Mountain Trail State Park—Birch Knob Section. www.pinemountaintrail.com.

Palmer, Arthur N. *A Geological Guide to Mammoth Cave National Park*. Teaneck, New Jersey: Zephyrus Press, 1995.

Ruchoft, R.H. *Kentucky's Land of the Arches*. Cincinnati, OH: The Pucelle Press, 1986.

Seymour, Randy. *Wildflowers of Mammoth Cave National Park*. Lexington, KY: The University Press of Kentucky, 1997.

Sides, S.D. *Guide to the Surface Trails of Mammoth Cave National Park*. St. Louis, MO: Cave Books, 1995.

Index